For the Love of Trout

For the Love of Trout

BY

GEORGE A. GRIFFITH

George A. Griffith

THE GEORGE GRIFFITH FOUNDATION
Grayling, Michigan

Published by The George Griffith Foundation
P.O. Box 502
Grayling, MI 49738

Printed in the United States of America

Library of Congress Catalog Card Number: 92-075561

ISBN 0-941653-10-2   Trade Edition
ISBN 0-941653-11-0   Limited Edition of 500

for
Peri

CONTENTS

FOREWORD

George expertly poled the AuSable riverboat into position, holding it against the current at the perfect angle for my flycast. "Try upstream of the deadfall, just ahead of that leaning cedar," he suggested knowingly. How many trout had he caught here over the decades?, I wondered.

He knew the river better than most guides. This was his river, the one with which he would always be connected. It was these waters where his passion for troutfishing first became his cause and later his legacy.

"Missed him!," I shouted. "I saw a 14-incher...more!...rise and turn just as my fly started to drag. It came from nowhere!" George knew better. He knew the trout was there all along and would be there again tomorrow. George did not seem displeased at my lack of skill. For him it wasn't the catching of trout that mattered, though it is always a thrill. It was having the opportunity to catch wily, wild trout instead of planted hatchery dolts that really mattered. Now *this* was genuine troutfishing.

For the Love of Trout is not just a book of memoirs. It is decidedly more. It is a charming book of America growing up and having to come to terms with how development affects the natural world. If the passenger pigeon was made extinct and the buffalo nearly so, what could keep the fragile trout from disappearing in the same way Michigan's unique grayling had? *For the Love of Trout* is the story of how one man gathered others to save America's trout fisheries and its trout streams forever.

George Griffith grew as an Ohio farmboy in the years before the Great War. His was a Norman Rockwell portrait of pastoral life in the American Midwest. Baseball, farmfresh food, and a loving family shaped his world. And, oh yes, there were those wonderful summer afternoons he eagerly spent fishing the local bass creek – until sudden spills from a local oil refinery killed the fish and the fishing forever.

George's early years were not unlike those described by Michigan's lumber baron from Saginaw, William Mershon. In Mershon's biography, *Recollections*, the frequent opportunities to hunt and fish are unsurpassed in the pleasure they bring. The pursuit of abundant wildlife and the adventure of stalking fish and game made life exciting and worth living. Both Mershon and Griffith as adults continued to enjoy hunting and fishing. Not coincidentally, they both became "conservationists" before the term had its modern meaning, with each striving to preserve for others the natural heritage that meant so much to them.

In the 1920s, George entered an Indiana business school and left early to work as a salesman. He was a natural. His instincts and good luck ensured him smashing success. During this age of *The Great Gatsby* and *Babbitt*, of Jazz intensity and Great Depression trauma, men of modest backgrounds rose to comfortable heights but they had to use their wits to stay there. Success did not come without risk or without talent, if it came at all. George's business acumen, his good sense, and his inborn pleasantness opened many doors and lead to many ascending stairways. They allowed him to survive and to do more when the situation presented itself.

If there is a calculation in George's career, it was to ensure his sales-territory was in that part of Michigan where he could continue to hunt and fish...to pursue his first loves. Other men choose the big cities in the states south, east, and west of Michigan. George chose the pine forests, cedar swamps, and pristine trout streams of Michigan. Graced with a job requiring he work only nine weeks a year, George spent most of his days in the Michigan outdoors.

In the late 1930s, Chance offered George a remarkable home on the banks of AuSable River Mainstream. "The Barbless Hook," as Joe Brooks would later name it, is still George's summer home. He remembers ruefully when there were less than a dozen homes along the nine miles of the AuSable's "Holy Waters," the section with the best troutfishing. Today, over a hundred cabins and homes line the banks of the Holy Waters. There are now more homes along the river than in the city of Grayling through which the river upstream flows.

As cabins went up, water quality went down. Breakwalls blocked natural springs from reaching the river. Bankside trees were cut. Natural banks were redesigned by naive owners. Deadfalls were cut to make canoeing easier. For years, the city of Grayling discharged under-treated wastewater into the great AuSable River. The river changed for the worse: Insect size became smaller.

Stoneflies, prolific in the 1940s when the water quality was purer, nearly disappeared and made way for caddisflies, which are less fussy about degraded water. Aquatic vegetation grew so prolific that it threatened to kill-off the entire troutfishery if the right, unfortunate, conditions were met.

Something had to be done. Some action had to be taken. Someone had to resolve the problem. So, George did it.

For nearly 20 years, George Griffith served the state of Michigan. He was a member of the Fish and Game Commission, the citizen-represented committee that oversaw the objectives and policies of Michigan's vast Department of Natural Resources.

Not afraid to have scientists debunk hard-held and ancient theories of wildlife and fisheries practices, George championed the scientific management of these renewable resources. New ways had to be tried as old ways were not working.

Throughout this period, George's first love, the AuSable River troutfishery, was in increasingly desperate peril. Fishing had declined along with the water quality. If nothing was done soon to save it, the river and its famous fishery would be lost forever.

So it was on that fateful summer night in 1959 at "The Barbless Hook" that friends of George and influential outdoorsmen were invited to create an organization to save troutfishing in Michigan. George told the group of the late George Mason's desire to create an organization for trout in the same way that Ducks Unlimited was created 25 years earlier for the preservation of ducks and duck habitat.

George Mason, president of the Nash Car Company and a relentless troutfisher, gifted the people of Michigan with 14 miles of some of the best troutwater in America, the South Branch of the AuSable River. Creating "Trout Unlimited" would be a fitting tribute to Mason's memory.

So started Trout Unlimited. Dedicated to the principle that hatchery trout ought not be dumped in every ditch and stream which if managed correctly could sustain their own trout populations, Trout Unlimited had an objective and mission avid troutfishermen readily embraced. Soon local chapters sprang up throughout Michigan and in other states. Scientific advisors directed Trout Unlimited's resource objectives. One hundred miles of special-regulation, quality-water sections of troutwater were designated. And hatchery trout were no longer planted in Michigan's Blue Ribbon trout streams....

Today, Trout Unlimited is an international organization with over 60,000 members in America. It is the world's leading coldwater fisheries conservation organization, protecting and improving the waters and watersheds where trout, salmon, and steelhead live. It is *the* spokesman for trout.

If George Griffith is not Trout Unlimited's spiritual father, he is at least its ethical father. The lessons Aldo Leopold taught us in his *Sand County Almanac* are the lessons George Griffith taught Trout Unlimited: There is an ethic of land-use and resource-use where we must live as part of the natural community. If we choose instead to treat nature as a commodity, as a thing to be used, abused, and discarded, then we will live apart from Nature and it from us. That is not Life worth living.

The Legacy of George Griffith is in his giving us the opportunity to preserve our coldwater heritage, the crystalline running waters where Mr. Trout dwells. Michigan's AuSable River is George Griffith's river, but he may more than any other man may lay claim to all troutwaters as being his rivers.

We should all be so lucky to have lead such a life and to have made such a contribution.

Allen Pienkowski
January 1993

INTRODUCTION

My grandfather Griffith died before I was born, but the family made continual reference to his love of nature, and his fishing and hunting trips were often the topic of conversation. His 640-acre homestead needed much attention in the 19th century. Any trip to any part of the property required a gun or fishing rod.

As a youngster, guns were off limits to me, so my dreams centered on fishing. Baseball and other games were important, as they are to all boys, but fishing became my real passion.

Upstream from our home, near Lima, Ohio a refinery discharged poison into one of my favorite streams and killed all the bass for fifteen miles. How could this happen? My father explained that the refinery created jobs and that a few bass were not as important as those badly needed jobs. I still wondered, "How could this happen?"

Later, in the early twenties, while traveling my territory in Illinois, I had occasion to meet many people who lived near the Illinois River, a major waterfowl flyway. Neither resident nor non-resident hunters would purchase hunting licenses, having been coached by "sporting guides" on how to avoid the fees. They went so far as to tell the "sportsmen" to leave ducks on the water if they suspected trouble – if they had no ducks in possession, they would not be guilty of any wrongdoing! This was also a common practice near Cairo, Illinois where geese were slaughtered on one of their major wintering areas.

This was extremely troubling to me, and in 1924 I joined the Izaak Walton League. Their wisdom and experience in the field of wildlife and resource management was eagerly absorbed as I actively worked for that organization.

I had hardly completed my move to Michigan when Jim Milliken and Opie Titus began training me and furthered the development of both my awareness and knowledge. MUCC (Michigan United Conservation Clubs) was in its infancy then, but they were destined to paint, with a wide brush, the sound management principles for fish and wildlife in the state of Michigan.

Since 1939 I have seen the AuSable River system in its early glory, witnessed its very-near destruction by overfishing, land development, and sewage, and the impact of resurgent concern over this and other treasured and magnificent trout streams.

I want to thank all those who have fought the good fight for so many years. The following is only a partial list of those who have been most active during the sixties and seventies with six or more years of continuous board service. My apologies for any omission are extended; my memory is not what it used to be.

Jim Beosey, Dr. Robert Behnke, Red Pittack, John Bailey, Martin Bovey, Roswell Burrows, Phil Bracewell, Hugh Chatham, Elliott Donnelley, Robert Evenson, Charles Fellows, Robert Foukal, William Fritz, Alvin Grove, Ira Gabrielson, Roderick Haig-Brown, Ray Kotrla, Harold Kleinert, Bud Lillie, Alvan MaCaley, Governor William Milliken, Dr. Gordon Guyer, Phil Orth, Leigh Perkins, Kenneth Peterson, Leon Martuch, Andre Puyans, Tom Reese, Lawrence Reno, Frank Richerdson, Willard F. Rockwell, Mark Rutlage, Alex Schenck, Ben Schley, Cornelius Schrems, Kenneth Sink, Tom Sopkowich, John Spencer, Dwayne Stranahan, Dr. James Hall of Traverse City and sons Jim Jr. and Tom, Governor G. Mennen Williams, The Honorable John Dingell Jr., Art Newmann, James Taylor, Howard Tanner, Otto Teller, Frank K. Smith, Pete Van Gytenbeek, O. L. Wallis, Casey Westell Jr., Carroll Wert, and Ebb Warren.

Today there remain many menacing issues for our attention. Trout streams are still facing the same threats, some in new disguises, and we need to remain vigilant and *active*.

This book was written as a reminder to a new army of conservationists that history does indeed repeat itself. Join the battle.

George A. Griffith
Grayling, Michigan
January 1993

* * *

GRANDPA'S LEGACY

"Well, where are the fish, George?"

Mom wasn't a big woman, but her eyes saw through me.

"Aw, Mom ..."

"You slipped out to that creek, didn't you? I was expecting a mess of fish for supper."

"But, Mom, the bass are all dead...all bloated up in that waxy stuff."

"Well, your Dad will surely be hungry. Get on out and catch me a fat hen."

Mom whisked me off with her apron. But I could hear her saying to herself once more: "I don't know what possesses that boy. Every day...more like his Grandpa Griffiths, always roaming off with that old rifle or his fishing pole."

I hung my head. I wanted to be like Grandpa Griffiths.

The chickens were flustered. I tripped between a broken rail and the coop, skinning a knee on the weathered wood. My heart wasn't in it as I picked up the axe.

But suddenly I was chasing a headless chicken around the yard. I grabbed the chicken and headed for the summer kitchen back of the big house. But I was with Grandpa at Sugar Creek. Winding the chalk line on his long fishing pole, I could hear him saying, "Boy, if you care about something, protect it."

What did Grandpa mean?

*   *   *

My mind flashed back to this morning.

"Be quiet, Chunky. You'll wake up Mom and Dad," said Emerson as he shook me awake in my featherbed.

I slipped into a short-sleeved shirt that may have been a plaid color many washings ago when my brother first wore it. I pushed my scarred, calloused feet through the shin-length legs of faded overalls and I was dressed. We didn't wear underwear in the summer, especially when we were going for a swim, and we only wore shoes on Sunday mornings from the day the bell rang school out until it rang school in again after harvest time.

My feet shivered in the morning chill of the wet grass as we walked down the lane which was pocked by the split hooves of the cows. "Get up, Spot," I said as I nudged the cow the others seemed to accept as their leader and then stood for a moment and warmed my feet as the grass where she had been lying all night sent steam upward into the cold fog overhanging the pasture.

Chum, our tan and white brindle dog, would go up and nudge the cows, but he knew better than to nip or rush them. Finally, we had all 14 cows, plus three heifers, on their feet and headed for the lane. I tried to choose my path through the cow beds, but the hard, cold ground sent me up on the balls of my feet after I left the last cow bed. The lane seemed slightly warmer but squishy as I stepped in the fresh hooftracks the cows left behind them.

Old Spot marched through the barnyard, which was a quagmire of sorts after the rain, and stepped onto the concrete floor at the east end of the stable side of the barn. I climbed over the wooden lane gate, slid open the west stable door, and met Spot as she stood in her place by the manger to be milked. We didn't have stanchions to lock the cow's heads into for milking as some farmers did. Emerson had skirted in the tall grass just outside the barnyard and was climbing the wire fence next to a fence post as he shooed the rest of the cattle inside.

I picked up a 10-quart pail and one of the four-legged milking stools we always used instead of the well-known three-legged stool.

"Think you can milk one of Dad's cows?" asked Emerson. I had milked four cows twice a day since I was six years old; Emerson milked six and Dad milked four after he distributed ground feed — ensilage from the silo in the winter. He also would check to make sure that we had stripped the last milk from our cows lest they dry up prematurely.

"I think so," I replied. "I'll take Old Spot. She likes me and she's easy to milk." She was Dad's favorite cow, if he had any, I thought as I placed the oblong stool beside her. I sat down, shoved the shiny pail under Spot, hugged it between my legs, and began squeezing milk from her front teats. Her udder was full of milk.

Soon I was stripping Old Spot's hind teats. I moved on to Flossie, my favorite cow. She turned her head, but kept munching the feed Emerson had just poured in the trough in front of her. Emerson's hands were slightly larger than mine, and he could milk much faster. But one of Dad's cows was dried up and due to calve soon, so Emerson would have only two extra cows to milk today.

"I told Dad he could sleep in and we would do the chores," said Emerson. "But I didn't tell him we were going to Sugar Creek." We each carried two full — and heavy — pails to the cold house and dumped the warm milk through a strainer into a 5-gallon can. Emerson lifted it into the cold trough.

"Pump, Chunky," he yelled out as I headed for the Red Jacket deep-well pump. He began stirring the milk with a long shiny rod with a disk on the end with holes in it that would let little streams of milk flow through each time he lifted it. The once-red pump cried with each pumpful and I could hear water splashing from the pipe into the 30-inch by 30-inch masonry trough that Grandpa had built as the cold building's refrigeration system. During warm months Emerson or I would pump fresh water into it no less than four times a day, eight on hot days. Many things were designed in those days to function with boypower, but filling the trough was one of the most boring jobs.

"It's cool," said Emerson, after dribbling milk from the stirrer onto his wrist. He shoved the cover down into the can.

"I'll meet you at the wood house," I said, remembering that I didn't have my jackknife. No boy would go anywhere without a jackknife in 1910. I ran back to the house, crept upstairs, back downstairs, and tiptoed past my parents' room.

I tried to quiet the screen door spring as it tried to sing a merry tune behind me. It was so hot and humid that the red oak frame of the door Grandpa had made from native lumber when he built the big house felt like a sponge. Northwestern Ohio had been hit by three days of soaking rain.

Dad was always up by five a.m., finishing chores by six and in the field by seven. But we knew that he would welcome an extra hour of sleep if we offered to milk, especially since the fields were all too wet to work. We had a hankering to fish and swim in Sugar Creek. All our chores were momentarily done. We had prepared the night before: The kitchen stove box was full of split oak and there was a small stack of kindling, and the always-thirsty reservoir that hung on the side of the big wood range was full of rainwater pumped and carried from the cistern to be warmed for washing. The soft water meant less soap to buy — Mom didn't make her own soap as Grandma had done.

We had good reason to hurry. A day or two after a hard rain, the creek would become muddy. But with the rainstorm just ended, the fish would be hungry until the feeder streams turned coffee-and-cream color and a banquet of worms washed downstream with the eroding farmland soil.

Emerson was two years older, a head taller, and much thinner than my then-chunky 10-year-old frame. I always had to run to keep up. As I spotted his long legs propelling him toward the wood house, I quietly stole into the pantry and summer kitchen adjacent to the big house, already full of hundreds of Mason jars of Mom's June peas and string beans. The building smelled with the distinctive scents of other vegetables hanging in the rafters from last winter and the ever-present herbs Mom grew in her garden and used to season our food.

I grabbed a handful of sugared oatmeal cookies Mom had left cooling on the wood range and headed for the 20-foot square brick cold building without giving the intimidating deep-well pump another glance. My interest was a bowl with four pieces of fried chicken I knew was sitting atop a milk can full of cream in the cooling trough. I stuffed them into a paper bag with the cookies. My ever-hungry stomach was growling and ready for the breakfast we were going to miss.

My thoughts again turned to Grandpa as I stepped out into the hot, humid air. I could see him at the blackboard in the upstairs schoolroom with its 11 desks filled, at first, with his own children and, later, with a number of neighbor youngsters in whom he instilled the first — and often only — formal education of their lives.

Emerson was already on his knees beside the 40-by-40-foot wood house Grandpa had built on stilts opposite the barn. He had unintentionally provided us a secret hiding place underneath the building. The north side had a distinctive odor of butter and housed the cream separator with its big metal bowl; the center had the odor of freshly split firewood, and the south side had grain bins already full of wheat. The batten-stripped red building had rusty metal chutes on the outside walls from which grain could be sacked for a trip to the grist mill to be ground into cattle feed or sold to buy the few foodstuffs we didn't raise.

Emerson's browned, bare feet protruded from faded overalls that seemed far too short for his scrawny legs. He tossed back a coarse, yellow mop of hair and looked up at me.

"Here's yours, Chunky," and handed out a nearly nine-foot hickory pole wrapped with carpenter's chalk line. Then he handed out a wooden bucket then withdrew an empty pail and his pole. "See if we got any worms left," he ordered, momentarily making me wish I were the older brother. I fluffed the rich loam, still damp from our last fishing trip, and several worms fought to return to cover. "We got some," I said. I wanted to fish, not dig worms. Fishing and swimming in Sugar Creek were our big breaks between a summer of threshing grain and chopping corn and filling the silo to feed the cows next winter.

*   *   *

Grandpa had come from Wales in 1846 to this area 60 miles south of Lake Erie with a deed written on sheepskin and signed by President James K. Polk that gave Evan Griffiths title to a square mile — 640 acres — of northwestern Ohio wilderness.

Although Grandpa's Welsh background may have been tainted with a bit of Irish, I could see his sparkling — you might say devilish — blue eyes and a full shock of yellow hair that still held most of its color, despite slightly graying temples, into old age. Grandpa's face had a gentle character with soft age lines and was tanned to the rich patina of fine shoe leather. He had a refined bone structure seldom seen in Welsh settlers and his well-formed hands must have seemed out of place on a two-man cross-cut saw clearing and often burning virgin oak and some native maple and hickory.

We walked past a section of stump fence and I recalled that, as he and his neighbors wrested the precious farmland from the virgin forest with teams of big Belgian draft horses, they had tipped those stumps with their many-pointed roots onto one side to form the fence and save always-tedious splitting of fence rails from logs with big-bladed broad axes. Crooked rail fences still zig-zagged across many farms, dividing field and pasture while creating edge homes for wildlife. But I didn't understand that — I only knew I could find birds and rabbits in fence rows.

Grandpa Griffiths' forefathers were woodworkers and furniture makers in

GRANDPA'S LEGACY

Wales. He had come from a scholarly background, but he knew woodworking, had blacksmithing tools, and could make bricks. With all these talents to teach others, he quickly emerged as the spokesman and leader of the small group of Welsh immigrants.

Neighbors provided manpower to help him build the big, square farmhouse with five second-story bedrooms crowned with another half story attic with bare hand-hewn rafters. He and his sturdy German immigrant bride, Hilda Ehernmann from Elida, a nearby village, had filled the house with seven boys — Samuel, Isaac (Ike), John (my father), Charles, Evan Jr., Benjamin and Alfred, and five daughters — Elizabeth (Aunt Lib), Alice, Viola, Ellen, and Carrie.

In those days only boys and indolent old men hunted or fished. But by 1860 Grandpa decided Sam, Ike, and John were old enough to work the fields. Without a care for his reputation, Grandpa would roam his square mile several times a week with a muzzle-loading rifle and he would go fishing for smallmouth bass in Sugar Creek whenever he could.

* * *

Down the lane, the Jersey cows were lying about the pasture and sleepily chewing their cuds. But now I barely saw them — I was swinging the pail as I walked beside Grandpa and shared with him my dream of catching a bucket full of smallmouth bass, rock bass, and sunfish from the creek.

Sugar Creek was relatively small, but older fishermen claimed it was one of the state's top smallmouth streams. I had never fished anywhere else.

My thoughts turned to the many times we had made this trek. I could see a smallmouth fighting me on the end of a chalk line attached to the hickory pole that I imagined had once been Grandpa's. Sometimes it would be a rock bass. But, while there must have been bad days, in my boyish enthusiasm, I never had to go home with an empty bucket.

When we were through fishing today, we would put fresh water on our bucket of fish and go to the old swimming hole, a wider, deeper spot in the creek downstream, shed our clothes and dive into the cool water. In cooler weather, we wore one-piece cotton union suits and blue denim windbreakers. But today wasn't going to be cool — by noon it would be hot and muggy and we would be thankful we had the swimming hole.

As I visualized Grandpa walking across his farm and a neighbor's place to get to the creek, I thought how different he must have been than Dad: 6-foot-2 and 240 pounds of raw muscle with big, calloused, hard-working hands — I never knew a stronger man — that had never known the thrill of hunting or fishing. Dad, like many of his generation, had little time for anything but work. One time he relented and, after supper, took us to Grandpa's favorite spot on the stream. He even stayed long beyond the time I expected he would insist we leave, apparently hoping we would get it out of our systems. When darkness came, he lighted a kerosene lantern and suspended it from a long pole out over the river so, we thought, the fish could see. Our fishing was good that night but we didn't know that the light attracted insects or that fish even would eat insects.

When he wasn't working, Dad was a tenor and sang professionally with quartets and choirs. He traveled as far as Minneapolis. He had yearned for a musical education, but he had stayed home to work the farm while four sisters and three brothers completed college educations. He met my mother, Evelyn Dennis of Kalida, six miles north of Vaughnsville, through music — she taught voice and piano. Singing school was a respectable place for young folks to meet in the late 1800s.

The family had farmed together until Sam and Ike built their own homes on farms carved out of Grandpa's land about 1890. Everyone got an education or an 80-acre farm. Grandpa promised Dad 120 acres because he managed the farm, but when he divided it, there were only 120 acres left — 80 acres for Dad and 40 acres for old maid Aunt Libby. Dad share-cropped Aunt Libby's land and married Mom six months later; he was 37, she was 25.

Threshing days were exciting for us. Men began coming from miles around at daybreak to go into the fields and load the shocks of grain onto horse-drawn wagons. Meanwhile, their wives would join Mom in the summer kitchen, cook hams that had cured hanging in the rafters of the pantry, peel and boil a mountain of our farm-grown potatoes, and bake apple pies. Noontime dinner for the hungry threshers was a well-earned feast and few men left the table without second helpings. The wives would always eat later.

GRANDPA'S LEGACY

Emerson and I would watch for the huge steam engine to pull the long threshing machine off the crushed rock road and up by the barn. I was fascinated as the engineer unhooked, backed off about 50 feet, and two men dragged a broad red belt from a pulley on the side of the threshing machine to a big, wire-spoked power-takeoff wheel on the side of the engine. Then the engine would spout a hot cloud of steam and back up until the drooping belt lifted off the ground and tightened. With a whistle and another cloud of steam, the wood and steel threshing machine would begin to shake. That was the signal for teams of horses to pull wagons piled high of grain up beside the machine and stand quietly as two men with three-tined forks would begin pitching golden yellow bundles of wheat into the seemingly starved machine.

As it shook, the threshing machine sent the grain down a tube on the side of the machine where two older men at twin spouts filled closely woven, once-white bags about two-thirds full of wheat. They would lift the bags — untied — to a wagon for a trip across the yard to the door of the wood house where other men would sling them over their shoulders, carry them inside, and dump the grain into the bins. But today the grain was in the wood house granary bins and, unlike Grandpa's first crop, which was so small that he carried it on horseback five miles to a mill to be ground into flour, there was plenty to take to town to sell at the elevator when we needed the money or when grain prices went up.

The scent of goldenrod, already in full bloom, wafted through our nostrils as we skipped across the slowly warming grass of the pasture toward a distant fence and our neighbor's farm through which Sugar Creek ran. Red-winged blackbirds flew across the pasture and one stopped atop a rotting stump of a once-proud giant oak — one Grandpa hadn't removed.

A barb from the top three strands pricked my bottom and hurried me over the wire fence, but I barely felt it. My thoughts were with Grandpa. While I was aware of Emerson ahead of me — as he always was — Grandpa always seemed to be beside me as I walked across the rich farmland he had wrested from the virgin forest and even more as I seemed to share with him our adventures in the out-of-doors. He was so close yet so far. I had never seen him except through the eyes of those who knew him, but with each bucket of fish we caught, I felt his

8

presence. He was always smiling over my shoulder. How I wanted to be like Grandpa; how I yearned to be a real hunter and fisherman.

Emerson reached the leaning stump ahead of me. He rested against it, jammed his pole into the soft soil of the bank and dangled a foot in the stream. But his toes barely broke through the surface. When I caught up with him, everywhere I looked the waterway was coated with a half-inch-thick waxy film.

Sugar Creek started south of Lima and the cool water meandered through some 11 miles of rich Ohio farmland before it got to us. It was cool and clear except during spring runoff when it would turn the color of coffee and cream. But it had never been like this.

I put a worm on my hook and dangled it over the stream, but it rested almost motionless on the surface, unable to penetrate the film. The usually clear shallows were turned an ugly, dirty tan that reminded me of giant candle drippings. We watched as something tried to poke holes through the surface — fish apparently trying to get air

"What happened?" we asked almost simultaneously. "Let's go to the beach," said Emerson. We hiked to our swimming hole, a wider spot in the stream, but it also was covered with wax. We weren't going to be able to swim either.

My heart was heavy and I dug the butt of my pole into the soft earth with each step as we made our way home. The empty metal fish pail seemed to make a hollow, mocking sound as Emerson occasionally struck it with his pole.

* * *

My thoughts were miles away as Dad handed me the platter of chicken. Mom had made a bowl of boiled potatoes and thick chicken gravy. I was quiet. The platter should be piled high with fish from Sugar Creek, I thought.

"George, tell your Dad about the creek." How did Mom always know what I was thinking? I guess Moms are like that. I choked back a tear and Emerson helped me explain about the wax on the surface of the water and the fish that must have been trying to poke through it and get some air. When he finished, we were both crying and Mom, who could be tough, seemed to be sharing our grief.

"That new Solar Refinery plant in Lima has been hiring boys off the farms since spring," Dad said as he passed the platter. It was his only response. Jobs were scarce. Neither he nor other farmers saw fishing as important. I looked down at my plate, but my thoughts again turned to Grandpa. Although he had died about the time I was born, Mom had told me about him and, at a time when boys are apt to create imaginary playmates, I always shared my thoughts and dreams with him. Help me, Grandpa.

My thoughts also turned to Lester Stone, a ne'er-do-well fisherman who counted on the creek for much of his food. Lester may have been kind of funny to some people, but he was my friend. He had a reel on his fishing pole, and a much lighter line and even three eyelets to run the line through. And no one knew more about the creek than Lester.

Mom cut the thick cherry pie. We always finished supper with cake or pie — during winter with mince-meat pie made of meat, apples, nuts and other goodies. Her pie tins were big, but she would always cut a pie into just five pieces to satisfy farm appetites. In the winter she would make up a dozen pies at a time and keep them frozen because we would often finish a hearty farm breakfast of our own sausage or ham, eggs and fried potatoes and pie.

About 8 o'clock, as Dorothy was trying to complete a puzzle on the dining room table and Emerson and I were playing checkers on Mom's oval hooked rug on the floor near the hard-coal burner, we could hear a familiar popping sound that stirred our appetites again. A few minutes later Mom appeared with a dishpan full of popcorn generously topped with melted butter along with a dish of walnuts and hickory nuts.

We raised popcorn, a farm delicacy also threaded and used to trim most farm and many small-town Christmas trees, in a patch by the garden. The nuts were home-grown, too. Emerson and I would put on old gloves and collect the olive-green husked black walnuts from a couple of big trees along the side road built for unshod horses. To remove the husks, which would turn almost anything black, we would pound the nuts through a board, with a hole about the size of a 50-cent piece, laid over saw horses. A friendly old shagbark hickory that stood sentry where the lane turned into the pasture produced hickory nuts. We would dry the nuts on the porches of the big house then put them into gunny sacks made of loosely woven burlap. The ever-producing old hickory, with its seeming plates of bark armor that Dad said might be 200 to 300 years old, always fascinated me.

"Chunky, clean it up," said Emerson as the shiny bottom of Mom's well-used dishpan began to show through the fluffy corn. Dorothy was done and Dad shook his head. Mom would seldom eat more than one dish. But as I scooped out another bowl, Emerson forced me into a jump on the checker board. As I picked up his checker, he jumped three of mine and crowned a new king. Why do big brothers always have to win? I didn't know.

"Play you another game of checkers," I said. But Emerson shook his head. "I've got to practice for music tomorrow night," he said. Emerson played violin with the Vaughnsville Methodist Church orchestra, and I had begun playing second fiddle — as it seemed I did to my big brother in everything in life.

Emerson and I went back again and again to Sugar Creek with our fishing poles. Occasionally, our cousins, Walter and Dwight Griffiths, and friends, Oliver and Harry Thomas, would go with us. But each time we would return fishless.

Then, one week in late summer, Sugar Creek seemed to recover her sparkling personality. I even caught a smallmouth about a foot long. But the other boys seemed more thrilled with a chance to swim. It was the last time. Fall, with school and shoes, was suddenly upon us, then came winter and the struggle against the weather. We forgot about Sugar Creek.

When spring came and we made our trek to the meandering mile-long stretch, Sugar Creek greeted us like old friends — fresh and clean as if nothing had happened. However, we didn't see or catch any fish. Then it was summer and Emerson and I headed for the creek. But once again, when I caught up with him at our favorite stump, he was shaking his head. The film had returned, thicker than before, and the stream was as quiet as the undertaker's parlor.

No one else seemed concerned. Solar Refinery had a waste byproduct and a waterway was a natural sewer to be used.

Again, we forgot about fishing. Two of the most enjoyable days of our year were upon us — the circus had come to town and, in only a few weeks, the county fair would follow at Ottawa, the county seat.

It was 1910, and the circus arrived in Lima at night aboard its own railroad train. It would take over a 10-acre site adjacent to the tracks, erect a big pole like a power pole, and set up the main and several sideshow tents. We marveled at the elephants as they would help raise the tents. But the highlight of the day was the parade. Many people would come just to watch the parade and not attend the show. For free they could watch as cages of lions, tigers, and other wild animals paraded with their trainers and colorfully dressed aerial performers and clowns all marched to the beat of a very peppy brass band loud enough to be heard blocks away. Admission was 50 cents for adults 25 cents for children, and $2 for a family. The acts were professionally good and worth it.

At the county fair, which we looked forward to for months, there would be motion pictures for five- or 10-cent admission fees. Like the circus, these were days that could never be duplicated. We could see the bearded lady for a dime, but we were always tempted by the shows on the other side of the midway that were as expensive as a quarter and were considered risque. Dad had no interest but we could usually find a stranger willing to allow a boy — even two — to tag along. We always emerged disappointed — the shows just didn't make sense to 10- and 12-year-old farm boys.

Even the real Buffalo Bill didn't impress us too much. He was on the bill with his Wild West Show with horses and real cowboys competing with real Indians. But his show didn't compare with the circus' aerial acts and wild animals. We were impressed, however, by his covered wagon, and we went home and tried to build one. When it didn't work, we decided to hold cowboy-Indian battles without circling the wagons. And I went to bed more than once dreaming of being part of the wild West.

Toward fall, I was curious. I made a trip alone to Sugar Creek, but the water was even dirtier. I met Lester, who told me that German carp had moved into a downstream section of Sugar Creek. The carp was a great game fish and would give quite a fight on dough balls. Mom made us some dough balls for bait, and Emerson and I went to a farm downstream Lester had suggested and we caught several good-sized fish. They were like logs to haul in. But we impressed the farmer so much that he went into Vaughnsville and bought some of the new cane poles and tackle the hardware store was selling to try fishing himself.

But as we arrived to fish again a few days later, the farmer was coming up from the stream. He was frustrated — he hadn't caught any carp.

"Sorry, boys, the creek is closed to fishing," he said as we started to go down the path. We'd never heard of anyone closing a stream. But he was sure we were doing something differently, taking all the fish and keeping a secret from him. We had told him how to make dough balls like Mom made but it didn't matter — he seemed to blame us.

Meanwhile, he and other farmers began digging shallow surface ditches in the flat farmland to drain spots left wet after a rain and to stir low spots into production. The drains became muddy ditches. Other farmers began installing underground tiled drains and started using chemical fertilizers in hopes of wresting even more crops from the soil.

With faster drainage, Sugar Creek, which used to dance like a prima ballerina through the meadowland, lost its fast ripples and became a dry streambed between now-lifeless pools during dry summer months.

Sugar Creek seemed to cry out after me for help. But I didn't understand. I'd never seen a stream die before. What could I do?

Then I suddenly felt Grandpa standing beside me. I began to glimpse a new meaning in Sugar Creek and the land around it . . . .

I sensed that a love of hunting and fishing and Sugar Creek were Grandpa's legacy to me . . . .

And someday I would know what Grandpa wanted me to do . . . .

* * *

TROUT OF KLACKING CREEK

We walked across the pasture with our fishing poles over our shoulders and a spring in our step.

"Where's the creek?" I asked as we stepped across tiny winding spring water rivulets. Two cows looked up from grazing then began chewing their cuds. The rest of the herd of about a dozen Jersey cows barely acknowledged our presence.

Tom grinned and ducked his head as he entered a stand of big Christmas trees. A low branch swished back and caught me squarely in the face and slapped the corner of my eye. I put my head down. The forest floor felt soft and cushioned my feet. I dug in my toe and found I was walking on several inches of dead, brown needles.

Looking back, Tom said, "C'mon. That's just duff."

I quickened my step as I saw light 30 to 40 feet ahead. I could hear water flowing. It sounded like Sugar Creek, but it seemed sort of muffled. Then we were in head-high brush.

"These are cedar trees," explained Tom. "The bushes are tag alders." I could hear the water — it was louder now — and I felt a cool breeze. Ahead I could see more cedars and the glint of the sun on the water. I parted the tag alders with both hands and suddenly it appeared. It was like a dream.

Klacking Creek was a woodland beauty, clad in a silver-sequined ball gown and shimmering in the morning sun, swaying from bank to cedar- and tag alder-lined bank, sparkling as she tap-danced in the sunlight, then swirled in a slow, flowing waltz through shaded runs.

I was in love.

The waterway was shallow and crystal clear. At its deepest, the water was licking at my knees. The sandy bottom felt cool and gentle on my feet, which were in shoes no more than six months of a year and used to a variety of surfaces.

"Drop your worm so it will drift down over that log sweeper lying across the stream," Tom instructed. "Stand still; don't splash," he cautioned. "A fish should be hiding just behind the log. Keep your pole ready to jerk up when he hits."

My pulse quickened as the worm drifted over the log. Then I saw a trout —

the first that I had ever seen — shoot forward and swallow my worm. Suddenly it was battling for its life, trying to entangle the line on stubs of branches long since rotted off the small log.

We had no nets. As the trout tired, I backed onto the shore and beached the fish. It was a 10-inch "brookie," Tom told me. It had beautiful colors. I was hooked.

*   *   *

It was 1916, and Frank Clevenger and his uncles, Frank and Tom, and Emerson and I had come north into Michigan in an E-M-F touring car, the forerunner of Buick, with a sturdy folding top and side curtains. We loaded the car with extra clothing, a picnic basket packed to the brim with fried chicken and loaves of Mother's bread for our lunch, and, because we had no refrigeration, we carried a home-smoked ham, four live chickens, a big tin filled with navy beans, and a big bag of potatoes.

The chickens were in a wood and poultry netting crate tied to the tonneau, a shelf on the back of the car. Mom never went anywhere on a visit without taking along some live chickens. The ham, potatoes, beans and two five-gallon cans of gasoline were strapped on the running boards. The car had a spare tire mounted just back of the front fender on each side.

After only a few miles in Michigan, we were thankful that someone had suggested we bring gasoline — few grocery and general stores along the 12-hour drive, mostly over dirt roads, appeared to have gasoline pumps.

The roads were flat and dusty for the first 60 miles to the Ohio-Michigan border, then we began going through hilly country and the farms grew larger and had more wood lots and wild land. As farmers, we noted the soil was obviously poorer. No wonder they had to have larger farms. Some of the hills were steep, but not so steep that we had to back up them as people often did with Ford Model Ts. A streak of dust a quarter-mile long trailed the car and everything was covered with clay dust. Thankfully, there had been no rain to turn the clay greasy. In low areas we would go through a wet, black soil we didn't have in Ohio.

"Black muck," said Uncle Tom, chomping on a cigar that he hadn't had lighted for a couple of hours. "I guess it grows good crops, but I've heard that you can sink a wagon and a team in it in some places."

Then we were going through cities, big cities — Ann Arbor, Flint, Saginaw, Bay City. The uncles drove through downtown, aware that this was our first look at big cities. We stopped in downtown Ann Arbor to stretch our legs and so Uncle Tom could take over the driving. In Flint I saw a streetcar — a single-car electric train that ran on a track down the middle of the street with two arms that reached up to suspended wires for power.

Despite taking turns at driving, the uncles were worn out when we finally reached a log cabin on a lake near Hale. It had a combination kitchen-living room and a bedroom with two beds. We were going first class. We built a fire in the little kitchen range.

"You'd better turn in, boys," said Uncle Frank. "We'll be going out about sunup." I went to bed, dreaming of fishing out of the boat tied up at a dock in front of the cottage. I had never been in a boat before.

Tom, our host's son who was about our age, greeted us at dawn with a bucket of eggs, a big loaf of bread, a dish of butter and what he called "bacon." It looked like smoked side pork to me. Tom picked up one of the three lids of stove, stirred the ashes with the lifter, and added a couple pieces of kindling, which soon caught fire.

Uncle Frank, who took pride in his cooking, soon had a pot of coffee boiling — "There's nothing like boiled coffee to put hair on your chest," he said — and ham and eggs, raw-fried potatoes, and some of that bacon sizzling in the heavy cast-iron skillet.

Tom, tall, blond, and blue-eyed, had a warm smile and a devilish sparkle in his eyes.

"I've got a boat to take you guys bluegill fishing," he said. I pretended to be knowledgeable, but no water has ever thrilled me in the same way that Sage Lake did that first full day of my first vacation that summer morning of 1916 in Michigan.

"You boys catch us a bucket of 'gills for dinner," Uncle Tom called out as he tipped the oars deep into the dark, quiet lake water. "We're going after the biggest northern in Sage Lake. Shucks, we might not even be able to get it into the boat."

TROUT OF KLACKING CREEK

Tom rowed us through lily pads, reeds, and other cover — a new world. We were only about 100 yards from shore when he tipped the oars into the boat and dropped an old cast-iron gear attached to a length of hemp rope overboard. The other end of the rope was looped under my seat and tied.

We all baited up and bluegills large enough to cover a supper plate began filling the bucket in the middle of the boat. They seemed plentiful and willing. I silently wished we could have fish like them again in Sugar Creek. Although our heavy tackle may have turned off the largest fish, we had a bucket full. We went ashore and proudly helped Tom clean them. It was already past noon and we knew the uncles would be in for dinner. In those days it was breakfast, dinner, and supper.

"Let's go trout fishing," suggested Tom as we were cleaning fish for supper a few days later. "It's more fun."

* * *

And now I was a trout fisherman.

The shorter pole with lighter line and smaller hooks was easier to handle. While Sugar Creek was in the middle of a pasture, with only occasional trees along the grassy water's edge, Klacking Creek was only 12 to 15 feet wide, and we had to be careful that we didn't catch a tag alder when we threw out our lines.

We waded into the stream barefooted and Tom showed us how to place our hooks, baited with small red manure worms, around stumps and fallen trees and along undercut banks where trout were waiting. The 10-inch trout Tom called a brookie had played cupid in a love affair I knew would last for the rest of my life. As we fished, I told Tom about Sugar Creek and he shrugged his shoulders. "We wouldn't worry about that in our country. If we fished out a trout stream, we would just go to another one." Imagine that, so many streams that they didn't care if one was destroyed because there always was another. How lucky can one be?

I was more elated with each catch, although some of the brookies were only seven- or eight-inch fish. I was a trout fisherman. And momentarily I thought of Grandpa Griffiths, and I was thankful that I had inherited his philosophy. If he could only see me. Another trout brought me back to the present. I savored the beauty of the clear stream and its woodland setting and suddenly felt a part of it

— it was all wrapped around me, gracefully swaying cedars, rustling tag alders, a blue sky, the shimmering water, and the sand that moved to cup my feet. What warmth. What beauty. I will never forget this day.

*   *   *

As I look back, days on the farm that Grandpa built were idyllic. Wrestling to keep the walking 12-inch moldboard plow peeling off and turning over eight-inch thick slices of rich, moist topsoil a foot wide behind behind our Belgian team, Jim and Ned, was hard work. But even when Dad bought a riding plow, I preferred the walking plow, perhaps because my bare feet were walking in the cool furrow. I always felt close to God and Nature when I was walking in freshly plowed soil.

As I was riding Nellie, our Morgan horse, a mile to the general store in Vaughnsville to buy some things Mom needed, I daydreamed of someday having a farm of my own. Farming was all that I knew. Except hunting and fishing. And no one made a living out of hunting and fishing. No one I knew, except Lester Stone. And he only made $25 to $30 a year from his trapline, enough to buy fishing tackle. Most people thought Lester was kind of queer. Everybody but me. I knew that no one around Vaughnsville knew more about the animals and the fish than Lester Stone.

I became a hunter just before my sixth birthday when I spotted a rabbit out in the apple orchard west of the house. But when I rushed inside and asked Mother for Father's rifle, she shook her head as if to say no. Then she smiled, took two cartridges out of the cupboard where I knew Dad kept them, and picked up the old gun leaning in the corner by the wood box. She shooed me ahead of her. Dad kept the gun ready to kill fox and raccoon that would try to get into the hen house, but I had barely ever touched the gun. And I had never fired it.

I showed Mom where the rabbit was sitting. She helped me lay the barrel of the .32 caliber rifle over the rail fence and wondered why she knelt behind me while I sighted it. But I was too excited. Carefully, I squeezed the trigger. The gun fired and the rabbit jumped high in the air and fell dead. And the great hunter, who had bounced back into the ready arms of his mother with the recoil of the gun, buried his head in his hands and cried on her shoulder.

I hunted on the farm throughout my boyhood, but that moment is etched in my mind. And I still hear Grandpa's reminder, passed on to me through Mom, "If you hunt, don't ever leave a helpless critter to suffer." For thousands of shots to come, I would hunt harder to find a cripple than a dead bird.

When I stopped crying, Mom wiped my face with her apron. She stood the rifle by the fence and walked with me to retrieve my trophy.

"I'll help you dress the rabbit, and I'll cook it for dinner," said Mom, leading me to the summer kitchen. "But after this, you're on your own — your Grandpa always dressed fish or game. If you want to be like him, you'll learn to dress game, too." Only Mom understood how much I wanted to be like Grandpa.

Emerson — he would go by F. Emerson in later life — and I would hunt for ever-plentiful rabbits whenever we could get away from farm chores. I was forever the little brother, although I grew to 5-foot-10, and I could never match him as a rabbit hunter. But he would always hunt with Dad's full-choke, double-barreled, 10-pound shotgun with big hammers that had to be cocked. It was hard to carry, but it had a definite advantage over Dad's rifle. I had to shoot a rabbit while it was sitting. Emerson wasn't supposed to shoot unless a rabbit was running, but it seemed he could always "accidentally" do something to make a sitting rabbit start to run just as I had the bead of the rifle on it. Sometimes big brothers are unfair, too.

Funny or not, I admired Lester. I watched him set his traps and, as most farm boys would do, I bought three traps and set up my own trap-line. But one of Lester's detractors suggested he must be removing muskrats from my traps. I finally trapped one, skinned it, and shaped a board to stretch the skin over, using little nails to hold it. It was my only experience as a trapper.

Meanwhile, neighbor farmers began installing tiled drains built with four-inch by 12-inch-long tile buried up to three feet underground. It was the latest in farming. Unlike ditches, the drains would help speed water from wet spots we couldn't farm and help produce more crops. The drains did pay for themselves within a few years, but then those farms began dying. And no one knew — and few cared — that faster drainage was polluting waterways with horse, pig, and cow manure and was drying up some streams.

In one of the first examples of conservation, several financially able men bought up "farmed out" properties and revived them to prove the folly of careless draining — without the use of chemical fertilizers that were becoming popular. An undertaker bought five 80-acre farms, the most difficult to make a living from. The investors found that they could rent the land to neighbors, leave game cover, and produce crops. But the renters let the land deteriorate again.

Solar Refinery had stepped up its oil production, but had stopped its discharge into Sugar Creek, I learned, because of growing public pressure. People were beginning to care. But the stream was now populated with carp, red horse, and suckers, and had few smallmouths.

The coarse gravel stream bed and the rocks and pebbles in the riffles, once covered with insect eggs, were now blanketed with moss, and once-abundant crayfish were gone, along with the bass. Much of Sugar Creek was now dry except after a heavy rain. Whenever I went there, my heart would escape to the sparkling cold water of Klacking Creek and fishing — as I told Mom — with Christmas trees all around us.

It was fall 1916, and Emerson was starting at Ohio State University. I took over milking three of his cows, and Dad took the others. I missed my big brother. I didn't mind the extra cows to milk, but I missed his companionship. Our room seemed lonely without him. But two months later he was home again — in a Marine uniform. He had lied about his age to enlist and was leaving in three days for Paris Island. I had gained a year in school and graduated at 17. Most of my schoolmates were 18. I decided to stay on the farm to help Dad. I would be exempt as a farmer, but I didn't look forward to becoming eligible for the draft the coming year.

Mom's two sisters, Emma and Florence, lived in Fort Wayne, Ind. Florence's husband, Uncle Herman Allison, was an executive with the Nickel Plate Railroad and a close friend of the president of Wayne Knitting Mills. Aunt Florence said Emerson had a job waiting at the mills. When he came home from France, he boasted that the day after the Germans heard F. Emerson Griffiths had landed at St. Nazarre, the Kaiser gave up and signed the Armistice. Emerson, would go to Fort Wayne, spend more than 40 years with Wayne Knitting Mills, and retire as general manager of the plant in Humboldt, Tenn.

TROUT OF KLACKING CREEK

Life on the farm wasn't all work and no play. Besides hunting and fishing, all three churches had baseball teams, and we had an excellent diamond complete with a small grandstand at the school in the town of 300 — a mile west of home. Vaughnsville was one of six small towns to have lights, and we played two nights most weeks as well as on Saturday.

We also had a semi-pro baseball team, including some good players who played into their 40s. Sid Collar spent a year as a catcher with the Cleveland Indians, but his strict upbringing was his undoing. He had grown up playing under a strict rule: If you didn't attend Sunday school or have a darned good excuse, you couldn't play baseball during the week. He wouldn't play on Sunday.

Chid Hidebaugh, our farmer-mailman, played for the seniors into his 50s. He could still hit well, but he jogged so slowly that he would barely get to first base on a hit that any man with good legs could have easily stretched into a three-bagger. He also served as first base coach and would use his boat paddle on the rear of anyone who didn't run out even a hopeless hit. Chid also organized our first Boy Scout troop and had many of us living by the Boy Scout Creed.

I played first base or center field and Frank Clevenger, with whom we had gone to Sage Lake, was a pitcher and continued playing after high school on a church team. Dad was a collector at ball games. There was no admission charge, but he would look every spectator squarely in the eye and wait until he contributed. Frank Roberts, our grocer, was a willing contributor and helped encourage other businessmen to give us the money needed for uniforms, baseballs, bats, and other necessities.

Competition was tough among the small towns. I recall one time we played Gomer, three miles away. I ran in toward home plate for a grounder then, rather than stepping into the baseline and touching the runner, I lost a race to first base — and took the snide remarks of the Gomer player.

We had girls' as well as boys' basketball teams but we lacked enough players for football.

Vaughnsville is seven miles north of Lima on the north-south Lima-Defiance Pike, the most-traveled road in the area. It had a crushed stone surface with a dirt side track for farm horses that weren't shod. Over half of the teams weren't shod.

Vaughnsville was centered on the intersection of Ridge Road and the Pike. Ridge Road was built along an east-west glacial ridge. The name has long since disappeared, and the ridge is subtle and barely noticeable. The best farmland is in northwestern Ohio, north of U.S. 40, which follows a major glacial ridge. South of Route 40 is poorer soil — mediocre in comparison with the northwestern Ohio farmland — and when Indiana experimented and planted thousands of tagged sharptail grouse, Hungarian partridges, and ringneck pheasants from Greencastle between Indianapolis and Terre Haute, game men found that birds planted as much as 35 miles south of the Route 40 ridge were never seen or shot south of the ridge six months later. Their theory was that the glacier had removed something necessary from the soil.

Soil types, I learned as we went north to Sage Lake, were severely affected by the glacier, and it took 120 acres of Michigan soil to grow as much as our 80 acres would grow. The glacial ridges, subtle as they were, also affected settlement of the West. Settlers who came by boat to Toledo would follow wagon train trails westward that followed the ridge while the next wave of settlers, who embarked from Pittsburgh, followed the Route 40 ridge 50 miles south that ran through Columbus, Ohio, Indianapolis, Terre Haute, St. Louis, Kansas City, and west into then-Indian territory on the Great Plains, where buffalo roamed to the Rockies.

But as idyllic as life was, we still got into minor trouble. It was smart for boys to smoke in those days. One time when we went to our swimming hole in Sugar Creek with cousins Walter and Dwight Griffiths and neighbors Oliver and Harry Thomas, we took along a sample package of Murad Cigarettes we had confiscated because we reasoned that Dad, who chewed, shouldn't smoke, too. Emerson, the eldest, took one for himself and handed cigarettes among us and, within a half an hour, we were all too sick to go swimming.

Farming apparently was going to be the life for me. I still had a vision of buying a larger farm next to ours when an ad for Fort Wayne Business College in Country Gentleman changed my life. I cut out the advertisement, filled it out, put it out in the mailbox, and watched as Chid Hidebaugh came by with his horse, Bessie. His enclosed mail buggy had a windshield and a door and window on each side until the Post Office made farmers put mailboxes on one side of each road. Bessie stopped without a word from Chid — she knew the mail route better than he did.

A few weeks later Dad and I were sitting on the grass in the front yard while waiting for a call to dinner. It couldn't come soon enough — Dad was beating me at a game of mumbley-peg with his jackknife. I heard a car and looked up as a Pierce Arrow touring car with top up turned into our driveway. A well-dressed man stepped out, straightened his tie, and walked across the yard, his black shoes glimmering in the noonday sun. He asked for me.

"I'm George A. Griffiths," I replied with as much grown up confidence as I could muster. Dad, who had gone over and sat down on the porch, was pretending to read the daily newspaper that had come in the mail, but I knew he was keeping an ear tuned to us, so I was trying to act especially grown-up.

"I represent the Fort Wayne Business College," he said. He went on, describing the school and its program and what an education there would do for me in the business world. He explained it well, but I sensed he was hurrying. I didn't know he was anxious to get to dinner in Lima, 11 miles away, and when he rushed me to sign an application, I resented it.

"My mind's not made up."

Dad interrupted as the man packed his brief case.

"Why don't you have dinner with us and we can discuss it further." The man welcomed the idea of a free farm dinner. He was smiling even more when he finished two servings and a big piece of apple pie. Mom was beaming with pride.

"Mrs. Griffiths, your cooking is outstanding," he said as he rejected a second piece of Mom's pie. "You must forgive me — I'm not used to such wonderful hospitality on the road. I haven't had such good apple pie since my mother died, God rest her soul."

We adjourned to the east porch, which was our sitting porch with two chairs, a swing, and Dad's favorite rocking chair. The man offered Dad a cigar. He surprised me by taking it. He offered the salesman his favorite rocker and sat down beside me on the swing.

"George," Dad said, "two families can't make a good living on this farm. Buying another farm with borrowed money is a gamble. A couple of years of education is always a good investment." The salesman smiled and lighted his cigar. Dad amazed me. The salesman reached for his case for a contract and a few minutes later I was signed up for business college that fall. Mom, who was listening from the screen door, said she would write and see if I could stay with Aunt Florence and Uncle Herman. It wouldn't be as close as the home of the widow lady whom the man said often took in college students, but it might be much cheaper than $10 a week — she could send along some ham, potatoes, and vegetables and I could ride the streetcar.

* * *

It was my first day in the big city. I was looking for somewhere to buy a bowl of soup for lunch when I spotted a sign on a restaurant window. Minutes later I had a job working an hour at lunch and two hours after school for my meals, and I would save almost a dollar a day. One night after I served a well-dressed lady, I found she had left two dimes on the table. I ran after her.

"That's your tip for good service, young man," she said. I had never heard of such things. Meals and tips, too!

I was too busy to do much except study. But I admit that I was lonesome when Dad and Mom came by train and spent Thanksgiving with me at Aunt Florence's. Mom had brought a couple of fat hens, and it reminded me of the farm. I wrote home that I couldn't bear being away from home for Christmas vacation, and Dad and Mom met me at the station in Lima with his pride and joy, a Ford Model-T. For me, I couldn't wait to show off some good test papers.

During my second year, I met Nina Putnam, whose brother was sales manager for the American Fabrics Co.

"We make trimmings of all kinds — laces for curtains, laces to trim lamps and pillow cases, but mainly fine laces for ladies' clothing from the skin to the outer garment," he said.

Proudly, I said, "I'm studying accounting."

"Salesmen make more money than accountants," he said with a grin. "And they have more fun out on the road."

"We're looking for a man to travel the Midwest," he said.

"Does that include Michigan?"

TROUT OF KLACKING CREEK

"Why Michigan?"

"Because I am a trout fisherman," I lied.

"So am I. In fact, I am going up to Traverse City, Michigan, this weekend to do some fishing," he said. "Would you like to go with me so we can discuss our business plans."

A few days later, he had a call to come to the factory at Bridgeport. Before the formal meeting, he told me later, he told company officials that he had a prospect for the Midwest territory.

"There was an odd silence," he said. "Then I learned that a fair-haired son had just been hired for the Midwest. Since you sounded good, they said they had an opening in the Mississippi Valley — Illinois, Iowa, Kentucky and Missouri."

No trout fishing. No Michigan territory. My interest faded fast, but that played into my hand. My lukewarm attitude, instead of hurting me, was making me more valuable.

Putnam said that every town of 6,000 population had one or more dry goods stores that sold floor coverings, and shoes for men, women and children, plus other lines that complemented the household. And that 90 percent of women's dresses were homemade. "That makes the mainstay of every dry goods store 'piece goods' — bolts of all kinds of materials for dresses and other needs," Putnam said. "With all the home sewing, trimmings, bias tapes, ruffles, laces, and elastic are in great demand.

"When I was on the road, I found that this is a neglected business — wholesale houses in Chicago and St. Louis buy American Fabrics laces, but their salesmen travel with large trunks by train and most neglect small items. We are the only people with salesmen calling on these stores."

He boosted his offers for both salary and expense account. I was nearly through school, and I did have a late model 1918 Ford coupe; I would need a job.

"All right," I said, and he offered me his hand. I quit school the next day, a term short of graduation. I was a representative of American Fabrics Co.

*   *   *

On the first day of my new career, I entered a small knick-knack shop for dressmaking and sewing im Momence, Ill., three miles north of Kankakee.

An older woman greeted me.

"I'm Mr. Griffith representing American Fabrics Co. May I show you our latest line of laces and trimmings?"

She smiled as I opened my sample case on the counter.

"Oh, these are just what I've been looking for," Mr. Griffith. "You are the first salesman to call. I've been having to take the train to Chicago for laces."

I will always remember her both for giving me my first order and becoming a valuable — if small — customer for years to come. Later that day I visited the only department store in Kankakee and found the salesgirls were desperately in need of laces — their summer light-colored laces were all gone. They needed both light colors and darker colors for women already thinking of Christmas sewing.

"Our merchandise manager is out of town, but I know the store manager will approve an order," said the woman in charge of the piece-goods department.

For the next three weeks, I worked my way through northern Illinois and into Tri-Cities — Rock Island and Moline, Ill., and Davenport, Ia. Everything was going well — I was averaging about $400 in sales a day.

Then I wrote a big order in a store in Moline — $1,200. It was the biggest order I had written and about 10 times as much as I had expected to write. I celebrated my good luck by taking in a minstrel show that night at the opera house.

But during the next two weeks I sold only a total of $400 in merchandise. It was after Labor Day, and people were changing over to fall clothing. Then I was notified by the company that they didn't ship the big order that had made me look so good. The store was in bankruptcy, but the buyer didn't tell me. He saw me as an opportunity to obtain wanted stock he knew he wouldn't be able to pay for. His credit rating was his undoing.

The next six weeks were rough. Then, despite a small depression dampening the economy, people began to buy for Christmas sewing. Fall set me to thinking of home and hunting.

As I began to develop my territory, I found many of my customers hunted waterfowl in the lower Illinois River marshes, which are part of the Mississippi

TROUT OF KLACKING CREEK

Flyway used by millions of migratory ducks and geese. A few customers, especially in lower Illinois, Kentucky, and Missouri, also had bird dogs. I bought a shotgun — I couldn't resist spending a day in a duck blind or afield in an area with the best waterfowl and upland bird hunting in the country, especially with customers.

But hunting began to limit my visits home to Vaughnsville on Christmas, Easter, and Thanksgiving. While I was doing some bass and bluegill fishing, I was now majoring in bird hunting. I wasn't going to get a sheepskin, but what a way to get an education!

One day a friend and customer in Pekin, Ill., startled me.

"George, two weeks ago I received a shipment of thirty dresses in popular sizes and they sold at nineteen ninety-five," he said. "We had thirty days to sell them or return them. They carried a forty percent discount, but they sold out on Saturday.

"We ordered another shipment by phone on Monday and they, too, sold out in a day. See those two carpenters in the piece goods department? They are making a ready-to-wear department out of half of it. Our piece goods sales are declining."

By September more salesmen were calling on my customers with ready-to-wear dresses. This was in the early '20s. Within a year I found several stores where half of the merchandise I had sold on my previous visit was still on shelves. At the end of two years, my variety store sales were down, too.

I was sitting in my hotel room and doing some serious thinking about driving 35,000 miles a year in my work when the phone rang.

"Hello, George, this is Phil Cantelon. I'm in Chicago waiting for my sales manager, George P. Hall, who has been interviewing prospects to travel Indiana and Michigan.

"I told him to stop looking," Phil said. "Catch the evening train from Peoria to Chicago and meet us at eight. Mr. Hall wants to take the ten-thirty train back to New York, and I've got him primed to hire you."

I met Hall and Cantelon in Phil's room. But I had learned — I was not the overeager, unhappy lace salesman looking for a job. Remembering my previous experience, I asked about future prospects, pretended to be weighing their offer.

"It might be helpful to spend December in your offices in New York," I finally suggested.

"Any other points?" Hall asked. "If not, we can finalize your contract and I will be able to catch my train for New York."

*   *   *

New York's Grand Central Station was crowded a few weeks later as I worked my way up to the counter for a ticket to Lima.

"Track five, car nine, compartment ten of the Twentieth Century Limited — right next to the Parlour Car," said the agent as he nonchalantly handed me my ticket.

I reached into my vest for my pocket watch. I flipped it open as I stepped aboard the legendary passenger train. It was 5:30 p.m. Dec. 24, 1925, and I was the Michigan-Indiana representative for Brown-Durrell Co., distributors of Gordon Hosiery. But it was Christmas Eve. I was anxious for the farm. I suddenly wished I were back home on the farm.

By six p.m., I was in the Parlour Car and an older man with a sophisticated background was helping me find my way through the jungle called big business.

"Three or more times a year I come to New York for two strenuous weeks. But making decisions where timing is important and fast thinking is required drains me.

"Watch," he said, "the world is moving." I looked out of the window and saw the buildings glide by — the 20th Century was on its way with perfect timing, perfect road bed, no bumps. We had gone a block and I hadn't realized we were moving. Our conversation made Christmas. The back page of the menu had an editorial entitled, "Yes, Virginia, there is a Santa Claus."

There was a religious atmosphere to our dinner — jovial but restrained. He led me to describe my life and the new job and complimented me on my love of trout fishing. He was a trout fisherman, he said, and had been active in forming the new Izaak Walton League.

"Always remember that being firm and also humble assures you of success," he told me. "Big men can sense your lack of experience and consider that in your deliberations because they also can remember that they started as you are."

TROUT OF KLACKING CREEK

His parting words would return to me time and again as I learned to choose unfamiliar paths, dodge predators and blaze my own trails through the jungle of business.

*   *   *

TROUT AND SILK STOCKINGS

Ladies' silk stockings lined my pathway to trout.

I was now a hosiery salesman. But most important to me, Michigan — with its thousands of miles of trout streams beckoning to come and fish — was now a part of my territory.

Look out, Klacking Creek, here I come!

But to get there, I would first have to face dreaded "plate glass," a term salesmen used to describe large department stores, and sell of lot of stockings. Both would be new experiences for me.

The greatest volume in the "rag business" or "glad rags," as the clothing business is sometimes called, was in the cities. With laces and trimmings, most of my accounts had been small-town stores that sold materials to local women and farmers' wives who sewed clothing for their families. I was apprehensive. The sign said "Welcome to Traverse City."

A bitter wind off the West arm of Grand Traverse Bay chilled my arrival at the old Park Place Hotel overlooking the bay. Heavy snow began blanketing my four-door Chrysler, barely melting on the hood after my trip from Manistee, and the dark brown car was soon transformed into white. It was cold.

I asked the desk clerk for directions to J.W. Milliken and Co. When he said the store was two blocks west, I decided to walk — and regretted my decision almost immediately. The wind cut through my heavy, dark blue Montanac overcoat and I buried my neck in the black velvet collar. I battled swirling updrafts with clenched fists for my black derby hat.

It was the first time I had ever felt cold while wearing the Montanac over my three-piece navy pin-stripe suit. A warm overcoat was a must in the Midwest and Brown-Durrell encouraged their salesmen to wear one of the best, a $125 Montanac, which stood out in a crowd like a Brooks Bros. exclusive. The fabric resembled modern ultra-suede. I also wore medium gray spats over my black wing-tip shoes and topped my costume with the "badge" of the day, the black derby that deserved — and got — respect.

In the plate glass front window, my face reflected almost as red as a traffic light. I opened the door of a vertical plank storm porch and the wind slammed it behind me. I mustered a bit more dignity for my walk through the six-panel plate glass revolving door. A Brown-Durrell salesman was expected to act in a very dignified manner, not like the farm boy that the storm door chattering in the wind behind me reminded me I still was.

A trim lady, who appeared to be in her mid-to-late thirties, met me at the hosiery counter. She wore a navy blue, ankle-length dress with a white lace-edged collar. Her dark brown hair was in a severe bun on the back of her head and was softened only by back-combed puffs over her ears. A gold locket watch on a chain gleamed as her badge of authority.

"I'm Florence Graser, the hosiery buyer. May I help you?" She had a warm, friendly smile that reassured me. Some of the buyers whom I had met on this first sales trip into Michigan plate glass had been somewhat intimidating.

"I'm George A. Griffith of Brown-Durrell Company," I said with all the confidence I could muster. "You are the lady I came to meet."

I had learned James T. Milliken was about to graduate from Harvard in 1912 when his father, J.W. Milliken, who had founded the store at about the turn of the century, died, leaving his son a business he would find himself running for the next quarter-century.

But I didn't realize that Jim Milliken was about to begin my education in merchandising. Or that, while neither a hunter nor a fisherman, he would surprise me with his knowledge of Michigan's fish and game and set me on the trail to becoming a trout fisherman, a ruffed grouse hunter, and a conservationist.

A sharp-looking, partly balding man in his forties walked past us wearing a three-piece blue-black suit and gleaming black wing-tip shoes. Mrs. Graser turned and called after him, "Mr. Milliken." He turned and subconsciously straightened his blue and gray tie and the fob that dangled from the gold watch chain that crossed his vest from pocket to pocket.

"Mr. Griffith, I would like you to meet Mr. Milliken, the boss," she said.

"Mr. Griffith represents Brown-Durrell Co. of New York City." (I had dropped the Welsh "s" from my name to make it easier for customers to pronounce my name.)

Mr. Milliken looked me in the eye, smiled, and extended his hand. His grip was firm and friendly. As he excused himself, he invited me to stop by his office before I left. That handshake was the beginning of a long friendship and a turning point in my business and recreational life.

I looked away from the hosiery department counter, which stood at the front of the store. I could barely see across the street through the plate-glass windows.

"The bay is churning up a blizzard," said Mrs. Graser, noting my concern. "I hope you're not going to go south tonight. The roads will be drifted until the plows get out."

"No, I have a room at the Park Place," I said. "I am from Indiana. This is the most snow I have ever seen."

Someone who had just come into the store said the temperature had dropped to four degrees below zero! That was also the coldest weather I had ever known.

"My two daughters will be home from school by now," Mrs. Graser said. "Since you plan to be in town, would you mind if we finished writing our order Saturday morning? We won't be busy."

"Of course. Will nine o'clock be all right?" I was thankful I had made plans to spend the weekend. I wasn't prepared to drive in weather like this. I headed toward Milliken's glassed-in office that shared the rear balcony with a small tea room and a kitchen beyond a swinging door. I saw Mr. Milliken motion to his secretary, whose desk was nestled next to the wooden railing.

He pointed me to a maroon leather-upholstered chair and closed the door; then, sensing that I was new and that his desk must be an imposing symbol of authority, he sat beside me. When I faltered, he pressed for details — drawing out facts about my company's line and graciously accepting my apologies when I lacked all of the answers.

The lights began going out in the store below us. It was nearly six p.m. and dark outside. We had been talking for more than an hour, longer than any store manager had ever spent with me. I felt a twinge of guilt as I started to put on my coat. I had come to provide information and I had gotten more in return.

Mr. Milliken removed a gold pocket watch from a left vest pocket and snapped the carved cover in a smooth movement with his right thumb. He subconsciously tucked the thumb of his left hand into the empty pocket as he studied the watch in his palm.

"George, it's dinner time. Unless you have other plans, would you be my guest for dinner at my home? Mrs. Milliken is away, so we can continue our conversation."

He introduced his young sons, John and Bill, who were politely outgoing. He did most of the talking, describing how he had become a merchant and his vision of opportunities for Traverse City in the future.

I learned he was a three-time mayor and of his efforts to get quality zoning for the city and to carry it out. He deserves much of the credit for making Traverse City glow in the eyes of people who appreciate quality. For a half-century or more, many influential families have passed large holdings in the area on to children.

Milliken was to go on and spend several years in the state Senate. I'm sure he could have become governor if he had been willing to sacrifice some of his principles. Despite representing the smallest city in the group, he also was a leader in the Michigan Retail Dry Goods Association that linked his store and others in Grand Rapids, Muskegon, Port Huron, Flint, Saginaw, Pontiac, Ann Arbor, and Lansing in a joint purchasing program.

"Are you a trout fisherman?" I asked Mr. Milliken. He smiled and shook his head.

"No, I'm not, but tomorrow I will introduce you to a trout fisherman who is a very active conservationist."

I tried to steer the conversation back to trout, but he avoided it, saying, "Tomorrow you will be able to talk trout until you are tired of the word."

Me? Never!

Billy, a nice boy of four, excused himself from the table after contributing his own tale of once catching a trout. How could I have dreamed that this youngster would grow up to hold the governor's office longer than any other Michigan governor — a nice guy liked not only by fellow Republicans but Democrats as well. Being too considerate was his only weakness as a politician. Yet, during the environmental decade of the 1970s, Gov. William G. Milliken would propose, support, and sign into law most of the state's environmental bills, including the Environmental Protection and the Inland Lakes and Streams acts.

During the coming years I would learn to appreciate the informal lessons Jim Milliken would teach me as a friend, including many of his own methods of which he was justly proud. During the next 25 years, I would spend at least 10 evenings a year with him as he pounded into my head what I needed to know about business. Despite his knowledge, he was always willing to concede a point and accept criticism. He was a natural-born teacher.

Brown-Durrell was one of the top organizations represented out of New York. My bosses knew the value of quality salesmen and were ready to help them set up local advertising programs for accounts and even to pay half the costs of ads. That would help me open many plate-glass doors.

My philosophy of selling changed drastically after I met Milliken. I realized that I was working with one of the most profitable departments in most stores and that "Gordon Hosiery for Ladies and Children" was a top line. In addition to a large investment, my line required a well-trained and experienced hosiery buyer or an honest and experienced hosiery salesman. Or both.

Jim exchanged sales figures with other stores and spurred an interest in his merchandising methods. Since hosiery accounted for 90 percent of my merchandise, his contacts opened the door for me with other new accounts, and it bettered my position with those already carrying my line. I had taken the giant step from laces and trimmings and small specialty stores to ladies' silk stockings and plate glass. Now Jim was helping me overcome my earlier apprehension.

After five years with Jim Milliken as my mentor, I would come to feel that I had earned an informal "doctorate degree" in innovative merchandising and that I had acquired knowledge I could never have obtained elsewhere. Jim was always full of sound business ideas.

For the moment, however, I could hardly wait until Saturday when I would meet his trout fisherman friend who was also a leading conservationist. But I wasn't sure I knew what the word "conservation" meant.

*   *   *

I peered through the hard-driving snow ricocheting off my hotel window

TROUT AND SILK STOCKINGS

Saturday morning. I couldn't see the long peninsula that bisects Grand Traverse Bay. I could barely see my dark brown sedan except when the wind swirled away some of the powdery white blanket. I didn't have a broom, so I decided to brave the bitter wind once again to walk to my appointment with Mrs. Grazer.

"Do you have a Mackinaw?" Milliken asked when he saw that Mrs. Graser and I had finished writing the order. I didn't know what he meant.

"Come this way," he said, as he led me through an archway that separated Milliken's from Hamilton's Clothing Store, and supervised as I tried on a heavy woolen red-and-black deer hunter's coat, similar pants and a heavy gray stocking cap.

Milliken smiled as I looked into a three-way, full-length mirror at my new image as a rugged outdoorsman. He gave his approval to my overshoes and went back to his office and put on a similar outfit.

I followed Jim to the back employee entrance. Through the plate glass of the upper part of the door I could see that the wind had calmed. The peninsula was now visible across the ice of the bay. His car's electric starter whirred and the engine coughed. He pulled the choke and this time it started despite the cold.

"The Boardman River," said Jim, answering the question in my mind as we crossed a bridge and a finger of dark moving water curled out from under the road into the bay. I noticed some big swans swimming about in the open water and waddling about on the ice, apparently picking up pieces of bread.

"There's something I'd like to show you," said Jim, as he drove to the East arm of the bay, and we walked toward a large camping area along M-72 that would become Traverse City State Park.

"What are those tents out on the ice?" I asked. The Bay was dotted with small, drab-gray tents.

"They're either ice fishermen or skiers," he replied, and he began to tell me about Harold "Opie" Titus.

"He was a sickly child," said Jim. "The doctors recommended that he spend as much time as possible outdoors. That meant northern Michigan outdoors.

"Opie is Michigan's foremost conservationist," Milliken said. He went on to explain that Michigan was the first state to have a Conservation Department overseeing fisheries, game, forests, and lands as well as having "game wardens," as conservation officers have always been known.

"The Conservation Department is overseen by a commission of seven laymen, each of whom has a sincere interest in our natural resources," Milliken said. "Commissioners are appointed by the governor for six-year terms — with no more than four members from one party to keep it non-political. That commission serves as the eyes and ears of the public on natural resources and develops policies to manage them."

Opie Titus was a member of the first Conservation Commission. (He served for more than 20 years until his health forced him to retire.) That aroused my interest, although I had no idea I would become known as a conservationist or that I would serve on that commission.

Jim guided his 1926 Oakland, a predecessor to Pontiac, along a gravel road that snaked around the west shore of the East Arm on Old Mission Peninsula, 22 miles of orchards that separate West Bay from East Bay. He nosed the car into a snow bank at the base of a high hill topped by a house overlooking East Bay.

Beth Titus welcomed us as though we were prodigal sons returning home. My eyes quickly circled the room and I suddenly yearned for Titus's way of living — a few mounted fish, a deer head, a couple of hides, two guns in a rack and many outdoor action photos, most, I learned, by his good friend, Walt Hastings, Michigan's first Conservation Department photographer.

As Opie took my hand, he looked at Jim and said, "I see what you mean." I didn't know that Jim had gotten Opie out of bed the night before to tell him that he had dined with a young man who was interested in trout fishing.

"What's new?" I learned Titus had asked.

"He represents one of the important firms I deal with and he's more than just interested in conservation," Milliken said.

I waited anxiously. This was the most exciting moment of my entire trip, and perhaps in my life!

"He wants to go trout fishing," Milliken told Titus.

Opie's face broke into an ear-to-ear grin. "Hell, I do, too, but the season is closed and won't be open until May 1st."

TROUT AND SILK STOCKINGS

We shared a hearty laugh and Titus mentioned some streams, including an upper stretch of the Boardman River, which runs through downtown; Acme Creek east of the city, and Silver and Cedar creeks, two small tributaries to Lake Leelanau.

"That's a prize smallmouth bass lake," he said.

As we left, Opie suggested I get acquainted with Mart Winnie, sports department manager at Hamilton's, before I left.

My schedule called for me to cross the Straits of Mackinac Monday aboard the railroad car ferry and go to Sault Ste. Marie on the northern shore of the Upper Peninsula.

On Sunday, Jim and I had a long walk and talk out on Old Mission Point. The wind had calmed even more and it didn't seem quite as cold despite the several feet of Lake Michigan ice piled up like miniature glaciers around the point. Somehow I had to meet Mart Winnie before leaving town, I thought.

"Who is your account in Petoskey?" Jim asked.

"I don't have one," I answered.

"It is a slow town in winter but a busy one in summer," he said. "Why don't you stop in Petoskey before you head for Mackinaw City?" He knew the schedule of the ferry, which long plied the Straits between Mackinaw City on the south shore and St. Ignace, five miles away on the north shore.

"Stores don't open until noon on Monday in Petoskey," he said as though he had been reading my mind. I could meet Mart Winnie Monday morning then drive around the East Arm of the bay and head north to Petoskey, the Straits, and the Soo.

I checked out of my hotel early Monday and was waiting as Mart Winnie arrived for work. He was like an old friend. Although the season was months away, Winnie said he would prepare a fishing outfit for me — a two-piece, eight-foot Granger bamboo fly rod with a Perrine automatic reel, a Halford silk line, a round aluminum leader-and-tippet box with a felt sponge plus all the other items I should have. My accessories included a steamed wood-frame landing net, various flies and spinners, and an all-important fishing vest.

"You must keep cat-gut leaders and tippets moist or they will become stiff," he explained. "And you should stretch your fly line between two trees every couple of hours and grease it with line dressing so it will keep floating."

He promised to have my trout-fishing gear ready when I returned in March. As I left, he called after me, "Subscribe to *Hunting and Fishing* and *Field & Stream* magazines. They'll help get you informed."

I made my way eastward, crossed Acme Creek, which I would come to know intimately, and headed northward along the east shore of East Bay and along Lake Michigan. Beyond the ice was open water as far as I could see! Could all that water possibly be filled with trout? Michigan was truly a water wonderland. Petoskey seemed to glisten like a jewel but it was, as Milliken said, a city far too large for its winter population. I made one call at the best-looking dry goods store, walked out an hour later with an order, and continued toward the Straits of Mackinac, the link between lakes Michigan and Huron.

Mackinaw City was a city in name only — a village that grew outside the sharp vertical logs guarding ancient Fort Michilimackinac, which — like Fort Mackinac on Mackinac Island — had seen Indian, French, English, and American flags. The fort, to be restored over the next seven decades, had been the scene of a vicious Indian attack that left virtually every Englishman dead. Braves who had been peaceably playing ball outside the gates suddenly took up the weapons squaws had concealed under their robes and captured the fort.

My car was number 11 in the line in a well-plowed parking lot that wrapped around the dock. I marveled at snow piled four to five feet high. I had never seen so much snow! And, for only $1.75, I was about to get a five-mile, 45-minute ride to the Upper Peninsula aboard the largest ship I had ever seen.

The ferry could carry about 30 loaded freight cars on parallel tracks in the middle of the deck plus 18 automobiles parked on each side. The railroad cars carried supplies from Detroit through Saginaw, West Branch, Roscommon, Grayling, and Gaylord. They would return loaded with cedar fence posts, I was told.

The crew had to distribute the automobiles to help balance the load of rail cars. After they had the freight cars balanced, they waved motorists to drive on board. During deer season, I learned, the lure of Upper Peninsula bucks would trigger five-mile backups of hunters' cars. But there was no crowd as I parked alongside the tracks on the legendary ferry.

I climbed a stairway to the heated cabin that overlooked the deck and felt as though I were inside a wood-paneled railroad station. Mackinac Island's Grand Hotel, the largest resort hotel in the world with its 400-foot-long porch, seemed to beckon to me. I watched the island for 15 or 20 minutes as the ferry passed it and I silently vowed to go there someday. Miniature icebergs of three-foot-thick chunks of ice bobbed in the 75- to 100-foot open channel in the wake of the ferry-icebreaker.

I was last to be waved to disembark on the north shore. I drove through the sleepy little village of St. Ignace without stopping and I saw only three people in two miles! I headed north between high banks of snow lining two-lane U.S. 27, which would eventually be replaced by the four-lane I-75 expressway. Here and there the top of a barn-red snow fence peeked through powdery snow.

The Upper Peninsula appeared to be an enchanted land of woods blanketed by deep snow I was sure concealed many trout streams. Occasionally, I would cross an open, flowing stream. I wondered how trout lived under the ice. A sign on my left pointed to Lover's Leap, a rock several hundred feet high from which two young Indian sweethearts plunged to their deaths because the tribe was going to separate them.

Sault Ste. Marie, affectionately known by Michiganians as The Soo, overlooks St. Mary's River and is the site of the famed Soo Locks through which ships from around the world carry freight to and from Lake Superior ports. Canada has one lock on the northern side of the rapids historically known as the Falls of St. Mary. Decades ago, Indians fished along the rapids for trout as Voyageurs portaged 40-foot freight canoes en route to International Falls, Minnesota, to exchange goods for Western trappers' furs, especially beaver hides for hats, in great demand in Europe. I checked into the Ojibway Hotel, named after the local Indian tribe. From my window I could see the lights of Sault Ste. Marie, Ontario. The river, which divides the United States and Canada, drains the cold water of Lake Superior southeastward into northern Lake Huron and, through lakes Erie and Ontario and connecting waters, into the northern Atlantic Ocean.

After dinner I took a long walk and located the store of M. Yalomstein, my account. We never sold to more than one outlet in any town. Four blocks from the hotel I found a ferry that crossed the St. Mary's to Ontario. The river was frozen over except for the ferry channel and people were walking across on the ice. In the distance I could see a small boat.

My fingers tingled despite my wool gloves as I hurriedly walked to Yalomstein's store the next morning. Bells were ringing. They became louder and louder. Suddenly three horses galloped past, pulling the first fire engine I had ever seen mounted on a sled. I heard someone say the temperature the day before had been 30 below zero but warmer weather was forecast for today — only 20 below!

Yalomstein's was a fairly large, high quality clothing and general store that had bought small quantities of stockings from my company. The hosiery manager was impressed with our new lines and even more when I told her I would be visiting four or five times a year. She called Mo Yalomstein.

"Mr. Yalomstein, we'd like to drop most of our lines and carry Gordon," she told the owner-manager. "Mr. Griffith has shown us how we can order small quantities from Brown-Durrell weekly and he has offered to set up an advertising program and pay half of the costs." Mr. Yalomstein seemed impressed, too, as he looked over my presentation.

I reached for my watch and snapped it open. It was obvious I wasn't going to finish in time to make the 3:30 p.m. ferry back across the Straits. I decided I would stay until Tuesday and catch the ferry the next morning.

On this first trip I had learned that no Brown-Durrell salesman had ever driven through the territory. A salesman would go by train to Lansing, Saginaw, and Muskegon, then would set up in the Pantlind Hotel in Grand Rapids and wait for buyers from stores in Alpena, Manistee, Cadillac and elsewhere, who were given a day to come and order.

"I'm sorry I can't spend more time with you," Mr. Yalomstein apologized, "but this has been a busy day."

"I heard that you are a trout fisherman," I said. I also was learning an old saying was true: If you meet an expert on a subject and want his good will, let him do the talking and ask questions only when the conversation lags.

"Are you staying overnight?" he asked. I seemed to have struck a chord of common interest.

"I have a room at the Ojibway."

"Good. I'll pick you up at three-thirty and take you over to Canada."

* * *

We walked across the ice, paid 20 cents each for a rowboat ride across about 20 yards of open water, and walked three blocks to the main street. Yalomstein turned into a bar. It had a distinctly French atmosphere with two drinking rooms, one for men and women, and another for men only. While not crowded, it was busy — the United States was in the throes of Prohibition.

"What will you have?" he asked. "What's your favorite?"

"Molson's Ale."

After a leisurely bottle of ale, my first in many years thanks to Prohibition, we walked through the three-block-long business district and stopped at a men's shop. Fee Devine had one of the finest men's clothing stores I had ever visited, and he offered England's best outdoor woolens. His clientele included many Michigan trout fishermen, he told me.

I strained my meager budget and started my outdoor wardrobe of woolens that day. Since I had purchased over $100, he suggested that a boy who worked for him but lived on the Michigan side could deliver my purchases to my hotel and save me 20 percent in customs charges. He was going to transform me into a well-dressed outdoorsman and save me over $20 more.

"Fee, I believe I owe you a bottle of Molson's Dark," said Yalomstein. "I want to settle the debt." I was beginning to love the far north. Over a tasty glass of dark ale, I pressed Devine for information about fishing camps on Canadian trout lakes.

"The resort owners will notify me when the ice goes out and I will send out a mailing to old and new customers," Fee said, "I'll put you on the mailing list." Mart Winnie and Ebb Warren, who also worked for Hamilton's Clothing store, were on the list, he said, but Warren was more interested in big game hunting than fishing.

"There is plenty of both," said Devine.

On my way south on Tuesday, I established contacts in Alpena and Cheboygan, which Milliken told me most salesmen ignored, and continued south to Bay City and Saginaw and back to Fort Wayne. But my thoughts were on trout fishing back in Traverse City.

When I made my trip in May, Winnie had a trout-fishing outfit ready for me and, true to his word, took me fishing. We went to the Boardman just downstream from Brown Bridge Dam west of Mayfield where he showed me how to cast small Colorado spinners with my fly rod. Winnie said he also fished two wet flies, one a dropper, tied together on the same tippet and told of earlier fishermen who had fished three flies.

Winnie almost had to drag me away — the hook was set in me. I began to plan sales trips so I could steal a day away from work to fish for trout. But the little spinners seemed very hard on small trout. I was anxious to try small squirrel-tail streamers.

During that May visit to Traverse City in 1926, Winnie also sold me my first pair of waders. Made by Hodgeman, they had rubber boots and waterproofed-canvas legs which snagged so easily that each pair was sold with a repair kit.

The Brown Bridge Dam area is recognized by a Michigan Outdoor Writers Association Outdoor Heritage Memorial as the birthplace of the famous Adams fly. As I heard the story, Mayfield fly-tier Len Holiday ran into Lorraine, Ohio, lawyer Lon Adams near Mayfield bridge. Adams asked Holiday what he was using and the veteran angler gave him the legendary fly with brown and grizzly hackle, grizzly wings, a gray wool body and three wisps of pheasant tail.

"What do you call it?" asked Adams, who would become a member of the first Trout Unlimited board of directors.

Holiday studied the fly, little realizing that it would become known around the world, grinned at the other angler and said, "Let's call it the Adams."

*   *   *

Milliken was to hit me with at least one new idea on each of my visits that were to become standard for the next 25 years. One was paying for his winter purchases after he sold the goods. In winter, cash was short in the resort area. Instead of paying by February 10 for January shipments, Brown-Durrell would carry him an extra 30 to 60 days. We didn't lose any money and the extra month only cost him a one percent discount at a time when his cash flow was very low.

"George, most salespeople sell many things about which they were never briefed and are unable to discuss the advantages of their merchandise over the competition," observed Milliken.

That led him to a compliment on the way I described my lines to his salespeople and set up his advertising program instead of just filling his shelves with items his staff had never seen. This was my greatest advantage over my competition.

"I got the idea of selling your salespeople on my products from you," I reminded Jim.

But I knew what he meant. Many stores sold goods purchased for them by a New York sales office which, while serving a good purpose, failed to give their salespeople any information about the products they were expected to sell.

As I headed home, I mused: Allah is good. I had a home base in Fort Wayne with Emerson for weekends. I was building friendships, and I was a member of the Orchard Ridge Country Club. I even had a social life.

Each July and December, I had to spend three weeks at the home office in New York City, where salesmen would see new styles and qualities and watch a style show or two promoting new merchandise and enjoy a generous expense account!

These were successful years for Brown-Durrell and its 100-person "family" — 40 stocking salesmen, 31 underwear salesmen, and sales and credit management. My sales were above average in my categories so I was much my own boss. I could be at home by Thursday night, if I chose, during slow periods — eight months of the year —and I only needed to make a real selling effort for four months.

It was late February and I was now a regular at Milliken's. Mrs. Graser met me to talk of problems she was having with the colors in different lines of stockings. She laid four heavy stockings out beside four lightweight sheers bearing the same color names.

"The colors don't match," she said.

"This is something we can't control," I explained. "The lines are made and dyed at different mills." While it disturbed color-conscious buyers, telling the truth elicited sympathy.

I was anxious to see Mart Winnie. A letter from him said rabbit hunting was good and that he had a good rabbit dog. I had brought my shotgun and hunting clothes.

Jim Milliken was now a Senator and in session in Lansing, where he would serve many years, and Opie Titus was on a hunting trip in Arizona. So I had two days to spend with Winnie and his beagle. He had a mellow voice on trail and he brought us some excellent shots on snowshoe hares. But my mind was more on the trout streams we occasionally crossed as we hunted. I could write poetry about them — even 70 years later!

Easter was in late April one year. Since trout season opens in late April, I would be visiting Milliken's to fill in stocks after Easter sales and for a changeover to lighter colors.

Mart was working, so I fished Friday afternoon on Acme Creek at M-72, near what is now Grand Traverse Resort. I saw no one and I hooked only three undersized fish. I decided to try Cedar and Silver creeks west of Lake Leelanau, but they seemed almost too small for fly-fishing.

When I returned to Acme, Mart was with me. I was fishing a small squirrel-tail streamer. He looked over my tackle, retied my leader, changed my fly, and stood on the bank while I cast. "You cast too often," he said. "Cast upstream and across the creek and let your fly drift downstream until it straightens out below you." He watched as I cast toward the bank. Once my streamer landed within two inches of the bank and I saw a trout following it.

"Try presenting your fly close to shore," he teased.

Mart returned within an hour with two trout, both over 10 inches. Suddenly I had a terrific strike. My line became entangled around my rod.

"Untangle your line carefully," he yelled. Carefully? I was nervous, but I did try to keep the line from getting too much pressure and it untangled itself.

TROUT AND SILK STOCKINGS

"Keep your rod straight up in the air and back slowly to shore where it's shallow," said Mart. He slid his net under the brookie. It measured 13 1/4 inches. How he got me off the stream that day, I'll never know.

* * *

I headed for The Soo in the morning. Yalomstein's salesgirls were excited. Their stocks were low and they wanted to re-order. From their $2,000 order — $3,350 at retail — they had sold over half. We were studying the figures and writing an order when Yalomstein walked in.

He looked at me, grinned and asked, "Been trout fishing?" I had to tell him about my 13 1/4-inch trout.

The girls waited patiently, smiling politely.

"Do these stockings of his sell?" he asked them. He was pleased with their enthusiasm but startled by the figures. "Are you sure? Let me see those figures." He went to his office and called for hosiery sales record sheets.

"Have a chair," he told me. "Do we have a large enough stock base? I want to say yes, but we have gone through Easter when stocks sell well. We also have Mother's Day coming up and this is a tourist town in summer.

"We also have a good business with the Canadians. Their stockings are too heavy and in poor colors. Let's add another $500 to our inventory — wherever you think it should go."

Yalomstein said he would like to take me trout fishing, but his club wasn't active before June 1. He might get someone to take me out in St. Mary's River for steelhead, but the rapids were dangerous. For once I was glad to be talked out of perhaps the trout trip of my life — if I lived.

Two weeks later, I was writing an order in Bill Gabriels' small ready-to-wear store in Owosso. He had long carried my line of stockings.

"A friend just returned from the U.P.," he said. "He had very good trout fishing on the Fox River, ninety miles from the ferry."

I looked at my watch.

"It's after one p.m. Do you think we can get Dixie and make the nine p.m. ferry?" Dixie Knowles was the advertising manager of the *Owosso Argus-Press* and his regular fishing companion.

"I'll call Dixie." An hour later we were on our way. It was Thursday and I was due in Lansing on Monday.

We stopped to eat. As we neared the ferry, Bill said we had only seven minutes. We pulled up to the loading dock at exactly nine p.m. as the ship's huge propellers began churning. The ferry slowly pulled away. The crew ignored my car horn and our yells.

We slept in the car at the dock. We ate breakfast at 6:15 and were on the seven a.m. ferry, ready to roll when we hit shore. We were fishing on the Fox River by 10 a.m. Bill and Dixie landed several but I had to settle for a nine-inch prize fish, one eight inches and a few smaller ones.

We were all amateurs mixing comments on business with talk about Colorado spinners, flies, and streams. We were having fun. Unlike the sandy soil of the northern Lower Peninsula, the eastern U.P. has a heavy clay soil that gives way to a rocky surface going westward. Since rock is a conductor of heat, many U.P. streams may have good steelhead spawning runs during spring runoff, but only ankle-deep warm water and a few small trout after mid-June.

On Monday, Howard Grimes, general manager of Lansing's J.W. Knapp Company, was envious as I related my weekend of fishing on the Fox. He led me to the hosiery department where eight girls were waiting to say hello.

"I've been waiting since Thursday for this fellow," said Grimes. "Give him the rough time he deserves for keeping us waiting."

I might take a ribbing now and then, but trout fishing was paying off — opening doors to business and building friendships on the streams — and often doing both at the same time.

I put my heart in my work for the next 10 days. Then came post-Mothers Day and post-Graduation Day lulls and 10 days to revamp my energy. There was only one way — I had to go trout fishing.

Mart Winnie was anxious to see me when I arrived in Traverse City.

"The ice has just gone out of the bay and the lake trout are in the shallows," he said. "They'll be leaving for colder, deeper water any day now. Bring a jacket. It will be chilly in the morning, but we have all the tackle. Be at my house at six-thirty."

TROUT AND SILK STOCKINGS

For pounds of fish, this had to be the greatest of my fishing experiences. The lake trout were moving around, a sign they were getting ready to go to deep water. Art Winnie, Mart's brother, who had a limited commercial license and could sell lake trout, made the tackle decisions.

Art handed me a casting rod armed with a spoon. We tried various spoons as we cast from his boat into six inches of water near shore and reeled outward. Art handled the boat and landing net. By noon we were all exhausted. Four hours of hard work had produced 18 trout from five to 30 pounds each — more than 200 pounds on the scale. No-kill regulations definitely weren't in effect that day.

In the afternoon, Mart and I headed for the Boardman River where we found trout feeding on a hatch at four p.m. Anyone watching me would have thought that the proper method was to see a trout rise then land your artificial on his head. I was fishing a small streamer — I didn't own a dry fly yet or know that Art was one of Michigan's best-known fly-tiers and creator of Winnie's Hopper. Both Art and Bert Winnie, another brother, had barber shops.

Mart spied on me.

"George, you must float your fly over the trout, not two or three feet below him. He is looking upstream." Then, as a trout fed, he waited a few seconds, dropped his wet fly on the water three feet or more above where the trout had taken an insect and set the hook as a nice fish took the fly. Mart's lesson made sense. I tried it and caught two legal fish after the hatch was over.

"Let's go, or do you want to fish all night?" he shouted.

He yelled again and a third time. I waded ashore with regret. I was sure if I had made just one more cast I could have hooked a trophy.

*   *   *

I went home to the farm from Fort Wayne for three days in September to help Dad finish husking corn. I was surprised my "citified" hands hadn't grown too soft for farm work. They held up well.

But what I had accepted as normal work as a boy seemed — after several years of city life — sheer drudgery. My parents were older and without anyone to help.

Dad's day still began at five a.m. with building a fire in the kitchen range before he went to the barn to feed, water, and milk five or six cows, and curry and harness the team of horses for the day's work. He had given up his driving horse for an automobile, but he still worked the remaining 80 acres with the one remaining team of Belgians.

In his spare time, he had wood to split and carry for the kitchen stove and coal to carry for the pot-bellied heating stove that had replaced the wood-burning stove in the living room.

Mom's day still began at 5:15 a.m. when she prepared breakfast. There still were eggs to be collected and packed in 30-dozen egg cases for the egg man. Chickens had to be fed and watched over, especially when it rained. Hatchery chicks would squat with their heads turned upward, and mouths open, and drown.

Mom and Dad kept a few hogs for their own use, but life had slowed from the days when she raised 500 chickens. Harry Thomas' order on Friday for "40 of your best" for a Saturday special at his fancy grocery store in Lima would mean coming home and working until 10 p.m. dressing birds and then getting up early to deliver them by eight a.m. She had even stopped making her own laundry soap from ashes, lye, and pork cracklings as she had learned from Grandma.

In the fall of 1928, they held a sale and disposed of all the machinery and stock except a small flock of chickens and a few hogs. Orville Benroth, a nephew, rented the fields. After a lifetime of hard farm work, Dad died two years later at 69, the only brother not to reach the age of 80.

One Sunday morning during one of my visits home, I took my fly rod on a sentimental trek to Sugar Creek. I found a ravaged skeleton of my old friend — 60 percent of the stream was stagnant and the only current was below the riffles. I cast a small streamer across the riffles and caught two seven-inch rock bass. A stone quarry I fished as a boy was nearly dry, and two aged farm machines and rusty tin cans and garbage were lying in the shallow water. I turned away, tried to swallow a lump in my throat and counted my blessings.

* * *

I was enjoying life in Fort Wayne and living on a higher scale and budget. I had fished more, yet my sales had nosed ahead of last year. Small-towns were booming. Everyone seemed happy.

TROUT AND SILK STOCKINGS

But I was concerned about the gloom that seemed to hang over big-city buyers. They were writing smaller orders and talking about shrinking inventories.

Just before Christmas?

This was 1929. This has been one of my best years, I mused.

"Next year should be even better."

* * *

THE GREAT DEPRESSION

New York Stock Exchange Prices Plunge said a boxcar-type headline across the front page of the early afternoon *Flint Journal.*

So what? I didn't own stocks. It was just another scare headline to sell newspapers.

I left the newspaper on the hotel dining room table in Flint and walked the few blocks to my appointment at Smith-Bridgman Department Store. A solemn secretary ushered me into the merchandise manager's office.

I found the usually confident executive as wide-eyed as a cornered animal. His hands were shaking as he shuffled a handful of papers into his desk basket. He quickly explained that he was a trader in the stock market rather than an investor in for the long term.

"I made a substantial investment on a hot tip," he confided. "If the market keeps going down, it's going to break me." Thoughts about his personal investments seemed to make him hesitant about writing an order. He finally settled on about one-half the amount he would normally order.

"I suppose women — or their husbands — will somehow buy stockings for Christmas." he said, trying to muster a feeble, twitching smile. "Women have got to have stockings to wear."

Only my largest outlets seemed to be suffering great losses. That would hurt, but my year's work was nearly over and by November I would be hunting quail back in Indiana and giving the stock market — and my accounts — time to recover. It couldn't last very long. Women who bought their stockings from my outlets would be decimating the stores' inventories by Christmas.

But the economy declined even further.

A telegram from George Hall, the sales manager for Brown-Durrell who had hired me, asked me to meet him that weekend in Chicago. Oh, well, I had nothing planned.

When I arrived at his hotel on Saturday, I was surprised to learn Hall had called in all of our Midwest salesmen. But I wasn't worried. I had a good sales increase for the year, despite the sudden pre-Christmas drop, and I was sure that my sales would again top off the company's annual sales chart.

But Hall's expression reminded me of an undertaker directing a funeral for which he doesn't expect to get paid.

"George, this is the saddest trip I have ever made."

"I'm sorry to hear that. What's happened?" I asked, wondering if he had some personal or family problems.

"George, we are in for a serious depression. Many firms are not going to survive."

He leaned over the hotel suite desk and rested his head on his hands as if he were going to share something confidential. "As you know, George, we have our largest inventories in October, November, and December to serve the Christmas season. We owe millions for those stockings. They are going to be worth about half what we paid for them by January."

"We are reducing our sales force regardless of ability. First to be released are all those unmarried, or married but without children."

"I've got no children and no quick way of acquiring any," I quipped. But my attempt at humor went unnoticed. He was serious.

"We will be continuing your contracts up to Feb. 1," he went on. "I am making an exception for you. We will offer you the big stores in New York City until something else opens up."

I knew something about that rat-race — it would mean taking orders every week from buyers I would seldom, if ever, see. I would never have an opportunity to show off and sell an entire line. The offer was no compliment. For Hall, it would be a means of keeping me in the wings until someone else left or retired. For me, there would be little or no opportunity for hunting or trout fishing. But it would be a job.

"How long have I got to decide?"

Hall was gracious. "George, January first is the deadline. I'll have to know by then. I hope you'll take it until I have something better."

It was a generous offer, I would come to realize. But I kept stumbling over my ego. There must be something better for a top-selling hosiery salesman despite the Depression.

Milo Hunter, who had several children and was safe for the present, called from Chicago to say he was driving to New York and suggested that I ride along and look for a job while he and Phil Cantelon were attending Brown-Durrell's winter sales meeting. He would pick me up in Fort Wayne.

I went with them. After all, I had an income from Brown-Durrell until Feb. 1. And I was optimistic, even though I learned the meeting was to be the beginning of a restructuring for the company, which would return to Boston as a regional distributor.

We stopped in Philadelphia and visited some of the several hosiery mills that produced Gordon stockings. Hunter, Cantelon, and I weren't newcomers — Brown-Durrell would take all of the salesmen to Philadelphia each year to mingle with the mill executives. Presidents of two mills told us they hadn't knit one stocking in 60 days and knew of no good mills that had knitted, which would mean all knitting machines would have to be re-adjusted when the mills resumed production.

"Our customers, including Brown-Durrell, tell us they're loaded with merchandise," said one president. "We have thousands of dozen pairs of stockings boxed and nowhere to ship them," said the other.

While we were at Shuykill Valley Hosiery Mill, we were introduced to Gus Waldmann of Philadelphia, who was visiting to see if he could sell packaging materials. In those days, stockings were shipped three pairs to a box and each pair was individually wrapped in tissue paper.

When mills were making good money, they weren't cost-conscious and they paid Gus two dollars a dozen pair of stockings for boxes and tissues — about 20 cents a pair. But the going rate had dropped to 50 cents a dozen, and Gus admitted to me he was lucky if he could sell any at that price.

"I've got an idea," said Waldmann. "Next week I'll be coming by train to New York." he said. Waldmann was one of those Philadelphia residents who would get on the train at seven a.m. and eat breakfast and play cards in the big dining car until they got to New York in time to open their offices at nine a.m. I couldn't quite understand that type — willing to spend four hours of the day and one or two meals on the train.

THE GREAT DEPRESSION

Hunter, Cantelon, and I were eating breakfast and just coming to realize how depressed the country had become. Milo and Phil said that since they still had jobs, they would remain with Brown-Durrell. But I still had no idea what I would do to weather the economic cloudburst. From the third-floor dining room window of the new Abraham Lincoln Hotel where we were staying, we suddenly realized we were looking down onto a line leading into a soup kitchen. It was tightly packed along the snow-covered walk and wrapped around the corner a block away. Men would enter one door and come out another with a bowl of soup and a spoon. But I still didn't realize the extent of the Depression.

"I can't visualize dropping down more than 20 percent of business," I said. "If I can make $200,000 to $250,000 in sales, I won't get rich but, at five percent, I'll get by. " That would mean about $12,000 with travel expenses. Then a funny feeling crept over me — if not Brown-Durrell, for whom would I sell $250,000 in stockings? I was unemployed for the first time in my life.

"I'm thankful I'm not a regular," said Gus as he stepped off the morning train from Philadelphia in Grand Central Station. "George, I've got an appointment with this big Wall Street banker. It wasn't easy to get. I wish you'd come along with me. Maybe we can work out something."

In pre-Depression days, silk stockings sold for $1.35, $1.65, and $1.95 a pair. We had learned that $1.25 and $1.50 stockings wouldn't sell and, when the top of the line was $2, women would flock to the store with $1.95 stockings — even though the $2 pair was the best buy.

We thought, if the mills are full of unsold stockings, perhaps we could sell some at a discount. But we realized that we would need a good cash flow.

I was impressed by Wall Street. The banker had the most gorgeous office I had ever envisioned and — until now — had dealt only with big business. He was round-faced and round-bodied. He sat in a leather-upholstered chair with brass hobnail trim behind a beautiful walnut desk, a modicum of a bank executive. But the vision of a bejowled bulldog guarding the bank safe ran through my mind as we sat down.

"I interview the few big businessmen who come in, but I'm bored all day," he growled. "What have you gentlemen brought to brighten my day?" He listened intently as we presented our plan.

Our plan was a simple one — I would write orders in smaller towns. Gus would buy the stockings from idle mills that had good reputations, have them packed in boxes and ship them to the purchasing stores Friday mornings. Gus would then take the orders to New York — two hours by train — where the banker would give Gus a check for 97 percent of the total value. After he paid the mills, Gus would send me my half of the profits.

"I will work with you for one reason — you plan to sell in small towns where stores are not overstocked," said the banker. "I see men every day who claim they can sell to the big stores. But they never mention the small towns. Guys like that are a dime a dozen."

Waldmann and I quickly formed Waldmann-Griffith Mills to sell high-quality hosiery at low prices and I headed back to Fort Wayne with Hunter and Cantelon. I wanted to spend Christmas and New Year's Eve at home.

When we returned Dec. 18, longtime friends Paul and Linda Sutter called.

"George, I'm so happy to reach you. We're arranging a holiday dinner-dance at the Fort Wayne Country Club," Linda said. "We've got blind dates for you and Phil. Your date is a nurse. That's all I'll tell you," she teased. My social life had suffered. I welcomed the idea as did Phil, who had only pretended to be married to keep his job with Brown-Durrell.

The country club was glittering despite the Depression and a Chicago band was playing. For Phil and his date, Marie Gehrke, a German girl, it was love at the first dance. My date was Helen Hall, a registered nurse at General Electric, who lived only two blocks from Emerson's three-bedroom house where I had a room when I was in town. Phil and Marie were soon engaged but, while Helen and I hit it off, too, I wasn't going to marry without a means of supporting a bride. I had friends whose wives were working, but I didn't want my wife to have to support me.

However, January, February, and early March brightened my outlook. I sold a ton of 59-cent and 79-cent silk hosiery — stockings that had been selling for $1.35 to $1.65 — and shipped the orders to Waldmann. Gus would take my orders to our banker, who would deduct three percent and give him the money to pay the mills. He would then split the profits and send me my share.

But when I made my rounds of stores again in late March and early April, many still had my merchandise on their shelves. They weren't selling any hosiery. Our visions of eventually selling big store bargain basements all the stockings the mills could produce dimmed under a dark cloud of reality. We dissolved Waldmann-Griffith Mills on June 1, and I returned to Fort Wayne.

I began to wish that I had taken Hall's generous offer of the big New York stores. But it was too late now.

"I'm depressed," I told my brother, Emerson. "I haven't hunted quail or grouse or rabbits or wetted a line in a trout stream since Brown-Durrell cut back eight months ago."

Like millions of other Americans, I was trying to think how I could make a dollar. My mind was sorting out ideas as I drove into a filling station. "Fill it up," I told Jack Hilts, the owner. "Charge it."

"George, I would like to, but I just can't do it," said Hilts, who was working by himself. "Everyone is asking me to charge, but I have to pay cash to the distributor. I'll make it half full."

"That will be $2.75, George," he said. "Please pay me as soon as you can. Meanwhile, here's your free glass."

"Glass? What do you mean," I asked, turning the glass around in my hand. Gas was 15 cents a gallon.

"I buy them from a guy in town," he said. "They're admittedly cheap, but if you break one, you have nothing invested."

H-m-m. As I revolved the glass in my hand, an idea came to mind. If filling stations were attracting customers with cheap glass, what would happen if I sprang a set of quality glassware onto them? The idea intrigued me. I'll bet I can do better.

I headed for Lee Hillman's china shop and arranged to buy some of the quality glassware he supplied to fine Fort Wayne homes — red- and blue-striped. Then I went on to a golf date with a Texaco-distributor friend at Orchard Ridge Country Club. Jack Hilts came from Pandora, Ohio, close to Vaughnsville. We met playing baseball during my late years on the farm.

I shouldered my golf bag. Caddies charged 50 cents a round and, if I was going to let my friend win a few holes at 25 cents a hole, I didn't have the money. I had deliberately hit the ball into the rough on a dogleg that would set him up to win a hole. On the next hole I appeared to be angry with my game and I missed a three-foot putt. A sand trap caught my ball at the edge of the 18th green.

"My game is off," I muttered as I handed over 75 cents. We headed into the locker room.

"Jasper," he called out to the valet who was alternately shining shoes and serving soft drinks at the bar. This was still Prohibition.

"Jasper," he called out again. "Would you bring us two glasses and some ice?" Without washing his hands, the young man scooped up ice and filled the glasses. Not very sanitary, but the corn liquor I knew my friend had in his locker would kill any germs — if it didn't kill us first. But during Prohibition you drank what you could get.

"What are you offering as premiums at your stations?"

"Nothing right now," my friend replied. He was nibbling at the bait.

"I have an idea."

"George, knowing you, I imagine you have half a dozen." He had a hearty laugh and spilled some of his corn liquor.

"I can supply you with a set of twelve quality glasses and a pitcher that will bring customers in thirteen times," I said. "You can give your customer an ice-tea glass and punch his card with each of twelve fill-ups then tell him when he comes again, you'll give him the pitcher in exchange for his card."

"I have the cards and punches," I lied, "and all your attendants will have to do is punch cards and hand out glasses. Your customer gets a set of quality glassware free and you make a friend."

I knew my friend liked quality things. The idea looked good to him. He sat back on the locker room bench and poured us another drink. It was a deal. We shook hands, a valid contract for many things in those days.

"Bring us some more ice, Jasper," he yelled. I had it made. I knew he had 17 stations in the Fort Wayne area. With them and a few independents, I might have something going.

THE GREAT DEPRESSION

But a few weeks later I realized I had been shortsighted. My glassware supplier-friend began complaining that he was always on the road delivering glasses to my customers.

"George, I'm supplying you good glassware at just above my cost," he groused. "You're making money selling my glasses and pitchers to filling stations while I'm spending all my time and what I take in buying gasoline and tires from some of the same stations."

The business lasted about six weeks then crashed just as I was thinking of offering him a higher price for his glassware. As motorists completed their sets of glasses and claimed their pitchers, they began abandoning my friend's Texaco stations for other stations that offered other premiums. I was caught short without another item to keep them coming.

The nation was thirsty. I dabbled in selling near-beer for a couple of months, but there were rumblings that Prohibition was going down in the next election. Whiskey-running gangsters had made fortunes, and thirsty, would-be beer drinkers had turned to making home-brew. Even corner stores sold the ingredients. But many who had seen their life's savings disappear were happy just paying the milkman to stop his horse and wagon and deliver a bottle of milk each morning.

In early July 1931 Milo Hunter called me. He was in the Keenan Hotel in Fort Wayne.

"Wayne Knitting Mills is reorganizing," he said. "Do you think you could sell stockings again?"

"Are you kidding?"

He asked me to join him at the hotel. It took me 10 minutes to get downtown. I was there till midnight.

"Wayne Knitting Mills has been bought by The Munsing Corporation, which now owns Munsingwear, underwear and hosiery manufacturers. They also own the Vassar Company, which makes the most popular young lady's girdle on the market."

"Both firms are making small profits, which is unusual in the fields today. By buying Wayne Knitting, they are adding the mill's past reputation for excellence

58

in leading department stores. With that good will and a couple million dollars to gamble with, they plan to modernize the mills and equipment."

"We plan to hit the trade with a new, high-style, high-quality line of stockings," he said.

Since most hosiery manufacturers were existing at a loss, there was a place for the type of stockings Wayne was planning. And, since the company had lost most of the style business, they planned to replace their present sales force with a younger, more aggressive, style-conscious staff. The salesmen trained by my former employer fitted their needs. Milo Hunter was their new sales manager and he had decided on dividing the Midwest, the best market, between Phil Cantelon and me.

I was cautious, afraid to appear too enthused until someone else told me the same story: Wayne planned to make stockings in leg sizes as well as foot sizes, the most-needed advance in the stocking business. It would give Wayne stockings a "leg up" with women.

Unfortunately, Al Crowder had the territory I wanted — Indiana and Michigan. I suggested a trade.

"He'll never go for a trade," said Hunter. "It would be like swapping a horse for a rabbit."

"Let me sell him." Crowder did not enjoy traveling.

"Al, you want to live in Indianapolis, and I want to fish for trout in Michigan," I told Crowder. "Why not swap and take southern Ohio and Indiana and you'll be home three nights of the week? I'll take northern Ohio and Michigan."

He went for the idea.

Hunter said John Kronenberg, chairman of the board, would be in Fort Wayne next week and Kronenberg wanted to meet Phil and me. A week later I got a call from his new secretary that Mr. Kronenberg wanted to see me at 10 a.m. — short notice but I was ready and early.

"I'm a very busy man, George. I want a background on you. What territory are you familiar with?"

When I mentioned Michigan, I nearly fainted at his reply.

"I have never been there, except Detroit, but I've been told that it has good trout fishing in the northern part."

"It's considered the best, my friends say."

"Do you fish?"

"Yes."

"Trout?"

"I try awfully hard," I said.

"Sounds like you could at times neglect your territory to fish. Do you fly-fish?"

"Nothing else," I said.

"How far is good trout fishing from here?"

"About 300 miles reaches the best fishing."

The phone rang and his secretary told him that the man he was so anxious to talk to was on the line. He looked at me. "This is going to be a long, important call. Hunter tells me you can sell hosiery. (Hunter had told him to refer to our product as fine stockings, not hosiery.) Hunter will be here Saturday to give you a contract."

We shook hands hurriedly and I got two warnings for speeding en route to the GE doctors' offices. Helen and I celebrated with the first cabaret evening we had had in six months. We had been going together for a year and a half.

Both Phil and I signed contracts on Saturday. We examined samples of the current styles of stockings, and Hunter assured us our Belle Sharmeer stockings would be a great improvement over the old line, but we would be unable to deliver the new style stockings for Christmas. We discussed Hunter's plan to sell available stockings, but both Phil and I disagreed.

"Milo, I don't want to show new customers our old Wayne Knit styles of stockings. I just want to show them samples of Belle Sharmeer and tell them new machinery is being installed to make these stockings in three leg sizes," I said.

Hunter called a general sales meeting for the day after Labor Day, but it was entirely different than those New York meetings. Instead of 100 men, we had only 16 salesmen. And we were meeting at the mill in Fort Wayne.

Hunter presented his plan to Kronenberg, Harry Bain, his assistant, and the salesmen. Bain's duties were never outlined by Kronenberg, so he assumed the functions of assistant sales manager. He had transferred from the never-profitable Far West combined Munsing and Vassar office in San Francisco to Fort Wayne.

When Hunter was finished, he asked the salesmen one by one for comments and how they planned to present the new line to accounts. Phil and I had experience with sophisticated meetings, but the others were at a loss.

"My plan is not how much I can sell in three months, including Christmas, but how I can plan on having a stock of Belle Sharmeer stockings for each store by Feb. 1, 1933," I said. I was concerned about not having quality stockings to sell while the company was installing new machinery. I wanted to get well acquainted and explain Wayne Knitting Mills' plans.

When Franklin Delano Roosevelt was elected president in November 1932, he promised a New Deal. He took office in January 1933, and one of his first major acts in February was to close all of the nation's banks.

I was in Saginaw when I read about the bank closure in the morning *Detroit Free Press*. When I went to pay my bill, the hotel refused to take my check.

"Mr. Griffith, I'm sorry, but everything is in a state of confusion. With the banks closed, we can't accept your check," the desk clerk said. Fortunately, I usually carried enough cash to last me through a week. I went on to Alpena, where I had an old-fashioned store that was selling a considerable quantity of Wayne Knit stockings. The owner was glad to see me and very interested in our new merchandise.

"I'm happy Wayne is coming out with a new line," he said. "Some of my style-conscious customers are beginning to reject Wayne Knit. How soon can you ship me a stock of Belle Sharmeer?"

While we were writing his order, he asked where I was headed.

"Milliken's in Traverse City," I replied. "But this bank closure has left me short of cash and unable to cash a check."

"How much do you need?"

"About $150 would allow me to finish out my week's work. The mill can't even send me any money," I said.

THE GREAT DEPRESSION

"We can spare that much out of cash we have. I'll be glad to cash your check."

Despite the bank closure, I opened four accounts that week — my best. My sales began to grow. By spring I began sneaking away for a few modest weekends of trout fishing in Traverse City. Bob Klaehn, an undertaker, Carl Hornberger, an independent oil distributor, and I would sleep in the car and fish the Boardman River or Acme Creek. It was great seeing Mart Winnie again.

We tried fishing an upstream stretch of the Jordan River, but I never cared for it. The stream was too flat and too shallow with little cover for fish. And it was hard to wade and only produced after a planting. This was about 20 miles upstream from the portion of the Jordan that would become popular.

But we seldom went to big streams; I don't know why except I was usually with anglers who had more money than I had and I let them make the decision. We also fished and explored the Black and Pigeon rivers near Gaylord, the Black River near Alpena, and another stream 25 to 30 miles south of Alpena also named Black.

My income was minimal when we started going together, so Helen frequently financed our weekend trips with other couples from her salary as a GE company nurse. I didn't expect my income to become stable for a couple of years. Helen said she wanted to keep working, but I told her no — not if we got married.

But by summer, business was promising. At 11 a.m. on a Saturday in late August 1933, Phil and Marie stood up with us at Wayne Street Methodist Church in Fort Wayne as we started a 43-year marriage. It was a quiet affair with about 10 guests. About 18 appeared at Helen's mother's home — her mother was an invalid — for a brief reception.

We went on a working honeymoon, spending the first weekend in Detroit where I had sold a lot of stockings to Fyfe's Shoe Store, a unique five-floor shoe store on Woodward and Grand Circus Park. The hosiery buyer was a sentimental woman and was pleased when I introduced Helen. I went on to Hudson's, who were buying far less stockings than they should be buying from me.

"We've got something radically different." I told Clay McDonald, Hudson's buyer.

"What's so different about stockings?"

"We are fortunate. For the first time in women's hosiery, we have leg sizes as well as foot sizes. No one else has it."

McDonald was too loyal to friends representing other hosiery mills to get overly enthused about my product. He bought only long and short stockings, no medium length, which we both knew accounted for more than 60 percent of Hudson's sales. I knew he stocked only a store brand in medium length stockings, but he was the buyer. I was confident his customers would demand my stockings once they realized he had leg sizes for short and tall women.

We spent three days visiting customers before we got to the Straits of Mackinac where we parked in Mackinaw City and took a ferry to Mackinac Island, a trip I had dreamed of making since my first ferry ride across the Straits to St. Ignace years earlier. But we were almost alone — although it was the last week of the season, just before the usually sold-out Labor Day weekend. Due to the Depression, there were only about 30 customers in the huge resort hotel with its 400-foot porch overlooking the Straits of Mackinac.

We golfed on the island for a few days then took the ferry back to Mackinaw City for our car — no automobiles are allowed on the island where horse carriages and bicycles are the only forms of summer transportation — and headed for Traverse City so I could show off my bride to all my friends.

"Honey, how would you like to go trolling for lake trout?" I asked Helen.

"Great!"

We drove north to Northport on the tip of the Leelanau Peninsula, birthplace of lake trout trolling, the forerunner to Michigan's charter salmon and trout fishing, and met a teacher who took people trolling during summer months.

He had advised us to eat a mild, greaseless breakfast because the water would be rough, and we would be tossing around in the boat. But I was confident my cast-iron stomach could take bacon and eggs — and anything Lake Michigan had to offer — when we left the dock at Northport Point for deep water.

Helen was enjoying the trip and getting acquainted with the guide, a middle-aged schoolteacher.

Then she noticed me.

THE GREAT DEPRESSION

"Are you all right, honey?" she asked.

"Getting along fine. How about you?"

"Swell, but your color is not good," she said.

"Never mind my color. Enjoy the scenery."

Two hours later I was forced to admit I was seasick. "But we are going to stay out here until we catch a trout," I said as I leaned over the rail again.

The guide was understanding, and he headed the boat through a spot where he frequently caught fish. A trout hit. I fought it for 20 minutes before he brought a 22-pound lake trout aboard, almost forgetting my seasickness. I was too busy to notice that he had been heading the boat for shore.

My foot felt as if it were encased in a lead boot as I stepped out of the boat. But after five minutes on solid ground, I felt as good as new. I took two Mother Fotheringill's Seasick Pills and we went back out and fished for a couple of hours in the afternoon. Helen fell in love with the Traverse City area and we spent many summers there.

Jim Milliken took us to dinner. Naturally, the conversation led to business. I sometimes disagreed with Jim, but we were never disagreeable about our differences of opinion. Through him I became associated with a number of top merchandising people throughout the state, including Clair Sperry at J.B. Sperry in Port Huron and Howard Grimes at J.W. Knapp Co. in Lansing.

One of my accounts was Jacobson's, with three fine-quality stores in Ann Arbor, Battle Creek, and Jackson, founded by Mose Jacobson in the 1920s after a brief start in the Clare area. Jacobson's was recognized as the top among stores selling top quality and latest, correct styles at moderate prices.

Jacobson's brother, William, a tailor, inherited the business, and William's son, Richard, became active in managing the store.

I had a $350 a month drawing account that covered all of my expenses, including eight- or 10-cent-a-gallon gasoline, and my contract called for a five percent commission on everything I sold, less my drawing account, at the end of the year. Hunter promised me a $50-a-month increase if I got married, which I didn't draw for the first three months after our wedding. Despite that, if I delivered $80,000 in merchandise, I earned $4,000. During the first year, Phil and

I were the only salesmen to sell more than $100,000.

By 1940, we had 21 salesmen, but I was the only consistent million-dollar-a-year man, and 11 percent of our total shipments went to my territory, which included the most large-city department stores. Phil was next; he had Chicago. We sold both Marshall Field and Carson, Pierie, Scott, a big store that competed with Marshall Field with not quite as high-quality merchandise. But the Chicago stores were made house accounts. Phil didn't get full commission, but he was happy.

My business jumped by 1935 and I was making $25,000 to $30,000 year, which was still in the Great Depression — the president of the mills was only making $80,000!

It was Friday, Nov. 14, 1939, and Helen and I were living in Fort Wayne where our mills were located. We were planning to drive to Columbus, Ohio, spend the night with Jim and Betty Simmons, and attend the Ohio State-University of Michigan football game on Saturday.

But at eight a.m. the phone rang. Harry Bain, my sales manager, said Mr. Rosenfeld from Jacobson's had called and wanted to see me in Jackson at 11 a.m. I called Richard Jacobson at his home, told him of the call, and asked, "Who is Mr. Rosenfeld?"

"He's a new man in the business," he said. "You were lucky to reach me. I was going out of the door on the way to my deer-hunting camp."

But he agreed to take time to call Mr. Rosenfeld and tell him I would be there at 11 a.m. as he had requested. It was my last time to talk with Richard. He left the business and died in an automobile accident shortly afterward.

It was about 10:45 a.m. when I walked into Jacobson's Jackson store. I went to the hosiery department where a salesgirl greeted me.

"Mr. Griffith! It's so nice to see you. But when did you start working in late November?"

I told her my mission.

"I'll tell Mr. Rosenfeld you are here," she said. "You are in for a surprise."

Nathan Rosenfeld was 5-foot-3 and weighed about 105 pounds. But I could sense a powerful personality behind the deep-set, dark, searching eyes scanning me.

THE GREAT DEPRESSION

"I have a temporary office on the fourth floor," he said. I was surprised as I followed him — the fourth was the fur and heavy coat floor. I was even more surprised to find his office was a dressing room with mirrors on two sides as well as a narrow table and chair on either side.

"First, let me tell you that I have bought Jacobson's stores. My plans are not to close them out but to make them a real factor in fine merchandise in Michigan.

"The first person I wanted to meet was the person who takes the largest check out of Jacobson's yearly. I can only see you for a half hour today, but I want to spend more time with you in the future.

"What is important to me now is to know that our Christmas stocks of your merchandise are complete," he said.

"Your Jackson and Battle Creek stores are covered," I assured him. "Your Ann Arbor department manager, Mrs. Handy, insists on ordering her stock without help and, as yet, we have not received her order. This order should exceed four thousand dollars."

"Mr. Griffith, I want you to place an order for her to make sure the store has adequate Christmas stock."

"Mr. Rosenfeld, I cannot buy your merchandise. First, I do not have your inventory, but that order is your buyer's responsibility."

He looked at me and smiled.

"I can see that we are going to get along."

I told him I would be in Jackson once a month or whenever he wanted me to come.

For then, my mission was over. I found Helen visiting with some of the salesgirls. We drove on to Columbus and had a wonderful weekend. At halftime, the score was 7-6, Michigan, and someone seated near us — apparently a Michigan fan — said the game should halt now. But Ohio State, which was favored to win, made a second half comeback and won, 20-7.

Nathan Rosenfeld was to become a friend and a teacher with whom I would discuss many of the things I would talk over with Jim Milliken. Rosenfeld would invite me to dinner at his home at least six times a year and, on two occasions, he and his wife, Marjorie, would be winter weekend guests at our Grayling home.

66

Within three years, Rosenfeld would replace the sign "Hosiery Department" with one saying "Belle Sharmeer Stockings," my brand, and I would take over Jacobson's hosiery department as *de facto* merchandise man.

His first points with me related to sales.

"When you see an item on sale at twenty to fifty percent off, ask yourself whether you would have bought the item at the original price if you needed it," he said.

Although I could never talk quite as freely with Rosenfeld and, like Milliken, he didn't fish, of my many friends, those two were to influence me the most businesswise. I learned almost as much about merchandising from Rosenfeld as I did from Milliken.

We were the first mill to get a significant quantity of nylon yarn. We made our first shipments of nylon stockings in June 1940 and, by July, nylon stockings were selling so well that silk stockings were gathering dust on shelves. We were getting ready for a big production of nylon stockings for Christmas sales, but the government declared our product non-essential to the war effort. After September, Wayne Knitting Mills was unable to get any yarn — the military, which had been using silk for gunpowder bags in big cannons, learned that nylon bags would burn completely while silk bags left a residue that had to be swabed out after each shot. Nylon also replaced silk for parachutes carried by Army and Navy pilots.

But Wayne Knitting Mills bought a no-brand mill in Georgia that saved the day for us. While we were allotted 60 percent of the yarn we had previously received, the new mill had a yarn quota, too. Put together with Wayne's quota, it would mean that we would be able to provide customers almost their average shipments of the previous five years — in rayon stockings.

"We're going to be guaranteed sixty percent of our five-year average of yarn used," said Kronenberg. "We're guaranteeing every customer — large or small — a fair share."

On Dec. 7, 1941, Helen, Forrest Nelson, another salesman, and I were fishing for bass and sea trout out of Crystal River, Fla. We stopped and cooked bass for our shore lunch then went out into the Gulf of Mexico and were catching sea trout. We had a long day. It was dark when we got back. The hotel was a madhouse. Japan had attacked Pearl Harbor that morning. We were at war.

The next day I called Guy Means, the Cadillac-Buick dealer in Fort Wayne, who had a winter home in Florida.

"Guy, my tires aren't in the best of shape. I had intended to order a set before we left Fort Wayne, but I was busy until the last moment. Can you get me a set?"

"George, I wish I could, but I just had a call from my office that tires were frozen this morning. I can't even get a set for myself. This damned war . . ."

We went on to Hollywood, Fla., Dec. 8 and spent about a month deep-sea fishing. Gasoline was still available. And when we went to rent a hotel, I told Helen a suite with a bedroom, living room, and davenport bed would probably be too expensive. I frankly expected to hear the woman at the desk say $100. To my surprise, she said $25 a week.

"What if three stay?" I asked. Nelson was going to stay with us until Dec. 15. Then we went to the dock and signed up for deep-sea fishing — $15 for a noon to five p.m. charter. We were enjoying prices that were surprisingly low because of the war. Of 18 units that had been sold out before Dec. 7, ours was the hotel's only rented unit. Yet, except for a minesweeper patrolling offshore, there was no hint that the United States was now at war. It was difficult to accept.

Meanwhile, Harry Bain and his wife, Jo, and Bud Rogers, a drug salesman from Grand Rapids, and his wife, Lou, were staying at a motel three or four miles away. The Bains' daughter was with them and Helen joined the wives while the men went fishing with me. There wasn't anything we could do about the war, so we enjoyed one of the best vacations of our lives, fishing daytimes — we learned later that the charter skipper was selling the mackeral and kings we caught — and spending every night at the dog races, which had only 25 to 30 spectators a night by the middle of December. We took the women on a float boat one day and I suggested a small wager — a dollar on the first fish, a dollar on the most fish and a dollar on the largest. Harry's wife, Jo, who didn't even know how to bait her hook, naturally won all three categories.

We hated to go home. Everything was plentiful and cheap and complacency was taking over. People talked openly — if the Japs hit Honolulu, would Hitler hit Palm Beach next? But no one seemed concerned if the Nazis landed. No one except the military.

When we got back, Phil and I found that we had been sold out — Kronenberg had volunteered us for the gas-rationing board.

"It isn't going to bother either of you because you never work anyway," said Kronenberg. "You bastards are making a lot of money sitting on your asses, so you can just go help the government."

There was more than a ring of truth in Kronenberg's remark — we were making three three-week trips a year, working nine weeks a year.

"Don't stay in a store more than an hour or you're going to be pressured," warned Kronenberg. I tried to follow his orders —especially since that gave me an opportunity to hunt and fish. We just kept acquainted while the mill had to pay our commission. But when the bosses complained, I reminded them that because of Phil and me — and others — they were in the 92 percent income tax bracket.

For seven years I had no orders — we just shipped each customer a quota of stockings based on purchases over the previous seven years. We would send Hudson's 1,500 pair of rayon stockings no one supposedly wanted and, without advertising, they would all sell within a day and a half. We had increased from 16 to 21 salesmen by 1940, but 11 percent of the total output of the mills still went to my territory.

Even the greatest of men make mistakes. After World War II, Rosenfeld wanted a store in Petoskey, which already had a few small stores that relied on the same fine clothing manufacturers. He wanted to go there because 64,000 people lived in the Petoskey trading area, according to a survey he obtained.

"There may be 64,000 people living there, but at least 60,000 of them get packages from Sears and Roebuck twice a month," I said. "The season lasts four months at best."

He ignored my warning. Jacobson's put a store in Petoskey. Four years later when he closed it out, Rosenfeld said I should have stopped him. The manufacturers that Jacobson's bought their fine clothing from already had loyal customers in Petoskey and refused to supply Rosenfeld's new store.

After the war, our job was to convince our customers that we had taken better care of them. As competition heated up, other companies began giving incentives.

THE GREAT DEPRESSION

But most of my customers said that we had been very loyal to them when stock was in short supply, and that made it easier to increase my sales. Smaller accounts said many suppliers furnished them virtually nothing during the war years and they were not going to buy from them unless necessary.

I quickly built my territory and, for 19 years straight, I shipped more than $1 million a year in merchandise.

*   *   *

DOGS AND HUNTING

We were approaching Fort Wayne ending our honeymoon trip.

"George…"

I looked over at Helen. Her eyes were twinkling, glancing at me and back to the road.

"Turn off at the next road. I have a wedding gift for you that I want to pick up."

I nodded, wondering why she had waited until now to tell me.

We bounced on a narrow gravel road, raising clouds of dust that permeated the car. After about a mile, I saw a small lake, typical of the many lakes surrounding Fort Wayne. Helen directed me to the driveway of a modest frame home. The well-groomed yard suggested an outdoor lover's place.

Helen got out, went to the door and knocked. A man in his forties emerged and wore a broad smile as he approached the car.

"Tom, this is George."

"Congratulations! You are a lucky man to get Helen Hall," said Tom as he offered a warm, sturdy hand.

I was still at a loss as we followed Tom to a small building with a fenced yard behind it. He went into the building and came out with an awkward English Setter pup.

Suddenly my mind clicked into gear. During our honeymoon trip, Helen had mentioned dogs two or three times.

"Do you like dogs?" she asked once. Yes I do.

Later she asked, "Did you have a dog on the farm." No, I didn't have a dog, but Dad had a couple of dogs on the farm as I was growing up.

"What kind?" she pressed me later. The first one was just a dog; the second was a farm collie, probably a mongrel whose bloodlines may have included some long-coated dogs, possibly a Collie.

So this was why she had been asking all those questions. And I, who thought I could almost read people's thoughts after my years on the road, was too dumb to take the fly.

DOGS AND HUNTING

The puppy was shy and ducked when I tried to pet his big head. He looked at me, then started to dash back toward the building. Helen grabbed him.

"Here, you're all right," she said. The puppy finally sat awkwardly as though he and his hind legs were barely attached. His front feet were crossed.

"Tom works at General Electric," explained Helen. She was an industrial nurse and she and the GE doctor cared for more than 200 patients a day with minor injuries, sometimes no more than a headache.

"I was treating Tom for a minor injury one day when he said, 'I wish our doctor was as good as you are. My daughter fell and bruised her arm on rough cement. I took her to the doctor, but the bruise isn't healing very well.'

"I told him to bring his daughter to the office. After a few visits her arm was healed. Tom wanted to pay us for treating his daughter, but I assured him that, as a GE employee, he was entitled to treatment for his family."

"I hear you are getting married soon," Tom said. "Is your husband a hunter?"

"He surely is."

"Does he hunt quail?"

"Yes."

"He told me that he had a litter of prize English setters and he had one picked out for me — or you."

"This is your wedding gift, George."

That was my introduction to Laddie, the first of 14 English setters in my life and probably the best dog a man could ever have. He sat with his haunches between us on the front seat of the car. Helen had her arm around him and his stick-shaped front legs fell across each other on her lap. But despite her cooing, I could sense him shaking. Obviously, he was scared.

I turned into a paved alley and drove up to the two-car garage behind the comfortable frame home we had rented. Although this would be our first night there, I had a warm feeling about coming home. This is a good neighborhood, I thought. I'm glad we have the fence for the pup.

But, as I stopped the car and started to get out, the pup broke away from Helen, leaped over my shoulder, and ran down the alley at full speed.

"Oh, George, catch him," I heard Helen...the pup's long ears seemed to ride on the breeze…he crossed the street…I was gaining…another street…now I have him…he's cornered between two fenced backyards.

I didn't have a leash or collar. I finally picked him up, legs seemingly protruding in every direction. I was breathless as I met Helen coming to help me. She petted him, cooed a few sweet words, and he settled back against my chest for the last half-block home.

It took some more cooing and petting, but we finally coaxed the pup into the kitchen. Warily sniffing the floor as if it might bite him, he slunk across to the kitchen sink and promptly lifted his leg against the sink.

"I'm going to go buy him a leash and collar," I told Helen. "The hardware must still be open."

Helen was unpacking when I returned. I slipped the collar on the pup and found it was too big. I made an extra hole with my jackknife and attached the leash. Helen sort of pushed as I pulled the pup out the back door. I could see Helen looking out the kitchen window as Laddie — that's what I decided I would call him — first leaped ahead then dragged backward, slinking one moment and seemingly atop stilts the next. After a half-hour, he reluctantly would walk at my side, alternately looking down then anxiously glancing upward at me.

"I think he's leash-broken," I told Helen. I was breathless again. Me, the ex-farm boy, breathless. It must be this soft life I had been leading. Or maybe I was just excited. The farm collie was my friend, but Laddie was the first dog I had ever owned.

We put Laddie down in the basement and went to bed. We immediately regretted it — he howled all night. Well, we still had the weekend. (We took him to a nearby farm and I turned him loose, especially since I had to leave on a sales trip on Monday.)

I kissed Helen goodbye. She had Laddie on a leash. I leaned down and patted him on his head. I heard him cry as I walked to the car. Helen waved and I could see her walking him around the yard as I turned out of the alley. He's her problem, I thought, but sort of envying her the privilege.

I learned later that she would walk him in the morning and at night, going several blocks each time. After a good friend told her how to teach him to heel, following at her left side, and to stop on command, she began training him in earnest.

It was 10 days later and I was driving down the alley. Helen spotted me and she came out with Laddie walking at her side. We walked together that night as she showed me what she had taught the pup. What a contrast! He was a pleasure now.

*   *   *

I was a boy again and I saw in the pup Bess, the farm collie, who would go with Emerson and me for the cows and — when she thought we dawdled — would meet us with the herd halfway up the lane. Bess would flush and chase quail, barking as if to scold them for being in our pasture.

And I saw once again Joe Collar's dog, who would point his nose at quail and stand there while Joe flushed the covey — including singles — and shot two or three. Joe would take the quail to Harry Thomas' grocery and sell them for 10 cents apiece, a lot in those days.

I was again standing in the kitchen telling Mom about Joe's dog. "Joe said he's a pointer." Mom shook her head as she bustled about, seemingly doing a dozen things at once. She wasn't impressed.

"Mom, these dogs came from England and Europe. There the game and fish belong to the king and he hunts and fishes with his friends. People like us are not allowed to hunt or fish."

"Go and fetch me a fat hen," said Mom, seemingly dumping all my words with the dishwater down the sink drain.

I recalled that Joe's days as a market hunter came to an abrupt end. In 1916 some farmer's wives persuaded the Ohio Legislature to classify the bobwhite quail as a songbird without any consideration for sport hunting — a big step for the always-plentiful bobwhite.

*   *   *

"Laddie's registration papers came today," said Helen. In those days it cost three cents to mail a one-ounce letter, but there was only a hint of the junk mail era to come — a pound of beef short ribs cost six cents at the meat market and eggs were 12 cents a dozen. Farmers' wives would take three eggs in with a letter.

We mused over the names of Laddie's ancestors, especially the famous Mohawk Speed Boy on his pedigree and took it to another dog man — a veterinarian who knew Laddie's background and had several dogs. He assured us that, indeed, we did have a valuable dog. But it was late August. He said the pup would probably be too young to hunt that fall.

Laddie was about nine months old when I took him on several short hunting trips. He ran around and showed interest. Then Homer Stambaugh invited me to go hunting. Homer lived across the street from Helen. When I mentioned that I had a new pup, he said, "Bring the pup along. It won't hurt him to be around birds and he won't bother my old dog — Joe has worked with untrained pups before."

To my surprise, Laddie pointed and flushed quail on his own but he had no interest in honoring the older dog's points. He was excited and wanted to go on and find more birds. I was embarrassed. My friend's dog was a methodical old pro, and my pup was always getting in his way as he checked old fence rows and even unlikely stone piles for birds.

On our way home, my friend noted I was depressed.

"George, don't worry. You have a good dog. Few pups his age would have shown as much interest in birds as he did today. Old Joe was just showing him the places to look for quail. Laddie will be a prize bird dog in the future."

I studied his face. He meant what he was saying. I was just too ignorant about the work of a bird dog to judge for myself. Other friends were patient and reassuring, too.

"The next year is important in his life," another hunter said. "You should send your pup to a good trainer if you don't have time to train him yourself."

It was Feb. 1, 1934, and I was working with a customer in Logan, Ohio.

"Did I tell you about my new dog?" I asked for an opener. I knew he loved to hunt. He had a shoe store and carried a few stockings he bought by mail until I began stopping in town.

"One of the best field dog trainers lives right here in Logan," he said "He's trained several top dogs." I invited him to dinner and pressed him for details. After dinner, he guided me out of town to the trainer's place.

I could see an older man through a cloud of pipe smoke over the porch railing of a one-story cottage. He was rocking slowly back and forth. As we reached the porch, he lowered his boot-clad feet from the railing and stood up. The house was on a low foundation, typical of houses in small towns in the South. And it was presided over by a quiet, friendly woman who seemed to hang onto her husband's every word but added little herself.

"I get a little stiff after running the dogs," he said with a grin as we were introduced. My mind flashed back to my days on the farm as I noticed his bib overalls. "Sit a spell," he said, leaning forward, elbows on his knees, and listening intently.

"What's your dog's bloodlines?" he asked over his pipe.

I described Laddie and recited what I knew of the Mohawk Speed Boy line of bird dogs.

The trainer, who was at least 65, explained that he had the privilege of training dogs on several miles of the very hilly scrub country with several varieties of berries and wild grapes that provided both food and cover for quail. But since Ohio had no open season on quail, the trainer said he had to fire a blank pistol over a dog on flush to give him some association between birds and gunfire.

He sat back, struck a match on the porch railing and relighted his pipe. "I don't take more than six dogs at one time," said the trainer. "But I could take Laddie in two weeks. A month should be about enough.

"Oh, by the way, when you come back, bring Laddie's pedigree with you," he instructed. "I like to know what I'm working with."

It was two weeks later and Laddie's growing frame was beginning to hide the passenger door window as he sat on the front seat looking out at the road. I introduced him to the trainer, who stroked the pup's arched neck and patted his chest as he examined him with knowing hands. Laddie seemed to accept the trainer as a friend. But cried as he saw me turn to leave. I couldn't look back — the dog was getting to me. He was a part of my little family. An increasingly important part.

Our little home seemed empty without Laddie. As I closed the garage door and headed down the alley, Helen waved from the kitchen window. But Laddie's fenced-in yard was empty. I was anxious. When I returned from this trip, the month would be up and I could bring the pup home.

A week later, I was back with a book full of orders and Helen and I would have a few days. But I had to use my key in the back porch door. Helen's mother was in the hospital. She suggested I leave Laddie with the trainer. I called and asked how the dog was doing.

"Laddie's doing very well," he said. "He's a natural-born bird dog, a joy to work. I'll be happy to keep him another three weeks if it will help you."

Twenty-one evenings later I was standing — out of sight — on his back porch as the trainer started putting Laddie through his training. I had promised to remain quiet in hopes he wouldn't get a scent of me.

The man threw a dog biscuit. Laddie started to go after it. "What a test," I scoffed quietly. "I can make him do that." Then the man commanded "Whoa!" Laddie stopped. When the trainer told him "Go," he moved up and took the biscuit. He put him through several other tests and he was perfect. I must be dreaming — in another world.

He had put Laddie and another dog in his car and told me to follow them down a lane to the field.

I watched quietly as Laddie pointed two coveys of quail. After the second covey flushed, the trainer put the other dog back into the car so Laddie could work alone on the singles that we had seen land along an old wire fence. I was speechless as Laddie found, pointed and was staunch as he flushed five singles from the fence row.

The trainer looked at me and shook his head.

"Mister, I don't know what you know about bird dogs but you have just watched some of the best dog work I have ever seen."

"Hold it, I am moved beyond words," I said, reaching for his hand. "I cannot express myself — I am amazed at what you have done with a green puppy."

I got out of my car when I reached his home. Laddie was standing about 20 feet from me and looking anxiously at my open car door when the trainer suddenly called him. Instinctively, he turned and took a step, then turned back to me.

DOGS AND HUNTING

"Generally, the dog picks me," said the trainer, somewhat deflated.

"What do I owe you?" It was over two months.

"Two months at…"

I stopped him "…$50 a month is an even $100. Best bargain I have ever had." He protested that it was too much. He had told me $30 a month.

"Your work is worth many times $100," I said as Laddie leaped onto the front seat. He was a top-notch trainer and he had more than earned his money. We corresponded for about two years until tramping the fields with six dogs a day became too much and he retired.

When Laddie and I reached Traverse City the following fall, Mart Winnie's nephew, Edwin Winnie, who trained dogs near Lake Orion, was there for the ruffed grouse opener. He had a female setter pup with him, a gift for Mart. We were going to see how the dogs worked together.

We were southwest of Traverse City in good territory. It was a bright but cool day and no other hunters were in sight when we released the dogs near Sleight's Crossing.

Laddie went right to work. Within five minutes he was on point under the top of a fallen oak tree. It was Laddie's first experience with grouse. I hoped he would stay. Despite his training, I knew he had not had experience with shotgun fire since quail season wasn't open in Ohio.

I moved in and two grouse flushed. My shotgun cracked twice. I was too anxious and my shots went over the rising birds. Then I remembered Laddie — still standing on point. Were there more birds? I took another step. Three more grouse flushed and this time I hit one.

Mart and Edwin heard my shots and came over to see what had happened.

"What's all the shooting about?" asked Mart.

"I missed four," I said as I held up my bird. "I was just too excited. Laddie stayed on point for two flushes. He had never seen grouse before."

A point by your dog is worth at least three by a companion's dog. Since Mart could step out his door and train his dog on grouse, I had prepared Laddie with a couple of training sessions on quail, the best I could do. I was excited as I repeated details of Laddie's points, but I did not realize that 45 years later it would still stand out as thrilling bird dog work.

They were complimentary. By 3:30, we had 15 grouse and six woodcock. But Mart was silent when we stopped at a tavern so I could buy a beer for the crowd. Mart's dog, Sue, had not been out before and was over-cautious. She was still over-cautious the next day.

I was puzzled, but I said nothing until after Edwin left for home.

"Mart, don't take this as criticism, but I watched both dogs work and it seems that your dog is worried when Ed is near." I didn't know where to go from there. "Let's hunt our dogs together tomorrow and see if your dog is more comfortable without Ed."

"You really think that, George?"

"Yes. First, your dog knows Ed much better than she knows you, Mart. Get acquainted with her. She needs your confidence."

After two more days and many compliments for Laddie, Sue was becoming a different dog. That afternoon when we stopped at Dingman's Bar, a landmark on M-72 between Grayling and Kalkaska, we celebrated with three apiece — too many for me but not for Mart, who liked beer. We had been hunting along Sunset trail, about two miles southwest of the popular tavern and eatery. After the second round, Mart opened up.

"George, the first day I was frustrated. Your dog got a fast start and mine never got started. Then when Ed started correcting Sue and you left Laddie alone, I was completely stumped."

After two seasons together, Sue became an average dog. But she was never able to equal Laddie.

One day Mart told me that Opie Titus had been in the store.

"He said he would like to see your dog. He owns several bird dogs." Titus and I had a few short enjoyable hunts for grouse, but I recall more of his discussions about the Conservation Department than the hunts. Michigan's way of managing wildlife, while not perfect, was much less political than most states.

Most of my grouse hunting was with Mart until 1935. That was the year we drove home from our vacation at Lake Leelanau and made an overnight stop at Edgewater on the AuSable River at Stephan's Bridge. Chet and Helen Kesler of

DOGS AND HUNTING

Fort Wayne and Helen and I floated and fished the river from Edgewater to Wakeley's Bridge from six p.m. to about 10:30. It was the first fly-fishing I had done at dusk and the best fishing for trout over 15 inches I had ever experienced. I was using Art Winnie's hopper fly. This was in late July, after the Hex hatch on the river was over.

Homer Stambaugh, who traveled for the Fort Wayne Drug Co., was a close friend and quail hunting companion. When he heard how well Laddie had worked in Michigan, he said he was anxious to see him in the field. He suggested a Saturday morning workout with his dog on Ed Hunter's large farm near Ossion, Ind. Hunter was an automobile dealer and his farm was in excellent quail country.

We spent three hours afield and both dogs worked well, but Laddie was in top physical condition and took the honors. Homer apologized because his dog was out of condition from lack of exercise. He lavished Laddie with compliments. It is painful for a dog man or hunter to see his dog outperformed.

Michigan's grouse season closed Nov. 1 but Indiana's quail opener was Nov. 11, giving us a chance for a hunting test. It was windy and the air turned chilly as the day wore on. It was a day when birds are usually hard for dogs to find and even more difficult to hold. Quail were flushing far ahead of the dogs.

One covey we located in a fence corner of a stubble field was apparently running ahead of us. After two false points — the scent was strong but they had moved again — Laddie ran far ahead in a wide buttonhook circle and came back in and held the birds until we were close enough to shoot and kill a couple.

I was still too much a greenhorn in bird hunting to realize how good Laddie was working.

Then I noticed Stambaugh began blaming his dog for not equaling Laddie. His frustrations seemed to be affecting his shooting; however, I thought we still had a good day.

But while driving home, Homer became very unhappy. I wondered if something I said had triggered him. He complained that I did not work as hard as he did and had more time to work my dog. And he blamed his being overweight for my getting to the birds before he did.

I stopped the car. We were good friends. Our wives were good friends. The four of us enjoyed playing bridge together. I was determined to preserve our friendship.

"Homer, let's talk," I said, and apologized. For me it was a lesson in humility. Laddie, never seeming to give a thought to the trouble he had caused me, slept with his head on his paws in the back seat he shared with Homer's admittedly fat setter.

I preserved the friendship, but it seemed we were both too anxious to please on future hunting trips. Stambaugh and Harry Stine, an insurance man, Bob Klaehn, an undertaker, and Guy Means, a Cadillac dealer, all from Fort Wayne and all dog owners, were my sole quail-hunting companions.

We also shot skeet together during the Depression. The Fort Wayne Wholesale Hardware Co. was the major distributor for much outdoor, fishing, hunting, and camping equipment and the Orchard Ridge Country Club Range was one of its major customers for lightweight 7 1/2 shot in all gauges, primarily 12, 20 and 28 gauge. They had the ammunition and skeet birds shipped by the carloads and a round of skeet, including 25 birds and 25 shells, cost members 81 cents.

But bird hunting, like sex, especially with dogs, is ideal for two. But with more it can be dangerous. Two men in a covert with high-powered guns is enough. Two can generally keep track of each other, but 20 other club members owned bird dogs and liked quail hunting. We shot on Sundays and most members were there from Nov. 15 through mid-March. Those who had dogs — and some who didn't — would always suggest hunting with our group. We avoided most because good hunting territory was hard to find and we compensated the owners of farms that had good quail populations. Our group could provide funerals, insurance, stockings, automobiles, and gasoline products, the latter through Carl Hornberger, an oil distributor with whom we occasionally hunted. We could help in most any way except change the baby.

We would have an annual dinner in the country club lounge with members providing the meat — duck rabbit, quail, pheasant, and sharptail were the most common. We exchanged monthly events with the South Bend Skeet Club and the Lake Forest (Ill.) Skeet Club. Good fellows, no fund raising, no art auctions no raffle tickets during those Depression days! Money was scarce.

But even my mother would keep an ear tuned for hunting opportunities. When a cousin, who lived on a farm at Connersville, Ind., visited her and noticed signs of a bird hunter, he mentioned he had dogs and good quail hunting. Mother somehow wangled an invitation to go home with him for a visit, saying I could come down to southern Indiana and get her.

I reached the farm Thursday night after working in Muncie, Richmond, and Indianapolis during the first part of the week, and we hunted Friday and Saturday behind his two pointers and Laddie.

All the dogs worked well the first day and it was a good trip. But we had been in a hurry to go out hunting Friday morning and I had not seen his kennel. As we were starting out Saturday, I noticed a beautiful liver-and-white setter in the kennel.

"What's with him?" I asked.

"George, I have been keeping him for a friend for several weeks. But it's not working. I just don't need him."

I was exercising Laddie about seven on Sunday morning as he was doing his chores.

"What did you think of that setter?" he asked.

"He is a beauty. How old is he?"

"Just past two. What would you give for him? While I would like another dog, my in-laws live with us and they don't like dogs. My health isn't good either, so when my pointers are gone, I will hang up my gun."

I did some serious looking and planning as we were called to breakfast. As I was loading the car, he followed me out to the car.

"Well, what about that setter, George?"

"I would love to have him but it wouldn't work out."

"Make me an offer."

"It would insult you."

"How much?"

"Twenty-five, tops."

I finally bought the dog for $25. His farm was not far from Cincinnati. Later,

I learned that Powell Crosby, who owned one of the first large radio stations in Cincinnati, was a sportsman and had dog kennels about 10 miles from Connorsville. And about nine months later, I learned another resident with a setter bitch had illegally bred her to one of Crosby's prize stud dogs and Crosby, who had heard about this litter, was trying to chase down these dogs. I suspect that was why, for only $25, Connorsville Jack became my second dog.

Tony and Kim were among English setters that followed Laddie and Jack and I came to have great respect for the noble ruffed grouse over the next 30 years of hunting.

Much of my education came from experienced professional game people, although I continued hunting quail. However, there was a great contrast — the best quail hunting was on poor or poorly managed, fenced farmlands. Our shoes were generally dirty or muddy, and the dogs were dirty as well as covered with burrs. It would take an hour to remove the burrs and to doctor cuts from barbed wire at the end of the day. In grouse hunting, we had no barbed wire, mud, or burrs to fight. And we never left shell boxes or empty shells where other hunters could find them and identify good grouse territory. At Babcock, a ghost town site on the Manistee River upstream from Sharon, which had two railroads plus five saloons in the 1880s heyday of white-pine lumbering, remains of one railroad bridge over the river was the last landmark.

A good road followed the river on the east side, but there were no roads on the west side for several miles where there were more than 2,500 acres of good grouse country. We would park our car on the east side of the river and cross the river by canoe while the dogs swam across. We were always careful to put the cartop carrier inside the car, leaving no evidence of our crossing.

"We" included Otto Failing, Dr. Ralph VanVleck, a chiropractor who lived on Lake Margrethe, and me. Our trick was based on Opie Titus' tale of how he and his partners would cut several small trees and leave them standing upright to disguise a branch trail road that led to good grouse country. That always worked.

When Failing, later Gaylord district game supervisor, wasn't along, we would keep records for his reports — barred markings across the base of the tail feathers identifies both gender and age of grouse. In dry weather, we would report grouse dusting themselves in rotten wood from early white-pine stumps.

Our best territory was in Kalkaska County from M-72 downstream nearly to Sharon on both sides of the North Branch of the Manistee River. It was also productive for woodcock. The Big Manistee River above the Mancelona Road, now in the Lake of the North development, had several square miles of prime grouse country and the lake had a good number of Canada geese. But when the developers bought the area and built several miles of roads and building sites, it was the end to good grouse hunting — all in a year's time.

From 1939 to 1943, while living below Wakeley's Bridge, it was not unusual to hear two or three different grouse drumming until eight a.m. every morning.

The first time I heard a grouse drumming, I asked a neighbor if someone was trying to start a washing machine motor. The neighbor asked more questions and got a real story out of me. Within a week, it seemed as if everyone along the river had heard the story and was kidding me about my washing machine grouse.

But that was an ideal grouse area. I could leave the house with a dog at four p.m. and be back at 5:30 after having flushed 20 to 30 grouse. At that time, a spot the size of a bedroom would have several deer tracks crossing each other. Two years later grouse flushes had dropped 75 percent.

I asked Otto Failing what had happened to the grouse. My neighbors blamed the great horned owl. Otto, who was first manager of Hanson's Game Refuge west of Grayling, answered simply: "Ground cover; it has disappeared.

"How many deer trails were there a few years ago?"

"Many."

"Too many deer have eaten all the ground cover," he said. "Grouse want small plants so they can dart from one to another while feeding. They are more afraid of aerial predators than ground enemies."

On a typical day four of us could plan a trip, such as to the Lake of the North, park on the lake shore, break up into pairs, and spend all day hunting in good cover.

While we are told not to feed a dog more than once a day, my dogs would have a light breakfast as I had a big one and, when we built a fire to broil our lunch hamburgs, they would be there for their share. And they always got a good meal at night.

I'll always recall Lady Kimberly. Kim was my last setter. One day in the late 1960s, Dudley Lea of Findlay, Ohio, and I were hunting in tall bracken ferns along the Manistee when Kim let out a low, moaning scream.

I was at her side in seconds and found her lying on the ground. She was a fast dog and, on a hot scent, she had jumped over an old log. A big limb about eight feet long with a sharp point had speared her squarely between her front legs.

Dudley took my gun and I carried the dog. We were at the car in three minutes. We drove to Gaylord where a veterinarian friend, Dr. Doug Hird, had a clinic. Doug was just getting in his car to go hunting. He took one look and told me to carry her into the office and put her on the table.

"She has bled very little," I said.

"For God's sake, George, she's bleeding internally."

"What are those little chunks?"

"That is part of a lung. You go home and I will call you. She has lost one lung and she will only hunt slowly if ever again."

At the same time, Helen was in Mercy Hospital in Grayling with a gallstone attack. I wanted her to know but I waited for news.

Doug worked for four hours cleaning Kim's lung and sewing her up. She was highly sedated and he would not let me visit her for two days. He feared she would get excited when she saw me.

But on the third day I walked her a few feet and she seemed comfortable. Helen wanted to leave her hospital bed to go see her. On the seventh day Doug called, saying he had done all that he could and that she would recover faster at home than at the hospital. Helen's room at the hospital was on the first floor facing the parking lot. When I parked, her room was 50 feet across the lawn and Helen was standing, looking out of the open window. When Kim saw Helen, she ran at full speed to the window and almost climbed into the building. Both she and Helen were in a world of their own.

Doug said it was a miracle that the lung had no infection and healed so fast. The next day — the eighth day after her accident — Kim hunted an hour and a half and made two points. I was lucky enough to hit one bird. Within another week she was hunting six hours a day. Meanwhile, Helen decided she would be better off at home, too.

I didn't ask Doug for a bill. But I had two Browning over and under, open-bore shotguns. Since I no longer hunted waterfowl, we packed the 12-gauge gun in a carton five times as large as it needed and Helen, Kim, and I took it up to Doug. I told him it was a clay pigeon trap and left before he opened it. Kim, who was four years old, continued to be a strong, fast dog through her ninth year.

Years later when he was 86 instead of 59, Mart and I had an evening together and Mart recalled Laddie.

"It's the hardest thing I've ever had to face," he said, "but that Laddie of yours was a wonder dog."

"Yes," I agreed. "That dog, Laddie, knew a lot more about chasing birds than I did. Many times I told him I was sorry when I thought I knew best. But he lived for fourteen years, had the best bed in the house, and good food."

The first time Kim was out with a gun, Bob Klaehn and Guy Means were with us. She pointed several woodcock and was surprised but didn't run when she heard her first shotgun report. Titus wouldn't let me send her to a trainer. "Take her out and let her chase them. When she finds she can't catch them, she'll stop." And she did. But I hadn't fired over her.

That was Friday. Sunday after they had left, I called Otto Failing and asked if he wanted to hunt a couple of hours. Previously she had seen grouse but never had any to paw over. She made a point and two birds flushed and flew down a tunnel through the cedar boughs. I hit both of them. She went on her own when the birds fell and kept rolling and throwing them up in the air with her nose, slightly sticking her nose in the feathers and filling it with scent.

She didn't learn to retrieve until we were hunting in the Lake of the North country with Bob Harrington, DNR photographer. He was waiting for the Wicksall brothers, Bill and Jack, who were Traverse City beer and wine distributors and ardent grouse hunters.

"Well, I'm not going to wait any longer for them," said Bob. "I'm going to go along with you."

"Have you got your camera ready?"

"Yes."

"You'd better. The dog is on point." We walked about 50 yards and flushed two sharptails. Kim had never retrieved a bird although she was four or five years old. When I shot one, she followed it, picked it up and brought it back.

"Did you get some good pictures?" I asked.

"My camera wasn't ready," said Bob, smiling sheepishly.

"I thought you said it was ready."

"It was, but it wasn't out of the case."

That was the first time she ever retrieved, although she had seen other dogs retrieve birds.

Dogs are keen observers and have a sense of what is right and wrong. One day Laddie was upset when it seemed to him a bird I had shot had been stolen and he stole it back.

We were hunting with Mart Winnie when his dog retrieved a bird Laddie knew I had shot. Mart had put the bird in his game coat, as I had told him to do, and we sat down on a log to have a cigarette. Laddie went over to Mart, stuck his nose in his game pocket, pulled out the bird, and brought it over to me.

"There," he seemed to say, "I found and pointed this bird and you shot it."

He looked me squarely in the eye.

"It's your bird, Dad."

If dogs were only running the world....

*   *   *

Me with dogs pointer Jeff and setter Tony, grouse in Manistee County, Michigan.

I show Harry Whiteley a ruffed grouse I just shot over the pointing dogs. The dogs enjoy a relaxing moment.

The picture of our farm home was taken in 1907. We were in our new Ford with doors for the back seat. Sister Dorothy and mother in the back, brother, Emerson in the middle, I'm in the driver's seat, and Dad at the left wheel.

Bob Summers and Lefty Kreh hold a prize mounted bonefish for my approval. Lefty is well-known and loved everywhere fly-fishing is available. He teaches fly casting and has written many books on fly-fishing and is world famous for his photography. His books on the subject are considered a must for the serious "camera hound."

Tying a Griffith's Gnat.

Tying on a long-shanked-hook Drake during a late-May hatch.

the Fly Box

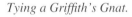

by Dick Pomeroy

Griffith's Gnat

July and August bring sun and heat to Michigan waters and hatches of our little summer midges or gnats. Fortunately, they don't bite as they come by the millions and trout gently suck in the

emergers or the floating adult as he is drying.

George Griffith, one of the founders of Trout Unlimited, originally tied the fly, now carrying his name, to imitate the emerging midge. Gary Borger in his

"Naturals" speaks of the Griffith Gnat as the "finest imitation of emerging midges I've ever used."

Robert Ervin of Paul Young, TU, and the Michigan Fly Fishing Club submitted its pattern and the Orvis award goes to him or to either club he selects. Bob loves the fly as much as his trout on any stream, during daylight hours, with or without hatch during July and August. His recipe:

Hook: Mustad 94840 #18-22.
Thread: Black mono 6/0.
Tail: None.
Body: Peacock herl (may need 2-3 strands).
Wing: None.
Hackle: Grizzly.

Elliott Donnelley entertains the TU Board of Directors at the Donnelley Fishing Camp at Coleman Lake in Wisconsin. His many talents were so recognized that we elected him president of TU. He was to play a strong role in TU's success for many years.

Ebb Warren, International Wildlife Photographer, with a 27-pound Atlantic salmon in northern Quebec. Most of the good photography in this book is his.

Ebb Warren spends an evening on the Upper South Branch near his home at Roscommon, Michigan.

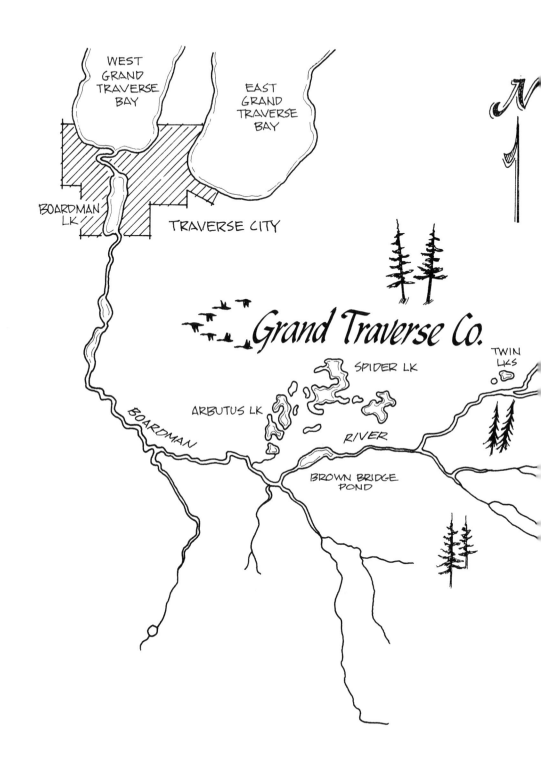

WEST
GRAND
TRAVERSE
BAY

EAST
GRAND
TRAVERSE
BAY

N

BOARDMAN
LK

TRAVERSE CITY

Grand Traverse Co.

SPIDER LK

TWIN
LKS

ARBUTUS LK

BOARDMAN

RIVER

BROWN BRIDGE
POND

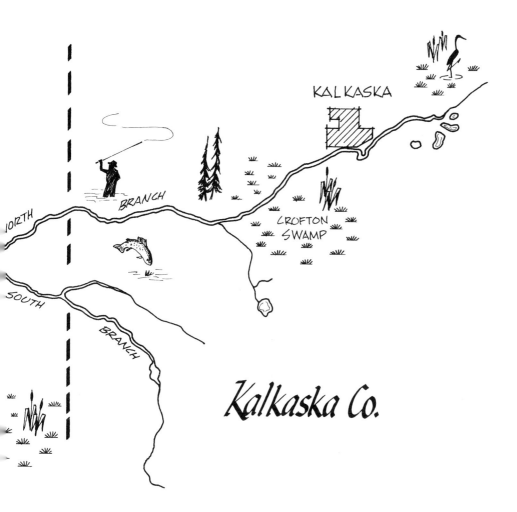

KALKASKA

NORTH

BRANCH

SOUTH

BRANCH

CROFTON
SWAMP

Kalkaska Co.

With John Kronenberg, president of Wayne Knitting Mills, my boss, on an opening day long ago. Due to a high fire hazard, trout fishermen were asked to carry buckets and shovels.

An evening's catch for two on the South Branch, which runs through the Mason Tract, another good reason for TU's growth through the '60s and '70s.

George W. Mason's cabin on the South Branch.

Two floating fishermen approaching the Barbless Hook dock.

Fishing and maneuvering an AuSable boat – it can be done.

A happy ending on opening day at the Barbless Hook, 1951. Seated: my wife Helen; Director Eddy; and Commissioner Shirley Allen, Dean of Forestry, University of Michigan. Standing: Fred Westerman, lovable Fisheries Chief; William Allen, Sales Manager of International Washing and Conveyer Co.; Dr. Leonard Allison, Fisheries Research.

A good motto to live by.

LET NO ONE SAY, AND SAY IT TO YOUR SHAME THAT ALL WAS BEAUTY HERE, UNTIL YOU CAME.

Vic Barothy, world famous light tackle saltwater fly explorer, Florida Keys, the Bahamas, and South America. I was fortunate to be a frequent visitor at all his lodges.

THE AUSABLE RIVER

The AuSable River is a sparkling, multifaceted, but ever-changing gem in a beautiful setting of northern Michigan forestlands east of Grayling.

Like a gemstone, the river reflects the sunlight. The cold, pure water of her springs glistens in millions of tiny wavelets as they dance over her gravel bars, reflects quiet but awesome strength in her deep-flowing runs, and cloaks itself in the mystery of her dark whirlpools.

Over centuries, the AuSable has served people of many eras — prehistoric Indians, explorers, trappers, loggers, farmers, dam-builders, and generations of guides, recreational anglers, and canoeists — all seemingly intent on loving her to death.

Until the early 20th century, the river offered food to those who would harvest her fish and, for all, a means of transportation. She swept away, ahead of the power of spring floods, logs cut from the trees that long shaded and cooled her waters. As they scraped the river bottom, the logs scoured grayling and trout redds from her life-giving spawning gravel.

Trout — and grayling before them — have contributed to the livelihoods of five generations since pioneer families began homesteading on the AuSable in 1875. Michigan has 874 miles of "blue ribbon" trout water among its 36,000 miles of inland streams. The AuSable — with her North, East and famed South Branch — has her share.

For hundreds of thousands of anglers around the world, especially the growing numbers of flyfishers, the river of their dreams is the world-famed AuSable. Her waters spawned Trout Unlimited to protect trout streams and, more recently, Anglers of the AuSable, who support no-kill regulations on the "Holy Waters," a 12-mile, flies-only stretch from Burton's Landing to Wakeley's Bridge.

That's nothing new. The lure of grayling began drawing people to the AuSable and other northern Lower Peninsula streams during the heyday of the lumber barons after the Civil War.

Over more than a century, the AuSable's fabled trout have lured millions to fish in her waters. In 1896, *The Wall Street Journal* advised

THE AUSABLE RIVER

readers, "If you want the best trout fishing, go to Grayling, Michigan, on the AuSable River. Look up the Stephans located near Stephan's Bridge. Should you have trouble wading a trout stream, they will take you in a boat ideal for trout fishing. Their knowledge of where and how to fish is also valuable."

Some descendants of early AuSable families are still guiding fly-fishermen, building boats, caring for fishing lodges, and providing services to trout fishermen more than a century later. This includes a growing number of fisherwomen.

The unique AuSable Riverboat was developed to the river's unwritten specifications through the craftsmanship of early guides. It was a design whose ancestors were polled downstream and back upstream by logging-camp cooks. The boat is a 22- to 24-foot vessel with a 30-inch-plus beam and narrower bottom designed to carry a fly-fisherman on a seat in the bow and a guide on a seat in the tapered stern. The long, narrow boats would still be capable of being polled upstream, but roads, cars, trucks, trailers and access sites have changed the need. Little alteration has been made in the basic design, except today's craft is usually built of thin marine plywood instead of pine, cedar or cypress, it is much lighter and each has its own trailer.

After more than 52 years on the river, I have come to be considered a master in managing a riverboat and, more importantly, respected for knowing what not to do. During my first two years, I turned over three times. Once it was my fault, but in the other swampings, I just wasn't in control of my fishing companions. Over the years I can name fewer than 15 men who have become masters at handling a boat. It takes a lot of experience.

At 92, I do not over-tire myself while guiding an angler-friend for an eight-hour day, but I no longer fish while handling the boat. I am less tired from a day's guiding than I am from a day's fishing. I am just as happy if I have a good fisherman in the bow seat. The boat, my second, was built by Jay Stephan in 1974 without a live well. It does the hard work.

Shore lunches break the day. I carry a bundle of 14-inch-long hard maple sticks split into about one-inch squares. Within 10 minutes, — long enough for a photograph and a Bloody Mary — we have a fire ready to broil the big hamburgers I carry. The meals we have cooked on an open fire are treasures. Yet it would be hard to identify the lunch spots used regularly by guides, except possibly for a few stones used to hold coals. We never take longer than an hour or have more than one drink.

*   *   *

I met the AuSable after our first vacation trip in the summer of 1934. It was love at first sight. Helen and I were enjoying terrific fishing for smallmouth bass out of Perrin's Landing on Lake Leelanau with Chet and Helen Kessler. He was a Coca-Cola bottler in Fort Wayne. On Saturday we heard there was good fishing for trout on the AuSable River. We were told to look up the Stephans at Edgewater Lodge at Stephan's Bridge.

It was late afternoon, but Mrs. Jorgensen, a descendant of pioneer Peter W. Stephan, said her son would guide us. We met a grinning, blond teenager at the Edgewater dock on the river.

"I usually get ten dollars. But it's after six p.m. I can take you on a four-hour float from Stephan's Bridge to Wakeley's Bridge for five dollars."

I looked at the boat. It was long and narrow.

"What about Chet and Helen?"

"I have a buddy coming who will take your friends."

It was late July, about three weeks after the hex hatch, and the Jorgensen boy suggested a fly I didn't have. I fished an Art Winnie's Hopper out of my fly box. There were rises everywhere. I had never cast from a seat in the bow of a moving boat.

"Cast to the side, Mr. Griffith," the boy advised. "Downstream at a forty-five-degree angle." I quickly got the idea. That also would protect both Helen, who was sitting on a seat midway from bow-to-stern of the red-cedar boat, and the guide from my back-casts. The boy quietly lowered a big chain drag anchor on a rope. It immediately slowed the boat. He steered with a pole.

"Fish on," I yelled as I anxiously horsed in a 10-inch brown trout a bit too quickly and netted it. I turned and showed it to Helen then released it. I false cast once and presented the hopper about six feet ahead of another rising fish.

"Another," I said, excitedly, as I brought an eight-inch brookie to the boat just as we were going under Stephan's Bridge, about 200 yards down-stream from the historic lodge. As dusk approached, fishing got better. I could hear Chet and Helen in the boat behind yelling as he took trout after trout. Nothing seemed to spook the fish. Fortunately, we had agreed that we weren't going to keep any fish — there wouldn't have been room in either boat for our catch that night.

"I never thought fishing like this existed," I told Helen as I released another nice brown. The Jorgensen boy was grinning from ear to ear. He knew he was in for a nice tip, and he wouldn't have to dress any fish when he was done. But he didn't realize that I was the one who was hooked long before we got to Wakeley's Bridge about 10 p.m.

"Wasn't that great fishing?" I exclaimed as we drove back to Fort Wayne on Sunday. "I've never caught that many trout." I continued talking about the wonderful trout of the AuSable most of the six-hour drive. Chet and Helen looked relieved when we dropped them off at their home.

"Helen, we've got to have a cabin there someday," I said as I turned into the alley and drove into our garage. Helen had a smile on her face, but it wasn't because she was listening. I had worn her out with my chatter; she was sound asleep.

*   *   *

The AuSable was born as the last glacier receded. It took with it Lake Saginaw, which covered most of the present-day two peninsulas of Michigan, and carved the five Great Lakes and interconnecting waters. She drains eastward and her riverine sister, the Manistee, drains westward from an epicenter located north of Grayling. Both have several major tributaries and countless feeder creeks injecting fresh, cold, springwater.

Collecting waters from her North Branch, East Branch and famed South Branch, the AuSable flows 240 miles from Stump Pond behind a dam in Grayling downstream to Lake Huron. But the Holy Waters and the 12 miles of the South Branch that flow from Chase Bridge to Smith Bridge, through the Mason Tract, are known to fly-fishermen around the world. Yet, to anglers' chagrin, some livery canoeists ricochet from bank to bank of this cool, liquid jewel as they float and paddle downstream on the Mainstream from Grayling or on the South Branch from Roscommon.

The stream compares in size with the spring creeks I have fished in the West. It is easy to wade and has a good gravel bottom that is rich habitat for the many insects on which trout thrive. The Pere Marquette, Boardman, and Manistee rivers, all tributaries to Lake Michigan, are similar in their upper reaches, but the Manistee carries much more sand from eroding high banks.

The next summer we rented a cabin from Grant Shaw in Shaw Park, a half-hour float from Stephan's Bridge, with a fisherman and sales manager from the Heddon Co., then makers of top-of-the-line bamboo fly rods in Dowagiac, in southwestern Michigan. Fishing wasn't quite as fabulous as that first evening float, but it was great. On my next sales trip to Milliken's, I excused myself while the hosiery buyer was preparing her order, and headed through the archway into Hamilton's Men's Store.

"Well, hello, George," said Ebb Warren. "How's fishing?"

I didn't answer. I had the AuSable on my mind.

"Ebb, I'm looking for something on the AuSable. Will you watch for a place that is available, preferably between Edgewater and Wakeley's Bridge?"

"I sure will."

Months went by, and suddenly it was winter.

"Ebb Warren is on the phone, honey," Helen called out. It was a cold February day in Fort Wayne, and I assumed Ebb wanted to remind me to bring my shotgun along on my sales trip. He would want to hunt for snowshoe hares.

Warren had other things on his mind.

"George, I think I've found you a place," Ebb said. "Bill Unger has lost his job, and isn't able to make twenty-five dollars-a-month payments on his cabin just below Wakeley's Bridge. The seller is foreclosing and, if he doesn't sell it, he's going to lose it. He'd like to get out what he has in the place."

I met with Unger then rushed through my sales trip and headed for Grayling to meet Mrs. Daisy Krause.

"Unger owes me $1,500," she told me. "If I take the cabin back and resell it to you, it will be for $4,000. The lot is 250 feet deep. I wanted to preserve the riverfront, so I built at the back end of the lot."

"I'll pay off his contract," I said.

The cabin was of big logs and was built into a hillside with an overhanging open porch. It was about 24 by 24 with two bedrooms. One served as a kitchen. There was a big living room that opened onto an open porch. It was simply a cabin with no water, no electricity, and an outside toilet that reminded me of my days on the farm. It had a stone fireplace and the porch looked like it could be closed in. It would mean a place of my own. I could wade into the AuSable and fish for those wonderful trout! I had hooked myself. Helen had told me to go ahead if I could buy it.

I gave Mrs. Krause a check for $1,500 and became a riparian — a riverfront landowner.

Over the next eight years we sank a well under the porch, built a walk-out block basement around it, and closed in the porch itself as a kitchen and bathroom. We installed a Delco generating plant in the basement, but it barely provided enough electricity for the pump and a few lights.

Helen and Chet Kessler came up to visit after we were settled. All she talked about was her fear of bears. One evening, as Chet and I came in from fishing, we had visitors, Bill and Helen Brand, who lived a short distance downstream. I drew Bill aside.

"Casually tell me that you heard at the bridge that a bear tried to steal Henderson's calf." Bill winked, knowingly. A short time later he began asking about our fishing, what flies we were using, and what was hatching.

"George, I was standing on Wakeley's Bridge today watching to see if anything was hatching when someone told me a bear tried to steal Henderson's calf. That must be a pretty big bear!"

Helen Kessler's face drained. She was obviously scared.

"Yes, I heard about it at the barber shop," I said casually. "Not much happens within twenty-five miles that old Bert doesn't hear about." Chet, who knew I hadn't been near the barber shop for several days, looked puzzled, but he said nothing.

"George, I'm going to turn in. It's been a tiring day on the stream. We'd better get out early tomorrow before the bear gets all the trout."

He was playing along.

"I guess I will, too. I'll set the clock for six o'clock. Good night, girls."

"Would you like a beer?" I could hear my Helen asking Helen Kessler as I headed for the bedroom.

"Yes, I would."

They were giggling over their beers.

"Helen, I'm awfully afraid of bears. Don't they worry you when George is out fishing?"

"Not really. I've never seen a bear around here."

More chatter. I almost went to sleep. I could hear Chet snoring.

"Helen, I've got to go out to the john but, with that bear around, I'm afraid," Helen Kessler said. "I wish Chet and George hadn't gone to bed so early."

"I'll take the flashlight and go with you," my Helen said.

The john was only 40 feet from the cabin but, in Helen Kessler's imagination, every sound was the bear. I could hear her telling my Helen to point the light here and there. It took them twice as long as it should have, but it gave me time to grab an ice pick from the ice box and run out behind the toilet.

The flashlight's beam emerged from the tiny window and danced around in the tree tops. Helen Kessler apparently had just gotten seated. I began scratching, lightly at first, on the back of the john with the ice pick.

"Oh, my God!!" I heard her yell as she jumped to her feet, rocking the structure. The door squeaked open and the light went out. I heard the flashlight hit the floor. Then a low beam swept erratically across the yard as they grabbed for the flashlight rolling around on the floor.

"Oh, I'm so afraid, Helen. Oh, I hit you. I'm sorry. Where's the flashlight?"

"You just kicked it. Stand still and I'll get it. I think he's gone. I think I heard him walking away."

I rushed back to bed. It was several minutes before I heard the door open. They had waited to make sure the bear had departed.

"G-e-o-r-g-e!" they yelled. "G—e—o—r—g—e!"

I was snoring, obviously too tired from the day on the river to wake up for a bear.

THE AUSABLE RIVER

"G—e—o—r—g—e!" It was my Helen, now. I may have overdone my snoring a bit, but she didn't notice.

"Oh, that man. How can he go on snoring?"

For months, mention of Henderson's calf brought a reminder of the night the bear scratched on the john. It was always good for a laugh because neither Helen ever knew the truth.

* * *

It was 1943, the middle of World War II, and I had virtually no stockings to sell. I was getting paid even though I was under orders to make only two, three-week trips through my territory a year. Although Phil Cantelon and I were on the gas-rationing board, lack of gas was limiting our trips to Grayling. We were always alert for someone with enough gasoline ration stamps to make the trip. When Helen and I drove north, we would stay longer.

One day I stopped at Earl Madsen's shop to buy some flies. Madsen, one of the historic guides and fly-tyers on the river, had a surprise for me.

"George, I know you've been looking for a place. I think I have the place for you. I'm the caretaker of the Whitney Camp just upstream from Wakeley's Bridge. My father-in-law, Art Wakeley, became caretaker of the property in 1926, and I took over from him.

"A man named Arland, a recorder in the U.S. Senate, built this place and the house next door in 1896 for his two daughters. One daughter never used her place and sold it. It's owned by David Whitney of the Whitney Corp. in Detroit. He said the corporation is demanding that he sell the camp, and he asked me if I knew any would-be buyers. I told you you might be interested.

"The place needs work," he added, "but it is on a hill overlooking the river."

That was the beginning of The Barbless Hook.

We hadn't eaten breakfast when Madsen arrived. Helen and I were equally excited. As we drove down the two-track trail that wound through the woods, Helen noticed the countless small windows in an otherwise beautiful cabin.

"The river's just at the foot of that hill," said Madsen. He pointed toward the rear of the cabin. We peaked down the hill at the stream, nestled between cedars, before we went to the door.

"If we had this, I'd be willing to give up our home in Fort Wayne," said Helen. That was what I had been hoping she would say.

"It would save a lot of driving and the expense of two homes. I could fish until this darned war is over when I will have Belle Sharmeer stockings to sell again. If we can only buy it."

"Mr. and Mrs. Griffith, this calls for a drink," said Whitney as he met us at the door. It was 8:30 a.m. Madsen grinned sheepishly. Helen shook her head no. I thought for a moment then nodded in agreement. I wanted to buy this place.

Whitney's wife brought out a bottle and poured a drink for Whitney and one for me. I edged my chair in front of the hard-coal burner that heated the building, hoping I would be able to pour the booze into the scuttle of Pennsylvania anthracite coal that sat beside it, but Whitney watched me like a hawk.

By 11 a.m. Whitney was drunk and, if I hadn't been so keyed up, I would have been, too. I didn't feel the liquor, but I was determined to buy the place, even if it meant getting drunk.

I gave a figure of $10,000 and Whitney mumbled, "Be in Nate Viger's office in the Whitney Building with a check at nine Saturday morning." This was Tuesday.

"You'll be there and have the money," he said, apparently forgetting and saying it again. I tried to say I'd have the money in about two weeks, but he wasn't listening. I was concerned because I didn't know Viger, who managed the Whitney estate.

I met Jerry Webber of the J.L. Hudson Co. while I was fishing. Webber was a member of the Rainbow Club. When he heard my problem, Webber wrote a note. "Give this to my secretary Saturday morning before you go to the Whitney offices," he said. The note said, "Give George Griffith a check for $10,000 from my personal account."

I tried to protest.

"If you need it, you've got it, goddamnit," he said. "Don't argue."

"Why can't I have your secretary call you?"

"Because I'll be fishing."

THE AUSABLE RIVER

I stopped to see Clem Feldman at his hosiery shop in Saginaw. He, too, wanted to help.

"I've just sold my home. Let me give you a check for ten thousand," he offered.

I also met Major Hawkhurst, who was with Norman-Huffman (bearings manufacturer) in Detroit. He owned a little cabin upstream from Club Thunderbird. He also offered a check.

"What will happen if that girl isn't in Webber's office on Saturday morning?" he asked. I shrugged my shoulders but said I was sure I wouldn't have problems.

I met Frank Richey, Hudson's merchandise manager, on Saturday morning and he took me to Webber's office. His secretary took the note and returned in a few minutes with a check.

Viger was abrupt when I met him in his office in the Whitney building.

"If you've got $10,000, we can do business. Meet me in the vice-president's office at Manufacturer's Bank at 11 o'clock."

I arrived at 10:45 and asked for the vice-president. He grinned when I handed him the check signed by Richard Webber, Jerry's brother.

"I'm glad you have a check, Mr. Griffith. Boy, is Viger going to be upset. Nobody can turn down your offer."

Promptly at 11 o'clock, Viger walked in.

"Well, Mr. Griffith, do you have ten thousand dollars?"

"No, he doesn't have it," said the vice-president. "I have it. Mr. Griffith, give me a check to cover the insurance and transfer, and it's a deal."

Viger's face turned from confident to sad. He whirled and walked out of the bank without saying another word. I found out later through Franklin Hills, who lived on the river and had wanted us as neighbors, that Viger had hoped to get the property for himself. Webber's check had been the deciding factor.

Arland's widow, who was living in the other house, showed us a photo of our home being built. It looked across the river for miles at a forest first stripped by loggers then scorched as the slash was consumed in subsequent cross-state fires. Heirs of the other Arland daughter are our neighbors today.

We moved to Grayling permanently in 1943. We wouldn't have electric service for five years. We installed a big Delco plant in what is now our mud room, just off the kitchen. It was noisy, its batteries were inadequate. It provided power for the pump and lighting only when it was running.

Fortunately, since I didn't have either the merchandise to sell or the gasoline to travel, I had time to fish, work on the place, and master my riverboat built by John Stephan. For six or seven years, during and after World War II, I made only two three-week sales trips a year just to keep acquainted and train the 50 percent of the salesgirls who were new to selling stockings.

I began remodeling the log house, much of it with hand tools. Then I hired an experienced carpenter to work with me part-time, partly because he had a gasoline-powered table saw that would save me a lot of hand-sawing. We spent four years remodeling because of a war shortage of materials.

Who you know and when often helped, especially right after the war. I took Milton Knight bowhunting and learned his family owned Knight Investment Co.

Although we stalked until nearly dark, Knight didn't see any deer. On the way back, I told him about our home. The next morning he stopped by to see our living room.

"It's just as you described it, George. How many of those little windows do you have?"

"One hundred and sixty-four."

"I can vouch for that," said Helen. "I subconsciously count them every time I clean."

"But as soon as possible, we won't have any," I added. "The previous owner told me he was afraid someone would look into the place, and that's why he installed so many tiny panes.

"We'd like to install Thermopanes — three by eight feet on the two sides and one five by six and two four by six panes overlooking the river," I said. "But they're hard to get these days."

"I'm going to see what I can do for you," said Knight. "When will you be in Toledo?"

"In two weeks."

"That will be on the eighth. Can you be in my office at ten o'clock?"

THE AUSABLE RIVER

"We sure can."

When we got to his office, I found he had called in the head of Libby Owens Ford Glass. The man was pleasant but distant. I didn't know that the Knight family owned more than 50 percent of the glass company, and that this was a command performance for the president and chief executive officer.

"Mr. Knight, I've asked our design engineers, and they say we're booked eleven-and-a-half months ahead."

"See if you can't get these out for George in five or six weeks," he said.

The man nodded and left. I learned later that the Libby Owens Ford engineers halted other projects to produce Thermopanes to my specifications. Then the company billed us for only $550. It should have been $1,500.

That day of guiding Knight paid off handsomely, even though Knight didn't see a deer. It seemed that everyone had an angle during and after the war years. Dyed-in-the-wood trout fishermen were no exception. Most got to Grayling somehow.

One Birmingham construction man, who was a trout fisherman, deliberately underbid a project at the Michigan National Guard camp at Grayling. Naturally, he won the bid. He lost money on the job, but the gas-rationing board gave him plenty of gasoline to come north to check on the project. Of course, he didn't tell them he came north only when he had a car full of friends ready to join him in checking the trout fishing.

Now that I was living on the river, I found I was making more business contacts while fishing, including Webber, than I was making during my twice-a-year trips. Jerry was a nephew of J.L. Hudson and Jerry's son, James, was married to Edsel Ford's daughter. Jerry was a member of the Rainbow Club and would fish for two solid months — May and June — with Earl Madsen.

Anecdotes abound on and around the river. These are true.

A harried part-time resident on the AuSable would fish one full day out of each of the weekends he was at his cabin. His hard work week, plus long drives up to the river on the weekends, was a little too strenuous, especially for his neglected wife.

In an outburst, she said his fishing was making their marriage a once-a-week event.

"Once a week is not enough!"

Her husband stood speechless for a moment as his interpretation of her outburst sank in, then he picked up his fly-rod.

"You're always right, dear. I shall start fishing twice a week," he said as he headed for the river.

No one blamed her for leaving him, but we all understood — fishing only one day of a two-day weekend just isn't enough. Not for a tried-and-true trout fisherman.

One day as he was cutting Ralph Redhead's hair, Bert, a popular barber, asked, "How's fishing?" His stock in trade included being an ask-all, know-all, tell-all town busybody and he might ask the same question 20 times a day, especially when there were strangers in his shop.

"Have you used Dad Hanson's green-bodied stone fly tied by Clarence Roberts, the conservation officer?" Redhead cupped his hand in front of his mouth as if it were asked in confidence.

"No. What size?" Bert whispered loud enough to be heard by anyone waiting in the row of chairs against the wall.

"A fourteen. Last night I had a half-dozen, but I lost all of them. Big trout."

I heard a couple of gasps from the pair next to me as Redhead smiled and his big hands spread out a good 24 inches.

"As soon as you cut my hair, Bert, I'm going over to Dad's shop and buy all the green-bodied stone flies he has in stock. Nobody can tie flies like Roberts."

The two fishermen compared their watches. One shook his head and they both quietly got up. From my chair, I could see they had gone into Dad's store, which was next door. Ralph smiled and Bert gave me a knowing wink. It had worked again.

After my haircut, I went to the grocery with Helen's list. Helen Redhead was shopping, too.

"Mrs. Redhead, how nice to see you. I just saw Ralph at the barber shop and he told me had a big night on the river."

THE AUSABLE RIVER

"Last night?"

"Yes."

"Did you believe him?"

"Of course."

"Well, forget it. We went to a dinner at the Legion Hall last night, and we didn't get home until ten o'clock. Ralph must have dreamed his great night on the river; he said he was tired and went right to bed."

I stopped in at Dad Hanson's shop for some leader material. I made a point of looking over the trays of trout flies. A tray marked "Robert's Green Stone Flies" was empty.

Dad saw me looking.

"Sorry, George, but I've just had a run on green stones. I had three dozen, but two fishermen from Dayton, Ohio, came in and bought all I had. It's kinda funny. I thought the green stone hatch was over a couple of weeks ago."

"They were hatching pretty good next door."

Dad smiled.

In the '40s, I had a boathouse on the river and, like others, I used a motor to go upstream. My first boat had a fish well with several inches of water.

"George, I've heard about these AuSable riverboats," said Bud, another salesman from Fort Wayne. "Is my fly-rod all right? What kind of fly should I use?"

And, obviously anxious to get started on his first float trip, he asked, "George, isn't there something I can do to help?"

I looked at the live well and handed him a small can I carried for bailing out the boat on a rainy day. Bud got down on his knees. He bailed and he bailed and he bailed.

"George, are you sure there isn't a leak in your boat?"

The last word had no more than rolled off his tongue when he reached in with his other hand and found the four holes drilled through the bottom. He was 20 seconds ahead of the five-minute average. He grinned sheepishly.

"Damn you, George. How many newcomers have you taken in with that bailing gag?'

I chuckled. I couldn't give an honest answer.

"Get in the boat, Bud. Let's go, but keep the bailing can —just in case the live well springs a leak. Or it rains."

Most fishermen do things that seem odd, like asking — especially in a group that included newcomers — if I had a reverse screwdriver or left-handed monkey wrench. Some business friends, who never learned they were being taken, would ask me later if I had found such a tool. Often, when I was trying to answer a question I hadn't wanted to be asked, some wise owl would come to my aid by saying: "George, you will need a reverse screwdriver to answer that one." Of course, we never let jokes interfere with fishing. Being the top rod of the day was serious business.

*   *   *

Change comes to everything, including the river. Often it is subtle, so subtle that it is difficult for a generation to accept new restrictions, size limits, slotting. Now it's no-kill, spearheaded by Rusty Gates, second generation owner of Gates AuSable Lodge at Stephan's Bridge, and the Anglers of the AuSable. Many river residents, and some guides, can't see the Holy Waters as being off-limits to keeping trout even though statistics in the late '80s showed 80 percent of the anglers were voluntarily returning their catches to the water by choice, not regulation.

Attitudes change, often with species and availability. Advocates like Gates can help bring about change. By the late '40s, I already was more interested in the life and hazards of trout than in catching a limit every day, or taking trout home. However, few then shared my growing concerns for the river. Bob Behnke, who has a clearinghouse for biologists' findings at the University of Colorado, wrote recently in *Trout* magazine about the "sportsmen," who looked down on the "fish hogs," who would take 100 trout. As Behnke says, they called themselves "conservationists" because they only kept their limits of 25 fish!

In the early 1900s, two fishermen reportedly fished the North Branch at Lovells and shipped 50 trout apiece every day to a saloon on Washington Boulevard in Detroit for its free lunch. Free lunches were usually laid out much like the salad bars are in many restaurants today. If you bought a nickel beer, you could help yourself to a free lunch, including fresh AuSable River trout shipped 250 miles by train from Grayling each day.

Jim Wakeley is probably the most-remembered guide on the river. He was one of a number of top guides, but he was of the younger of the two generations guiding when I moved to Grayling in 1943. Guide's Rest, on the old Marshall property the Stranahan sons gave to Trout Unlimited, was dedicated to Wakeley because of Dr. James Hall of Traverse City. Hall got the idea of Guide's Rest, including the plaque on a big rock and three tables used daily by guides, and began collecting one dollar per person. I wish it could have been done on a larger scale and dedicated to all of the people who have guided. After Jim's death, Wakeley's widow married Don Feldhauser. They live at Wakeley's Bridge just downstream from my home.

*   *   *

Michigan had only two native trout, the lake trout, which was widespread in the Great Lakes, and the brook trout, which was supposedly a native of the Upper Peninsula, despite early reports that the Jordan River had both grayling and brookies. Four streams — the AuSable, Little Manistee, Boardman, and Pere Marquette — are numbered among the nation's top 100 trout streams, said Dave Borgeson, assistant Fisheries Division chief and trout fisherman, who nominated the foursome.

The Baron von Behr strain of brown trout so cherished today was imported from Germany. Fish culturists at the U.S. Fisheries Service hatchery in Northville didn't know what to do with the brown fingerlings they had raised, so they seined them out of hatchery ponds and shipped them north by train in milk cans. The first introduction was less than memorable. The train stopped on a trestle over the Baldwin River, the north branch of the famed Pere Marquette River, and the fingerlings were unceremoniously dumped, says Don Ingle, a Baldwin outdoor writer.

Popularity was long elusive for the browns. They were first blamed for out-competing the grayling, and then they were said to be out-competing the brook trout for spawning gravel and food. About the time of World War I, Eastern fly-fishermen finally discovered Michigan trout, including the rainbow or steelhead trout imported from California.

Virginia Secor Stranahan of Perrysburg, Ohio, recalled it was the heyday of the brook trout when she started coming to Wa Wa Sum as a little girl about 1914. Wa Wa Sum is one of the old rustic log fishing palaces on the Holy Waters.

A daughter of J.K. Secor, one of the four Toledo, Ohio, founders of the 90-year-old fishing lodge, she rode the train to Grayling and then traveled by horse and buggy the several miles downstream to the camp she and a step-cousin, Frank Bell, donated to Michigan State University in 1980.

"In those days a guide would pole his AuSable riverboat upstream to Grayling at night to meet his client on the four a.m. train," she said. "It was one guide, one fisherman per boat. A guide would be on call for twenty-four hours for three dollars."

Kevin Gardiner is a third-generation caretaker of Wa Wa Sum, now operated as an MSU conference center, and a fifth generation relative of AuSable pioneer Peter W. Stephan. He said that the camp was started in 1897 by Rubin Babbitt, son of another pioneer who was a guide and early Grayling conservation officer. It was named by Chippewa Chief David Shoppenagon in 1905 for the clear-cut, burned-over plains vista on the south side of the river.

"The big lodge was built from red pine with tamarack base logs that Ed Kellogg, who lived on the North Branch, cut on the Manistee River near the site of the one-time logging town of DeWard, from 1921 to 1923," said Gardiner. "Kellogg hauled the logs twenty miles on big sleds pulled by horses during the winter months." The lodge, built on a hill overlooking the river and Thendora Road, is still intact and TU chapters and groups like the Royal Order of the Trout use the camp and donate toward restoration work now underway.

Generations have earned their livelihood from the AuSable's fishery, directly or indirectly. Clare "Skip" Madsen's grandfather, Thorun, settled on the river in 1875. He didn't guide, but his son was my friend and neighbor. Earl Madsen, Skip's uncle, guided all of his life, tied flies and created Madsen's skunk fly. He helped design the AuSable riverboat.

Skip's father, Clare Sr., also guided during the Depression of the '30s. Skip doesn't guide for hire. He and his wife, Gail, have served anglers from their

THE AUSABLE RIVER

Skip's Sport Shop on M-72 just west of Grayling year-round for 25 years. Skip officiates over the Grayling buck pole during each firearm deer season.

Chief Shoppenagon also was an early river guide. He worked on other nearby historic fishing camps — Camp Shoppenagon, Twin Pine Lodge, Club Thunderbird, Edgewater, Recreation Club, Rainbow Club, Ginger Quill, and Paw Wah Nee. Paw Wah Nee was owned by the Marshalls, but purchased by Mrs. Stranahan's sons and, except for the lodge, given to TU.

Gardiner says Peter W. Stephan settled in the Stephan's Bridge area in 1876 after the timber barons stripped it bare in hopes of developing a power dam. Failing, he turned to farming. After he found farming impossible because of poor soils and summer frosts, he turned to fishing. He worked until 1879 to get the money to move his family, originally from Prussia, to Grayling from LaHavre, France.

Jay Stephan, who has been trying to retire from guiding during recent years, and Lacey Stephan Jr. are among descendants of Peter W. Stephan who still float fishermen downstream in home-built boats in the ways of old. Jay Stephan has guided the same party on opening day for more than 30 years.

A Michigan Outdoor Writers Association Michigan Heritage Marker placed near the old Grayling Fish Hatchery commemorates Grayling as the birthplace of the AuSable riverboat.

Jay Stephan said that loggers had trim boats that camp cooks used to go for supplies. The cooks learned early that a long, narrow boat could be more easily poled back upstream. From that boat evolved the AuSable boat.

The beautiful slate-blue Michigan grayling with its long dorsal fin disappeared in the wake of the log drives and the devastating fires. Rube Babbitt, famous AuSable fishing guide and early conservation officer, in a 1929 *Detroit News* interview, said few fishermen knew what the grayling was when he was a boy.

"The grayling lay like cordwood in the AuSable and it was no trick to catch them on a fly tied with the feathers of a blue jay or highholder, or a squirrel tail."

* * *

Good companionship makes a good hunting or fishing trips better. Dudley

Lea, who built self-lifting piano trucks and heavy hand trucks in Findlay, Ohio, became one of my best companions.

Dudley, whose father and an uncle started the business about the turn of the century, and his wife, Mary, had a cabin in Shaw Park. When we bought our first cabin downstream from Wakeley's Bridge, mutual friends from Fort Wayne told us we should look up the Leas. We finally located them a few miles upstream through the post office.

He was an experienced fisherman and hunter, and Helen hit it off with Mary, who is still living in Findlay. Since our wives played bridge socially, Dudley and I had plenty of time to chase both birds and trout, especially since the product I was selling — nylon stockings — was declared non-essential to the war effort from January 1941 to 1947. My two three-week trips a year were to keep acquainted for when the war ended. I wouldn't announce I was coming; in their desperation to find extra stockings, merchandise people would be waiting to plead for an increase in their monthly shipments.

Despite purchasing the no-brand mill and having 60 percent of its normal output, we couldn't supply enough of the once-hated rayon stockings our accounts needed. To be fair to all, we distributed our production on a quota based on stockings customers purchased between 1935 and 1940. I couldn't afford to play favorites.

Dudley also had his business arranged so that he had much free time to spend on the river or in grouse country, if gasoline had not been so scarce. The average person was allotted enough stamps to drive about 140 miles a month or so during the war and early post-war years. We would often include a third hunter who had a car and gas stamps.

I never longed for a different face in the bow of my riverboat. Or in the stern. Dudley was a good fisherman, but unlike most, he could guide the boat so I could sit in the bow seat and fish the productive spots we both knew on the river. I cannot count 10 fishermen capable of guiding a riverboat, but that is a matter of experience. All who mastered the art fished often.

Dudley might have been embarrassed if I had singled him out as a conservationist, but he attended 25 of the first 30 Trout Unlimited annual meetings. Although he was never a TU director, he sold as many or more memberships than most directors.

I would always be in charge of broiling our big hamburgers, and Dudley would be the provider of the attitude adjustment potion, always a generous one, but only one, during our shore lunches. Bad weather hit as he made a trip north in mid-July 1988. We made a date to float the river later in the month and he returned to Findlay to see his doctor. It was to be his last trip to the river he loved. Dudley died a few weeks later. Before his death, he had contributed $10,000 to TU and another contribution was made in his will.

Fred Bear, who began building bows while working in Detroit, founded Bear Archery and moved his factory to Grayling to be near the deer he loved to hunt. While he became world-famous as a bowhunter and would kill a polar bear, cape buffalo and elephant with his bow, he also was an excellent fly-fisherman and made many river floats with us.

Carrol and Sally Wert came from Hillsdale County with a love for the outdoors. He was at home in the woods or on the stream and was the best bowhunter I ever knew. Bear said Carrol could read tracks, conditions, and other signs as well as any bowhunter he knew, and he always made sure Wert was the first to try any newly developed product for the bowhunter. Wert's opinion was tops with Bear.

Carrol also was excellent at reading trout water, and his fly would seldom land in an unlikely riffle. It would always be presented in the logical spot. Always....

Carrol and Sally had built the log building that became Wert's Lone Pine Inn in 1947. She served as the popular restaurant's hostess and manager for 21 years. Carrol, meanwhile, broiled all of the steaks and chops over charcoal. He paid for it in later life with emphysema.

About that time I was looking for a fisherman to rely on several days a week. Wert became my regular companion.

Most of our fishing was on the Mainstream, downstream as far as Parmalee Bridge, and on the South Branch from Steckert's Bridge to where it enters the Mainstream. Starting in the mid-'40s, those waters had become popular to the point of being crowded. We knew that the trout of both the Holy Waters and the Mason Tract had been offered several flies before our flies floated over them.

Since much of the river from Smith Bridge on the South Branch to McMaster's Bridge on the Mainstream had much less pressure, Carrol and I adopted it and were catching a large number of 12-inch to 16-inch trout, much better than fishermen were doing on other parts of the river. I had already given up keeping trout and my boat had no live well, but on some days Carrol would say, "I'd like to take a mess home."

The most overworked phrase on trout water or among anglers is "How's fishing?" We would give the usual answers and, when we were asked where we had fished, we would never mention our area. When someone asked us about the stretch of river, we would simply say that some of it was good, but most of the water was too deep and too slow and that we merely paddled through much of it.

One day, however, we passed John and Maggie Hinkle as they were cooking a shore lunch while spending a day floating. Then we noticed several boat trailers were parked at McMaster's Bridge. Our secret was no longer a secret.

While Carrol did not carry a camera most of the time, he was an excellent photographer and, with Sally's help, became a professional and was the Grayling school photographer. He also did outdoor cinematography for outdoor shows. Wert was probably the best Grayling booster I ever knew, and he served TU as both a board member and a leader.

Carrol was also a fly-tyer.

"Here are some more of Wert Fancys," he said one day as he handed me four new trout flies, usually tied on No. 12, 3X long-shank hooks with deer-hair bodies. Many of his flies would also have deer-hair wings.

I'll always remember the first time Wert said, "Try these," and handed me some of his all-deer-hair flies. He smiled as the fly surprised me on my false cast, but I was in for an even greater surprise. When the fly landed, it floated like a duck. It probably would have been a great night fly during the hex hatch, but neither of us was as agile as we once were, and we always fished daytime using dry flies.

Our best fishing would usually be after June 18 or later, several days before the first Hex hatched on the Still Water, a three-mile stretch of wide, slow Mainstream water that resembles a lake more than a stream. We would float it at the slow stream speed and see possibly six flies hatch per mile. Homeowners along the Still Water often would be opening their cottages for the Hex hatches.

"Have you seen any big flies?" we would ask innocently.

"Not one," was the usual reply, even though we had seen single flies hatch within 100 yards of them. We would mark the spot, float within casting distance and frequently hook a prize.

One year we fished on a Friday, Saturday, Sunday, and Monday. On the first three days we had good fishing. On Monday, we saw the normal number of flies, but caught only two trout each, all under 12 inches.

"I'll bet you that a big hatch of Hex will hit this water tonight," said Wert.

"Where did you get that prediction?"

"We have had four good days from interested trout. Today we caught only small trout because a lot of nymphs are moving under the water and getting ready to emerge. He was right.

"The flies were crazy last night," a Still Water resident told us on Tuesday. "But while there was a blanket hatch, the trout fed for less than ten minutes." He did not know the fish had been feeding on emergers that were easier for them to catch. Carrol had found out what scientists knew, but had not put into print. Wert's game theories were also his own, but today they are recognized as fact.

Clarence Roberts of Grayling, conservation officer and close friend, also was a member of our senior fishing club. He also was the best fly-tyer at the time in Grayling, and he taught me many outdoor lessons.

One day in 1953, as Stan Madsen and his crew were cutting seven acres of over-mature aspen on our property. I was burning the brush as Roberts drove in.

"George, some large browns are feeding on the river just out of town. Get a rod and a couple of streamers."

"Stan, tell Helen where I've gone." The smoke of burning brush is nothing to compare with rising brown trout.

We had barely launched Robert's canoe when a sleet storm hit. I couldn't see, so I removed my glasses. I cast a streamer along a log, but as the fly went forward, I sensed that I had over-cast the log. I made an irregular back-cast to try save the fly and, instead, put the big streamer into my right eye.

"Oh-my-God, George," said Roberts. "Don't touch it. Let me cut the leader. We've got to get you to Hennig's office and get that out. I couldn't see but I could sense sleet forming on the shank of the hook. From out of somewhere came Carrol Wert.

"George has got a streamer hooked in his eye," Clarence told Wert. "I've got to take him to the hospital."

"Leave your canoe and tackle and I'll take care of it," said Wert. "Good luck, George."

Fortunately, we were very close to our car. We were in the car within 10 minutes. Roberts drove me to the office of Dr. Moe Hennig, surgeon and a member of our fishing group. Hennig took a quick look at my eye and immediately called Dr. Jack Bell in Traverse City.

"George Griffith has a hook in his right eye," he told Bell. "I'm sending him in an ambulance. He'll be at your office within an hour."

"It's all my fault," said Roberts, as I emerged — already dopey from the shot Hennig had given me.

"N-o-o-o, but can you tell Helen?"

Bud Sorenson, the local ambulance owner, went along. I could sense we were going fast, but I was becoming numb from the shot. Everything was a haze.

I had met Bell, who also was an archer, twice at Fred Bear's home on Stump Pond, and I had seen him making movies of deeryards during winter.

"Why did you take your glasses off, George?"

"It was sleeting and I couldn't see."

Bell took a pair of tweezers and retrieved the fly.

"We are lucky. I could have spent two hours getting that out." After bandaging the eye, he sent me to Munson Hospital.

Bell was in my room at 7 a.m. the next day.

"I had a call from [Govenor G. Mennen] Soapy Williams while you were on your way here from Grayling. He said, 'A good friend of yours and mine is on the way to your office. Do your best.'"

THE AUSABLE RIVER

He took a careful look at my eye through the bandage and closed it up.

"There's a danger of infection. If that happens, the eye must be removed within three hours or you will lose both eyes." He said I had a 50 percent chance of infection.

My good luck prevailed. For 10 days I couldn't see with my other eye. It was hot weather and I could hear boys playing baseball outside my window. It made me think: Suppose I lose my sight, what kind of books can I find on record? "Reading" will be by ear rather than eye. I was hospitalized two weeks.

After I lost my eye, I enjoyed paddling as much as fishing. During our last few years together, Carrol and I seldom both fished at the same time. We usually fished Monday, Wednesday, and Friday. On Tuesday and Thursday, Carrol would fish in his 13-foot canoe from Stephan's to Wakeley's Bridge while I played golf or "worked on the books," a favorite expression by John Libcke, another fishing buddy, that described a do-nothing day.

Carrol built fly rods and hunting bows in addition to tying flies and could have made a living, had he chose, doing any or all three professionally. He and Sally joined Peri, whom I married after Helen's death in 1975, and I for a three-week trip to Montana in 1985 and had a most enjoyable time fishing and sightseeing. When we reached home September 25, we returned to fishing the AuSable and hunting in the grouse coverts.

That was Carrol's last fishing and hunting. A few weeks after Peri and I arrived at our winter retreat in Florida, Sally called to say that Carrol had made his last float. He had thoroughly enjoyed his life on earth, and he had left it better than he found it.

John Libcke — General Libcke — was a unique member of our group. He always wanted to do more than his share of guiding, and usually gave us a quiet lift. But he could be the life of the party.

Libcke, who was raised in Gaylord, had a special assignment during the war. When the enemy had been pushed back, General Dwight D. Eisenhower's quarters had to be moved forward to a new position. It was Libcke's job to explore newly captured areas and scout for castles and other buildings large enough for the Supreme Allied Commander's headquarters.

When the war ended, John was called to Washington, D.C., for a special honorary banquet.

"When I heard my name called, I was the most surprised man in the world," he recalled. "And when I got up to the speaker's platform, I was even more surprised — I was promoted to general."

When he returned to Detroit, Mayor Louie Mariani was waiting for him. His honor wanted Libcke to serve as city tax assessor. John accepted and served for several terms. Louie, who later rented an apartment from me in Florida and became a close friend, told me that "John Libcke moved mountains for me." He satisfied a lot of complaining taxpayers without costing the city a cent in revenues.

We met at the Grayling Golf Course just after he moved north. I was looking for a partner when he came in as a newcomer. We were partners for more than 10 years.

I bought enough marine plywood and other materials for three riverboats and Jay Stephan was supposed to build one for me and two for him. But when Libcke saw mine and learned that there was another one available, he quickly bought it from Jay and soon became a senior member of our fishing group.

Hennig, who averaged seven operations a day, would fish with us on Fridays, his only day off. Just for the day. He was on call Saturdays and Sundays. Now retired and a neighbor, he fishes three or four days a week, once with me.

Ironically, I never fished with George Mason, who donated the famous Mason Tract on the South Branch and who started me on the road to founding Trout Unlimited.

But his ghost floats the South Branch.

*   *   *

SPORTSMAN TO COMMISSIONER

Otto Failing became my friend, teacher, and hunting and fishing companion, and he played a key role in my transformation into a conservationist.

We first met briefly in 1938 at the Grayling Sportsman's Club, an affiliate of the Michigan United Conservation Clubs, which he attended as game supervisor at Gaylord. Later, we met again in February 1939 at Dr. Roy Van Vleck's cabin on Lake Margrethe just west of Grayling.

One winter night I asked: "Otto, just what do you do in the woods?"

"Well, I just look around."

"In the cold and deep snow?"

"Yes. Winter is a critical time of year for deer."

"I'd like to spend a day with you someday."

He momentarily looked away, then eyed me squarely.

"Do you have snowshoes?"

I nodded. Luckily, I bought the only pair Dad Hanson had last week.

"Meet me at eight o'clock tomorrow at Dad Hanson's shop."

*   *   *

Grayling was just waking up as I stopped in front of Dad Hanson's shop. It was precisely eight o'clock. A couple of pulp-cutters carried their Thermos bottles as they headed into the restaurant. Failing was waiting in his car. He motioned for me to join him. Much of the town was closed for the winter. My parked car wouldn't deprive Dad of any business today.

Failing turned west off U.S. 27 onto what is now M-72, and stopped just beyond the Bear Archery plant, within the Grayling city limit. I followed him a few yards into the forest. Just out of sight from the road, spots of blood on the snow told a story I didn't have to ask him to explain; a few yards farther the carcass of a half-eaten fawn was lying amid countless dog tracks. "Too damned many dogs running loose around town," he growled, as we walked back to the car. "We have too many deer for the winter food supply. The fawns are weak and vulnerable. This one was dying, but that was no reason for it to be chewed alive by a pack of dogs. If I tracked them, I'd probably find every one had dinner waiting for him at home. Every owner would swear his faithful pet hadn't been off the porch all day."

A few miles northwest of town he stopped his car again, This time he took his snowshoes and handed me mine.

"This is the Strong's property. It is a few thousand acres and it has a deeryard back in a cedar swamp." I may have passed the area a hundred times, but I had never been in a deeryard in winter.

Failing watched as I struggled with the stiff straps to buckle on my obviously new snowshoes. His looked like old truck inner tubes with holes and a bit of lacing around the toe. I knew he sensed that I was strictly a beginner, but he started off at a near-run for about 400 yards then stopped on a little hill and looked back. I was out of breath when I caught up. He started off again at the same pace. I struggled to keep up, but with each step, one rawhide-webbed hickory frame kept getting in the way of the other.

"George, why do you have to be such a klutz?" I silently asked myself as I nearly fell — my right shoe was firmly anchored by the tail of the frame of my left shoe.

Failing stopped after a short sprint. He grinned as I trudged up to him. "See those tracks, George? A raccoon came out of hibernation, climbed down, and took a walk to look around. He didn't like what he saw, so he turned around and went back to bed in his den up in that hollow tree."

It was the first of many lessons in practical biology I learned from Failing as the self-trained game supervisor had learned in Nature's own classroom. I circled the tree. Otto smiled as my eyes finally focused on a hole in the trunk of the oak.

It was a cold mid-February day, and my glasses steamed up. I was out of breath. I had been out of breath all morning. I was sweating as I never had in winter. I was determined to master the damned snowshoes. This time I watched Failing. I spread my feet and walked faster. I stopped tripping. I was learning an art I heard most Indians learn as soon as they can walk.

We stopped short of the cedar swamp. I could see deer rearing up to reach cedar bows. None of them had horns.

"Where are the bucks?" I asked. Before Otto replied, I smiled sheepishly and answered my question with another question: "They've shed their horns, haven't they?"

"Antlers, George. Deer have antlers. Animals with antlers generally shed them; animals with horns don't shed them." Failing was becoming a bit more patient. I hadn't set any snowshoeing record, but somehow I had covered a half a mile of snow.

A smaller deer reared up and grabbed for a lower bough, but its mother grabbed the tasty cedar branch for herself. Failing saw me watching.

"A doe doesn't care as long as her own stomach is full," he explained. "Many fawns can't reach the lowest browse once winter sets in. It's Nature's way of culling the crop by starving the smallest, weakest animals first. Our battle sometimes seems hopeless. We're fighting Nature and hoping to carry as many fawns as possible through until spring because those that survive will be the 'yearling' bucks most hunters will kill in the fall. Unfortunately, they have a long, rough time ahead until spring green-up."

"Isn't there anything you can do?"

"The department could try to sell some stands of aspen near the yard to pulp-cutters, but that takes time and a market for the pulp. The deer are so hungry they will follow pulp-cutters and stand almost within reach until they can feed on the tender tops.

"Someday, we may be able to kill some does and fawns during the fall season so we won't have so many deer going into the winter. It's better to have fewer going in and having more healthy deer in the spring."

"But the deer are eating cedar. Do they like popple?"

"When they're starving, they'll eat anything. Aspen, especially. Cedar is difficult to regenerate. They'll pull up the seedlings almost as soon as they appear. With much of the cedar gone, aspen is becoming number one."

"Hunters say the Conservation Department should feed the deer. I heard that the Game Division is against it. Do you feed them?"

"No. It won't work. Oh, they'll eat hay or even corn, but it won't do a starving deer much good. A deer has to have certain microorganisms in its rumen in order to digest the food. By the time these deer could develop the microorganisms, they would be dead. No, it's live or die with the food available in the yard."

Another lesson. Failing estimated the herd and made some notes.

"Let's head back, George. It's past eleven."

My snowshoes seemed more obedient on our way back, and Failing was content to walk at my pace. He pointed out various trees and shrubs as if answering questions I was hesitant to ask. "How about going somewhere for lunch?" I asked as we neared Hanson's shop. "It's the least I can do for your putting up with me and my new snowshoes."

Otto grinned. He flipped his watch open, then shook his head. "Thanks. I wish I could, George, but I'm got several days of reports to get in the mail this afternoon or Mr. Ruhl will be ready to nail my hide on the Game Division wall. I'll take a rain check."

"I have to be on the road for ten days," I explained. "When I get home, could I go with you again? I didn't like what I saw — especially fawns starving — but I learned something."

"You did all right for the first time on snowshoes, George. You're the first hunter that ever asked to go with me, but I can see you're really interested. You're welcome to go with me anytime."

He took off his glove and offered his hand. He had been suspicious. And for good reason. There always was a cloud of politics over the department. He was warming up and letting down his guard. I was going to hold him to his promise.

Ten days later, a smiling Otto Failing picked me up at my home.

"I've never been able to locate the yard in Connor's Flats Marsh," Failing grumbled. "Let's see if Earl Madsen knows where it is." Madsen was my guide and also my friend and teacher.

"He's probably at his fly-tying vise," I suggested. Madsen guided full time during the season and tied flies for his clients during the winter. He lived only a couple of miles from The Barbless Hook.

"Hi, Otto, George. Come on in. I'm in the midst of getting a batch of flies out. How about some coffee?"

"Thanks. I need your help," Otto explained. "I want to find that deer yard down in Connor's Flats. I was hoping you could guide us in to it?"

Earl shook his head, regretfully. "Otto, I'd like to, but my customers are on me to ship these flies. They start getting nervous a couple of months before the trout opener. Sit down and I'll give you directions."

Earl began describing the yard, which was about two miles east of his place and just off the Mainstream. His report on the deer seemed complete, but I could sense that Failing wanted me to see the starving deer for myself.

"I can draw you a map so you won't get lost," offered Earl. "It's pretty thick in that yard."

$$* \quad * \quad *$$

Our friendship warmed as Otto and I headed into the cold marsh. He set a pace I could match. It seemed like we snowshoed several miles. We tracked one deer several hundred yards as it averaged a bite of browse every 25 feet. Not good browse, Otto grumbled.

"He's burning up more energy than he can get out of this stuff," Otto pointed out. "He would've been better off staying hungry in the yard. It's a life-or-death mathematical equation —calories in have got to equal calories burned or the deer begins to starve." One more lesson. As a hunter, I'd only been interested in where I could find deer.

As I pressed Otto for explanations, he relaxed even more. When we got into the swamp, I suggested it might be easier snowshoeing on the edge.

"George, there is no easy snowshoeing," Otto replied gruffly.

We neared the yard and several deer spooked, but some floundered in the deep snow and many appeared too weak to run. Larger deer that were strong enough were balancing on their hind legs to get cedar boughs that the packed-down new heavy snow had brought within reach. Does ate while their fawns tried to grab a few morsels. Many were so weak they could barely stand. Nature is cruel. A number of deer were lying dead in the snow.

"When the foresters got the fires under control in the late twenties, the forest produced deer food beyond belief," explained Otto. "By 1935, the herd was snowballing, but there were warning signals. It was growing faster than the food.

"We need to harvest more deer, but few people can understand that the herd has exceeded the carrying capacity of the range. We need a Conservation Commission in tune with the deer problems."

"Opie Titus is on the Commission. Can't he do something?"

He shook his head in disgust.

"Not by himself. I've tried to get the Conservation Commission to come into the yards and see starving deer, but sometimes I think Opie Titus is the only commissioner who has ever been in the woods. He went once with me. He supports Ruhl's ideas of scientific deer management, but he stands alone. We could use some more guys who know something about deer."

"How do you get appointed?"

It was 1945. Otto explained that appointments were little different than they were when the nation was founded in 1776. Elected officials paid off political debts with appointments. Yes, the Conservation Commission was set up to keep the department out of politics. However, the only real safeguard was that no more than four men could be from the same party. With 6-year terms, the most a governor might have to appoint during a 2-year term was one or two.

That might be fun, I thought. I might help bring about this scientific management of deer. However, I wasn't a politician, and I was on the road too much of the time. Some people assumed I was a Republican because I was in business; others were sure I was a Democrat because I was a member of the Michigan United Conservation Clubs and a charter member of the Izaak Walton League. If I were to call myself anything, I thought, I would have to be accepted as an independent.

By going into the deeryards this winter, I had a developed a new insight into growing deer problems, I recognized that few people knew me. Why would they want me?

I joined the Grayling Sportsman's Club, and I attended regional MUCC meetings. I joined other clubs, but I didn't run for office. I tried to get acquainted. I wanted to know what the sportsmen thought about deer. It was more difficult than selling stockings. The stores knew what I had to offer.

Members of sportsman's clubs didn't know me and most weren't interested in knowing me. Everyone was skeptical. How could a newcomer snowshoe into the deeryards one winter and become an instant expert? I asked myself the same question, then I remembered what Otto said. None of them had seen starving deer!

I tried to discuss deer, but most of the members just wanted to enjoy a few beers, recall a hunting trip or two and cuss out the "damned Conservation Department" for not having more deer in the woods or planting more legal-sized trout.

Then the winter began to ease her fury. Otto's dead deer surveys included searches for beaver ponds. He needed to know their locations, but I soon realized that he made note of the ponds so he could share the information with Doctor Van Vleck. I didn't know the retired chiropractor and ardent bird hunter was also a beaver-pond fishing nut.

"I'll go anywhere to catch trout," explained Otto, "but beaver ponds aren't my favorite."

"Nor mine."

He drew a detailed map before we headed back to the car.

"This one will make Van Vleck happy."

* * *

You never know how good a pond will be and few, if any, will be good for more than four or five years. However, I had heard that beaver ponds warm up before the rivers and often provide excellent opening-day brookie fishing opportunities for those like Van Vleck who knew how to fish them.

"How about going along for the opener?" Van Vleck asked. I accepted.

Van loosened the ropes and we lifted his 13-foot canoe from his car top. We placed our rods and gear in the boat and carried it through a half a mile of thick brush. Suddenly, I saw several aspen stumps gnawed to a point as they were felled by the flat-tailed little dam builders. We were at the pond.

The doctor pointed to a path around the dam. We maneuvered through brush and we were upon his rustic launching site. There were only a few inches of water. We could see dark, deeper water a few yards farther out.

We launched the canoe and climbed inside. I settled on my knees in the bow and began paddling.

SPORTSMAN TO COMMISSIONER

"This pond is pretty typical," Van explained. "It's relatively shallow except for forty to fifty feet directly above the beaver dam. Sometimes I pick up some good fish who are waiting by the inlet for a fresh supply of nymphs and worms after a hard rain."

Fish weren't rising. I threaded my tippet through the eye of a squirrel-tail streamer on a No. 10 long-shank hook. Van chose a wet Cahill that tended to float until he jerked it under in his retrieve. I watched. I made a short cast. On my second jerk a fat, but small, brookie took my streamer and was momentarily airborne. It was nine inches long. I didn't care if I kept any fish, but Van had a taste for brookies. I preferred a hamburger.

We drifted toward the dam. Van Vleck made a 30-foot cast and placed his fly within a few feet of the dam. He stripped in his line in short jerks. Suddenly it was sucked under the surface. He had a good fight for a few minutes, then lifted a brookie that was slightly larger than mine and the largest of our 10-trout limits.

"Good eating size," smiled Van Vleck. He knew I would give him my catch when we got to his cabin. I seldom took fish home. It was more fun to catch trout than to eat them, and I was becoming more interested in the life and perils of a trout than in bragging about the number I caught.

Despite his love for eating trout, the doctor was a conservationist. I was pleased with the way he treated young fish that took his fly. If the number of strikes suggested a pond's population was declining, he would return every fish he caught so there would be enough trout to spawn.

* * *

I called Otto a few days after the opening-day beaver pond trip with Van Vleck.

"Otto, this is George Griffith."

"Oh, George, how was your beaver-pond trip with Van Vleck?"

"Good. I was wondering if you could get away for a float down the Mainstream."

The phone was silent for a long time and I wondered if I had been disconnected.

"George, I do have to check on some nesting woodcock along the river. I guess that would justify it. Yes, I'd like to get away for a day. It will be different. We can count as we float. I'm sure Mr. Ruhl wouldn't mind."

"I'd like to meet Mr. Ruhl someday. I've seen him at some MUCC meetings, but I've never had a chance to really meet him."

"You will."

Otto could have been a prize trout fisherman, but he was satisfied. Match the hatch or no, he caught trout. A No. 14 was the smallest fly he had in his box, and the 2X tippet he always used was strong enough to anchor my AuSable River Boat. Few fishermen then carried flies smaller than the No. 16 Griffith's Gnats I tied.

"What do I need, George?" Otto asked. I tried to explain, then I realized that he didn't want to learn how to identify river insects. All he had to do was ask me. Turnabout was fair play. It was noon when we put in at Stephan's Bridge and the beginning of the first of many pleasant afternoons of drifting and fishing. Otto made notes on game. By five o'clock we were nearing my place.

"Boy, I can't wait for that hot toddy Helen promised," said Otto, as he put his rod down in th boat. I had already learned that Otto wasn't a drinker; he drank only when everybody drank. His limit was two drinks — he never drank three.

At a time when college degrees were beginning to float around the Conservation Department, I sensed that Otto felt lucky to be one of the last game supervisors without a sheepskin, Nature was his religion and he was a high priest worshipping at her altar. He loved the woods and streams with a tenderness most men reserve for the women they love.

On another float, Otto surprised me.

"George, pull ashore," Otto said as trout started feeding. "Let me handle the boat while you fish. You're a better fisherman, and I'd like to have a mess of trout."

Otto was one of fewer than 15 men I knew who, while not owning one, could handle the boat well. However, unlike me, he wouldn't fish and pole the boat at the same time.

Rises were suddenly all over the water.

"What are you using, George?" Otto asked.

SPORTSMAN TO COMMISSIONER

"Just an Adams dry fly. It resembles several flies. When they're feeding like this, you don't have to match the hatch."

* * *

Our friendship grew. We exchanged knowledge. I questioned him in the woods and he asked me about flies, but I sensed that we could rely upon each other far beyond a mess of trout or brace of grouse.

It had been a cold day. I was pleased to see my boathouse, as we rounded a the bend. Otto laid his rod down in the boat and rubbed his hands together as his breath floated over them like a miniature cloud.

"It's been a chilly one, George," he grinned. I knew he was savoring the thought of the hot toddy Helen always had ready for us. When we put the boat away, Otto saw Helen and rushed up the hill.

"Thanks, Helen, you've made our day," he said as he wrapped his hands around the steaming mug.

"You're welcome, Otto. You're welcome to fish with George as long as you don't bring him any onions."

Otto raised onions in his garden and he knew that I enjoyed them. Helen never served onions. Otto didn't understand that I smelled like an onion field for three days after last week's float.

* * *

It was nearing 4 o'clock as Tony, my English Setter, retrieved Otto's grouse and brought it to me.

"Damnit, George," he grumbled, "That dog of yours makes nice points and retrieves, but he thinks every bird we shoot belongs to you. Well, I guess it's time to quit, anyway."

"Why? We've got an hour of good hunting left."

"There are some fellows coming up tonight. I want to take some things over to the cabin and do a little cooking. We'll spend the evening talking game. How about coming along? You'll like these guys."

"Well, Helen isn't expecting me. She's playing bridge with the girls. I'll call her as we go through town."

Otto's cabin was on the Hanson Game Refuge and was often used as a Game

Division retreat from telephones and politicians.

I was helping Otto with dinner as I heard a car stop. A somewhat portly fellow walked through the door followed by two others. Otto confidently greeted the leader.

"How are you, Mr. Ruhl?" So this was Ruhl. I had heard that Otto was one of the only field men who talked back to him.

"Mr. Ruhl, this is George Griffith. He's the guy who went into the deeryards with me last winter. Last spring, he took me down the Mainstream in his river boat to check on woodcock."

"Otto, you rascal, you'll always find a way to hunt or fish when you're supposed to be out counting game," Ruhl chuckled. "Well, I guess that's being resourceful." I liked his laugh. With his dominating personality, I sensed that this was a man who knew how to get things done.

"Do you hunt, George?"

"Bird hunting with English setters is my sport, but I like to hunt deer, too."

"What do you know about grouse or deer?

"I know that we find grouse in high-bush cranberries, wild strawberries, wintergreen and thornapples. I know that our deer herd is eating itself out of house and home."

Ruhl's eyes lighted up. I sensed that the latter had been the right answer. Otto had told me Harry Ruhl almost ran the Conservation Department, but he was facing a big challenge. Because of politics, he couldn't get the Conservation Commission to vote for scientific deer management rather than the traditional bucks-only rules then popular with most deer hunters. The others were Dr. Stan Whitlock, his deputy, a one-time medical doctor who went back to school and became a veterinarian, and Ralph A. MacMullan, a game researcher who jumped from a bachelor's degree to a doctorate. Whitlock was Ruhl's deputy and MacMullan, who would become director, was in charge of the Houghton Lake Game Research Station.

After steaks, a pot of Mona Failing's beans and Otto's famous salad, we gathered around the pot-bellied stove that heated the cabin. Tony, my Setter, was fast asleep in front of the burner, probably dreaming of the grouse he had pointed and retrieved during the day.

Otto again caught me by surprise.

"Mr. Ruhl, George and I have spent many days on the stream and in the woods and deeryards over the past three years. He shares many of our concerns about wildlife."

Suddenly Ruhl began grilling me. He was friendly, but I sensed pressure in his probing questions.

"George, have you ever held public office? Are you active in either party?"

Ruhl fired one question after another without waiting for an answer.

"Are you well known in your community? Church? Do you attend church regularly? Are you a member of a service club?"

"I'm an independent, Mr. Ruhl," I explained. "Many people consider me to be a Republican because I'm in business. Yet, because I'm active in MUCC and a charter member of the Izaak Walton League, many Republicans think that I'm a Democrat. I never reveal to anyone how I vote."

Ruhl turned to Whitlock and MacMullan. I sensed that they wanted to talk over something private. Perhaps it was time to get out of the way. Tony passed some gas as he gave a high-pitched, soft bark.

"Excuse Tony, gentlemen. I think it's time he went for a walk.

* * *

The October evening chill was penetrating my flannel shirt. Tony was tired and impatient to go inside, but I stomped out my cigarette and lighted a second.

I puffed nervously and talked to Tony as we walked — yes, I admitted, this means a lot to me. I stepped on the butt, and ground it under my boot. I was lighting a third cigarette as Otto emerged.

"George, you passed with good grades." I couldn't help but smile nonchalantly as if it were a foregone conclusion, but I'm sure Otto could detect my sweaty palm as he shook my hand.

Tony led us back into the cabin and stretched out beside the stove. Ruhl was smiling. I knew that he probably had several potential candidates floating upon political winds. However, I didn't realize how few people of either party were willing to challenge the generations-old, bucks-only trend.

"B-r-r-r, it's getting chilly out there," I said as I rubbed my hands and walked toward the stove.

"George, sit down," said Ruhl. "I want to know more about you. What do you know about deer?"

He didn't wait for an answer.

"Otto tells me you've gone into some browsed-out deeryards with him. What do you think of the herd?"

"I've hunted deer, but I realize now that I didn't understand the effects of winter on whitetails until Otto and I went into Connor's Flat Marsh. I'm not sure exactly how many dead deer we saw, but a high percentage was fawns.

"There just isn't enough food within reach. I saw a few deer standing on their hind legs, trying to reach the lowest cedar branches. Some fawns that tried were too weak to reach the food. The does eat what their own starving fawns might have reached."

"What do you think about scientific management of deer?" pressed Ruhl. "Especially if that means hunting does and fawns to reduce the herd to the carrying capacity?"

"I don't like to think of killing a doe and even less about killing a fawn. However, I realize that habitat is the controlling factor.

"Yes, I guess I can accept hunting does," I continued. "Fawns, too, if they're going to starve to death anyway."

Ruhl pressed on: "For many hunters, I think it will be a sort of test of manhood. Do you think it would make you feel less of a man if you killed a doe or fawn?"

"I don't think so. I don't know anyone who admits to having killed a doe or fawn. Frankly, as with trout, I've become more interested in learning how deer survive rather than how I can kill the biggest buck."

"That's what I hoped you would say," said Otto. Ruhl was smiling.

"Yes, Otto, I think you've found a man who understands something about deer management. George, have you ever thought of being a conservation commissioner?"

"The Conservation Department has a seven-man commission with no more than four from either party," Ruhl explained. "Their duties are to set policy, but at times, especially with deer, they can't resist the temptation to try to manage the department. Some people think the Legislature should have complete control of the deer herd. We're looking for candidates with an understanding of the problems we face with managing deer.

"There may not be an opening for awhile. The governor appoints men every two years for six-year terms. But you need to get yourself known for your positions on the various divisions, Game, Fisheries, Forestry, Lands, Parks and Law Enforcement. Otto can help you with that.

"The commission is hard to work with. We have some members who are very opposed to killing antlerless deer. I think others feel that they represent their geographic areas and, like politicians, oppose scientific deer management."

The evening went on. I mixed drinks. Ruhl wasn't much of a drinker. He asked for Scotch and 7-Up. MacMullan and Whitlock offered occasional questions when Ruhl wasn't grilling me.

"George, have you ever worked on committees? Do you feel comfortable arguing. When you argue, do you enjoy the argument or do you try to avoid it?" The grilling continued.

"I think Otto can tell you I enjoy a good argument anytime about almost anything."

"I can vouch for that," Otto interjected.

I pulled a chair near the stove and sat down. Otto was smiling. He nodded approvingly.

"I've been interested in the Conservation Commission since I met Opie Titus about twenty years ago, but I never thought I would get an opportunity to be a commissioner. How do I go about getting on the commission?"

"First, we have to get you known. Then we have to build up some support and convince the governor that you're the best man for the job, better than any Democrat or Republican. The governor is always looking for a good party worker.

"In 1940, we had 500 square miles of browsed-out deer yards. Now we have 8,000 square miles," Ruhl explained. "Something must be done soon or we're going to lose entire crops of fawns during rough winters. At least in the U.P., where winter is longer and more severe."

Nomination was slow in coming. There were no openings nor any expiring terms. Generally two terms — 12 years — was the limit for a commissioner at that time. I joined three other sportsman's clubs to become known and, frankly, to have more patches to sew on my jacket. I talked with members informally, but I avoided making formal proposals from the floor. I avoided running for office. I just wanted to know them better and to be better known.

Outdoor writers were invaluable.

Jim McKenna of the Grand Rapids Press and I met at a meeting and began talking about conservation. His articles were also published in Booth Newspapers in seven other Michigan cities.

"I'll be in Grayling next month," said McKenna. "I want to do a story on the AuSable trout regulations." Flies-only rules had been proposed by the AuSable Rivers Property Owners Association.

"That's a topic that's close to my heart," I said.

"Well, would you mind if I look you up when we have time to talk? I have to excuse myself now to write a story and call it in to the desk."

"That would be great. I'll draw you a map. Give me a call. I'll take you on a float down the river. I have a boat and I'm pretty good at handling it. You can have a first-hand look."

* * *

McKenna phoned a couple of weeks later and he agreed to meet me at The Barbless Hook.

"I wish I had time for a full-day float, George, but supplying all eight Booth newspapers with outdoor copy is time-consuming."

"A half a day may be all you'll want with the hatchery trout they've put in here."

"How can you tell the difference?" he asked, trying to draw me out. Of course, that was what I wanted. A chance to explain what I knew about fish and wildlife.

We became good friends, after I convinced McKenna that I was developing a well-rounded knowledge of conservation. That fall he came up to hunt grouse and woodcock behind Tony.

"I've heard that dog of yours has a real nose for grouse," he said, "and that he retrieves as well as most retrievers. Is it true?"

"Tony is getting older, but he makes up for that with his bird knowledge. He's never failed to retrieve a bird, including woodcock, which many dogs won't even touch."

That afternoon Tony proved those weren't just idle words. He had six finds, including two woodcock. McKenna was a good shot and Tony retrieved every bird — to me.

"Tony thinks I kill every bird, and I haven't tried to tell him otherwise."

McKenna got out a Speed Graphic press camera and shot two photos — both sides of a 4 by 5-inch film holder. The first flash bothered Tony for the second. Then he carried a grouse up to McKenna's camera.

"Could he do it again?" asked Jim.

"Sure." I stood behind McKenna as Tony proudly carried the bird to him like the polished veteran he had become.

*　　*　　*

I was itching to get a fly-rod in my hand. The spring opener was a few days away and there had been trout feeding on flies. The opener might be the best yet.

"Honey, it's Jack Van Coevering of The Detroit Free Press," yelled Helen. I climbed the hill from the boat house. I knew who Van Coevering was, and I had given him an invitation to fish.

"George, I understand you have some pretty strong opinions about hatchery trout," said Van Couvering, who was one of the Michigan Outdoor Writer's Association's most respected members.

"Come up and see for yourself. My boat has a seat waiting for you anytime."

"How about next Thursday? I'd like to see the river from Burton's Landing to Wakeley's Bridge if we can do it in a day."

"It's a date. Can you be here by 8 o'clock? I'll have everything we need, including a fly-rod you can use, unless you prefer to use your own."

On Wednesday, I saw the fish hatchery truck making its semi-monthly run.

Jack would get to see dumb hatchery fish at their worst — hungry but barely able to catch enough food to stay alive in the wild environment of the river.

"Yes, we made a heavy planting," said Hans Peterson, superintendent of the Grayling Fish Hatchery. "The fish were legal-sized browns raised at the Paris Hatchery," he explained. I knew Hans had about as much love for hatchery trout as I had, but he didn't have much choice but to plant them. In the post-war, plastic rod era, everyone had to be able to catch a trout.

We had drifted only a few hundred feet when Van Coevering placed a fly in a big run. We watched as a trout rose, then chased the artificial down the river, and returned to his feeding station.

"Cast to him again, Jack," I suggested.

Van Coevering looked puzzled, but he shortened his back cast, while I held the boat, and placed his fly adeptly on top of the trout. The fish rose, but again his untrained reflexes made him no match for Van Coevering's floating dry fly. He chased and struck the fly just as it stopped moving with the current, something no wild trout would do.

"What kind of trout are these, George?" he asked as he netted a somewhat lifeless blob and released it. "That wasn't like any brown trout I've ever caught before."

"Hatchery fish. Until yesterday his greatest chase was for fish pellets sprinkled over the raceway at the Paris Hatchery."

About then we passed a nesting woodcock Otto had checked during our fishing trip a day earlier. I pointed it out, explaining the male woodcock's spring sky dance, even though I knew Van Coevering probably knew as much about woodcock.

"What do you think about raising legal trout in the hatchery?" asked Van Coevering. He didn't know that was the question I was hoping he would ask.

"Ernie Borcher, a longtime guide and owner of a canoe business, says they're not sporty or interesting to catch.

"I've been watching the planted fish for several years. They barely know enough to come in out of the rain. No self-respecting wild brown trout would have missed your fly or, if he missed it, chase it downstream.

SPORTSMAN TO COMMISSIONER

He wouldn't have looked at your fly a second time."

*   *   *

The death of Bob Champion of Lapeer created an opening on the Conservation Commission in October 1949 — and pressure on Gov. G. Mennen "Soapy" Williams from candidates for the job. Outdoor writers, including McKenna and Van Coevering, and Vic Beresford, executive director of the Wayne County Sportsman's League and a power in the Democratic party, all urged me to become a candidate.

Most of the executives in the stores I sold stockings were trout fishermen and were members of private trout clubs. Many also hunted and enjoyed other outdoor activities. They and others wrote the governor. Many sent me copies of letters. Several told me that they had talked to Williams about me.

The governor's office called and asked me to meet him on a Sunday afternoon at a ski club.

I was green in political ways. I called Opie Titus and he told me to contact Tony Nielson, chairman of the Crawford County Road Commission and the county Democratic party. Nielson agreed to go with me. He had his own reasons for meeting the governor.

The governor wanted to know why he should appoint me.

"Are you a registered Democrat or Republican?"

"I traveled all of my business life and usually voted an absentee ballot," I explained. "I haven't had time to be active in either party. I consider myself an independent."

"Nice to meet you," he said walking off.

"I don't think you've got anything to worry about," Nielsen said on the drive home.

A few weeks later I called Helen from Columbus, Ohio.

"You've just been appointed to the Conservation Commission!" Helen exclaimed. "I heard it over the radio."

En route home on Thursday, I headed for Lansing, hoping that I could get in to see the governor. About 8 o'clock Friday morning, I called Williams' Capitol office from my room in the Olds Hotel across the street.

I was lucky; he could see me.

"Governor, I want to thank you for appointing me. I want to assure you that I will make every effort to do the job the way it should be done."

"From the supporting letters you have, I'm sure you will," he said. "You realize that I wouldn't have appointed you if I had a good Democrat."

*   *   *

SOAPY AND THE COMMISSION

My 12 years on the Conservation Commission were at once the most satisfying and most frustrating days of my life.

My confirmation hearing as an independent appointed by a Democrat was more horse-play than the ordeal faced by Democrats. But I had to be careful. While the committee was dominated by Republicans, there was one Democrat on the committee who might report any mistakes I made back to the governor.

"Mr. Griffith, could you get me a permit to hunt from my car," asked one able-bodied senator.

I grinned and shook my head.

"I would like a permit to fish with a net in the AuSable River," laughed another.

I chuckled and shook my head again.

And then the clincher:

"What's your opinion of Soapy?"

"Why, I moved to Michigan to be governed by him."

That brought a round of laughter, even from the Democrat, and a motion to confirm my appointment.

"Anyone who moved to Michigan just so he could be governed by Soapy deserves an appointment to the Conservation commission," quipped one senator.

I was in.

* * *

Within 24 hours after I was appointed the pressure started:

The Secretary of the Bay County Democratic Committee invited me to be a guest speaker.

An elderly, well-respected judge from Gaylord called to ask me to have brook trout planted in his favorite section of the Black River. He described the stretch of streams, including stumps and log jams. Could I meet him there tomorrow night?

There were others. If I had accepted all the requests, it would have taken every day — or night — for a month.

Ben East of *Outdoor Life* magazine, dean of the Michigan Outdoor Writers

Association, gave me a list of what he called the "most asked" questions:

"Are you a Democrat?"

"Are you in favor of the department's land-buying program?"

"Do you favor feeding deer?"

"Do you think we should plant more trout?"

"Do you think we should charge for campsites?"

I had a safe answer for Ben and anyone else who wanted me to say in advance how I would vote:

"Ben, suppose you were just appointed to this job. Don't you agree that I need at least a few weeks to ask those questions from the staff and the division chiefs?"

I had phone calls three times a week from Joe Rahilly, a commissioner from Newberry, telling me how to answer these questions.

"If you need help, George, don't hesitate to call me," he offered. I thanked him. I doubted that I would accept his offer.

*   *   *

During the first several months I noted that our primary task was to rubber-stamp generally good decisions, many of them land purchases, already made by Conservation Department division chiefs and approvedand signed by Director P.J. Hoffmaster.

The director was a parks man. He deserves the credit for establishing the principle of purchasing wild lands nobody wanted for state parks and forests. He didn't stand in the way of Harry Ruhl's proposed game land purchases.

During my first year, Hoffmaster urged the chairman to appoint me as chairman of the Parks Committee. He had no interest in hunting. When Haven Hill, the Edsel Ford estate, became a park, it would have provided good rabbit hunting for hunters from Pontiac. Hoffmaster was opposed. Several other southern Michigan parks given to the state also could have provided nearby hunting needed especially to provide Detroit blue-collar workers an outdoor experience close to home, but we allowed Hoffmaster to ban hunting in all state parks.

Some parks got rougher use than they would have from hunters. Hoffmaster had to order picnic tables secured with buried chains, but a fellow hooked onto a table with his car and drove down the road with the table and the rock it was chained to bouncing along the road behind him.

Hoffmaster loved trees. When George Mason gave the state 40 acres on the South Branch of the AuSable and said he would give a total of 29 such parcels to be dedicated as a sanctuary for trout fishermen, Hoffmaster was enthused. We visited the nucleus of the future Mason Tract.

"George, how wonderful this will be for thousands of people who seldom see a tree to walk through here."

I said nothing but, to myself, I vowed: "You won't have thousands of people ruining this sanctuary if I have anything to say about it."

Meanwhile, George MacIntire, Forestry Division chief, was having trouble keeping regenerated timberlands. After they were logged and many burned, big timber owners had allowed them to revert to the state for taxes. Shore-to-shore forest fires that burned the slash loggers left behind were brought under control in the '20s. The scorched forests regenerated and MacIntire and his staff were bringing $1 million a year into state coffers to the envy of those who said such valuable land shouldn't be in state ownership.

Game land purchases were under different rules. They were purchased with Pittman-Robertson federal wildlife restoration funds from taxes on sporting arms and ammunition. Our share was based on Michigan's percentage of the total number of hunting licenses sold in the nation. Many times the state received more than $1 million for game lands and habitat. In later years, the Game and Fish Protection Fund monies helped buy and build recreation areas and some parks where hunting was permitted except, of course, campgrounds where dogs were required to be on leash at all times.

* * *

The commission met on Thursdays for an informal session to hear division chiefs as well as the public. Action on the agenda during the formal session Friday mornings seldom took more than an hour.

One Thursday I opposed something that another commissioner was determined to pressure me to approve. I stood my ground. I said I would not vote for his proposal.

"Have you changed your mind?" he asked me as we were walking back to the Olds Hotel after the informal session. "You know the governor wants this?"

I doubted that. I moved to table the measure during the formal meeting. As soon as the rest of the agenda was passed, I headed for the governor's office to ask him.

"George, I know that members of some other commissions come to Lansing once a month, see a few legislators and have a night on the town at the state's expense. Then the next morning, they listen politely and pass the secretary's complete agenda in one action.

"I appointed you because I had confidence that you would make good decisions based upon conservation of our natural resources."

That was my answer.

Soapy loved to hunt and fish. He had an honest concern for the state's natural resources.

"I'm busy, but I always have time for you," said Williams on one wintry Friday morning. "Sit down.

"George, while flying around the state, I've come to look for patterns in land use. I see many areas without trees. Is that good?"

"Well, Governor, we need some grasslands, and we need some wetlands."

"How much do you feel is enough?" he asked. "Do you own any wild lands? Probably commissioners should."

I pondered the governor's suggestion on the drive to Grayling and barely noticed the bitter west wind blowing snow and trying to heave my car off U.S. 27. Perhaps he was right.

Stan Madsen was standing outside Dad Hanson's shop as I drove into town about 3 o'clock. I stopped.

"Stan, where can I find some land with a fair stand of timber on it?"

"I know of a section [640 acres] with good timber and a fifty-acre lake in Kalkaska County."

I had my wool hunting clothes and snowshoes in the car. I called Helen to make sure she didn't need me. Her lifelong battle with high blood pressure had taken a toll on her health.

"I'm OK, honey," she said. "I'm feeling good today. I'll have dinner ready for you when you get home." I didn't mind cooking or housework, but I was worried when I was away.

An hour later Stan and I were snowshoeing from east to west just north of Cub Lake, which was on the property.

"Who owns it?"

"Uncle George Burke." I knew Burke. He was the Ford dealer. He had served three terms as mayor of Grayling and I had heard that he owned about 4,500 acres of wild lands. Most of it cost him $5 to $10 an acre.

I paid Burke and now I could tell Soapy I owned a square mile of wild timberland. It proved to be a good investment. For several years, I sold oil exploration rights to Shell Drilling Co. During the fifth year I sold the aspen pulp. I finally subdivided the lake frontage at a good profit and sold the rest. My experiences were good training in understanding land values.

* * *

I found Williams, whose picture had been on the cover of *Time* magazine twice that year as a likely presidential candidate, as strong a competitor in the duck blind, in a fishing boat, or in gin rummy as I had come to realize he was in politics.

Several times Soapy and I fished for pike in a boat on Reed Ranch north and east of Mio.

"George, when I'm out here, I'm 1,000 miles away from Lansing," he said quietly. He cast another red and white Daredevle and a northern struck.

"That makes seventeen," he said as he released the fish. "I'm still one pike behind you, George."

"Soapy, I'm willing to forget that last hammer-handle I landed."

"No, you won't. I'm going to at least tie you if we have to stay here all night."

Soapy caught one more pike. It was so dark I couldn't measure it.

"I've just lost my Daredevle, Soapy. I concede. Let's go ashore — if you have any idea where shore is."

SOAPY AND THE COMMISSION

He chuckled. "You're a tough opponent, George."

"You, too."

Another time we fly-fished for plate-sized bluegills over on their spawning beds in a private lake on 4,500-acre Camp Tampico in Kalkaska County. Soapy didn't own a fly-rod, but he did remarkably well. We cleaned a couple of dozen for him to take home but fed the group hamburgers AuSable style. He ate two and drank a quart of milk.

We also took the governor on a float through the Mason Tract on the South Branch and on the Holy Waters of the Mainstream to show him the heavy canoe traffic. On another trip to Drummond Island to fish for smallmouth bass, Nancy and Soapy's brother, Dick, went along. We fished in 30 feet to 40 feet of water with 5-pound to 8-pound bass swimming around us in the clear water.

"Sometimes bass can be as uncooperative as a Republican," the governor quipped. However, of the six we took, three were his. We were fishing on a small lake later in the afternoon. Soapy and Nancy in one boat and Paul Webber, his press secretary, was with me in a second. A car drove up to the shore and stopped. A man with a megaphone yelled that the governor had an important call. Paul said he would go in and answer it.

"It's a sad day," he said when he returned a half hour later. We carried the message to the governor that Blair Moody, a Washington correspondent and Soapy's candidate for the U.S. Senate, had died while recuperating from an operation. Williams was running for re-election and had to stay neutral. Paul and Soapy were in a heated argument as they left me in the hotel. I heard Webber saying, "I cannot allow you to ..."

It was after 2 a.m. when Webber, who shared a room with me, came to bed.

"Where have you been," I asked.

"I can see that you are a political infant," he laughed. "With Blair Moody dead, we have three weeks to get a replacement candidate on the ballot."

One time when the commission had a vacancy, Soapy asked me to help him decide among eight or 10 candidates.

The first letter was from a forester. It was letter-perfect, far better than I could write. Pure bureaucratese.

"I didn't read beyond the third page, Soapy. This guy is too professional for the commission."

* * *

I was often at odds with Rahilly, a Democrat who ran a grocery store in Newberry. Rahilly was for anything that meant sending money to the U.P. Although I never saw him in outdoor clothes, he adamantly opposed Ruhl's game management plans.

At one meeting, we had a request for a one-mile-long road to be built from the end of the state road into a proposed state forest campground and picnic area.

"It will be costly to build and receive marginal use," Glenn Gregg of the Parks Division told the commission in the department's official analysis approved by Hoffmaster.

"We recommend against building it," Gregg concluded.

We debated and debated. I knew Chairman Hal Glassen opposed the road as too expensive. I did, too. Glassen was forced to call for a vote. Rahilly won. It was approved 4-3.

A month later, a similar proposal came up in southwestern Michigan, except the southern park served more people, the proposed road was only a half-mile long, and it would be easier and far less expensive to build and would receive considerable use, Gregg explained.

"If the state needs the road, then Highway Department funds should build it," Rahilly declared.

"Mr. Chairman," I addressed Glassen, "I would like to make a motion to rescind commission approval of the road we voted last month, then I want to make a motion that we approve both roads in one motion."

"You are making two motions, commissioner. Is there a second on the motion to rescind..."

"Mr. Chairman," said Rahilly, "I'll make a motion..."

"Just a minute, Commissioner Rahilly, we have a motion on the floor. Is there a second to Mr. Griffith's motion?" No one said a word.

"All right, Mr. Rahilly, go ahead with your motion." Rahilly had seen the light. He moved approval of the southwestern park road. The vote was 7-0 — without debate.

Pete Hoffmaster's fatal heart attack in his office in 1951 shocked the commission, which included Glassen, a Lansing lawyer, hunter, and dog breeder rising in the ranks of the National Rifle Association, a longtime Republican; Don McLouth of Trenton, owner of McLouth Steel Co., a Republican; Dick Fletcher of Bay City, owner of a string of Texaco gasoline stations and Bay City's "Mr. Republican"; Lawrence Gotschall, a Baldwin schoolteacher then dabbling in real estate, a Democrat; and Pete Calcatera of Norway, a beer and wine distributor in Iron Mountain, a Democrat. Rahilly was the third Democrat, and I was the lone independent.

Rahilly went to Lansing and urged the governor to replace Hoffmaster with Dorias Curry, former conservation officer and Region I chief from Marquette. Soapy asked my opinion.

"Curry is a friend of mine and a good candidate, governor, but there are other good men in the department who are not from Law Enforcement."

"Who do you think we need?"

"My choice would be one of Harry Ruhl's capable assistants."

But since I was regarded as a Ruhl man, I had to hold up. We spent nine months before we finally had four solid votes for Gerald Eddy, chief of the Geology Division, to succeed him. We had too few candidates and should have had a national search. Eddy was a great guy and a good geologist, but seniority rights gave him a poor staff and made the job a heavier load. After I left the commission in 1961, Rahilly made Eddy's job even more difficult. He resigned and returned to the Geology Division as chief.

District field offices were at first manned only by conservation officers and the Law Enforcement division became known as Field Administration. When the regions formed — Marquette, the Upper Peninsula, Region I; Roscommon, the northern Lower Peninsula, Region II; and Lansing, southern Michigan, Region III, Field Administration encouraged law chiefs to tell district Game, Fish, Parks and Forestry people that the regional Field Administration chief was in charge of the region. That occurred before my days on the commission, but it fueled conflicts for decades.

I learned that Rahilly had stonewalled for his two candidates, Dorias Curry for Region I, Harry Aldrich for Region II and "whoever Hoffmaster wants" for Region III. Curry was a good man and a hard worker when I went on the commission; Aldrich demanded a, "good morning, Mr. Aldrich" from everyone in the regional office. He pressed me throughout the nine-month vacancy to support him for director.

Ruhl couldn't accept the setup. Fred Westerman, the Fish Division chief, was nearing 80 and tended to say "whatever you want, director" and "whatever you want, commissioner." George MacIntire, the Forestry Division chief, was a good fighter but, ironically, foresters were not as well known in the woods as were game men.

Someone set up purchase of a piece of land from the state with the Baldwin District forester. When he walked into the district headquarters, he forgot to mention the forester's name. Karl Kidder, the district Field Administration chief, took the would-be buyer out to see the tract, a job the district forester should have done. This was typical of conflict between divisions, especially in the field.

Nevertheless, when I attended meetings of the Wildlife Management Institute and the National Wildlife Federation, I found that Michigan led the country in progressive natural resources management. It still does.

* * *

In 1950 I was the Parks Committee chairman. Don McLouth was chairman of the Fish Committee. I became Game Committee chairman in 1951, and held that until Don's death in 1954.

In the late '40s, we organized the AuSable Rivers System Property Owners Association. I was very active. Dr. Leonard Allison, fish pathologist, and Dr. Albert Hazzard, in charge of the Institute for Fisheries Research at Ann Arbor, gave us good information on which to build our proposal for flies-only regulations on the stretch that became known as the Holy Waters. Dr. Justin Leonard and his wife, Fanny, and others found that the state was depending on hatcheries to keep streams stocked with trout and was neglecting both fish habitat that produces trout and water quality. They told us the fish hatchery program was costing almost twice the entire operating costs of the Game Division.

SOAPY AND THE COMMISSION

The Conservation Department's largest source of income, and the bulk of Game and Fish Protection Fund monies, then came from sales of deer licenses. Deer hunters were subsidizing fishermen, especially those who fished for the hatchery trout released in the state's best trout waters.

Marsten DeBoer, who was Westerman's hatchery management chief and made many of the decisions the Fish Division chief should have made, had woven hatchery costs into the fish budget.

We began our own stream experiments on fly-hooked and bait-hooked fish. Franklin Hills, who overcame being crippled to become an excellent riverboat fly-fisherman, kept records as a guide floated him down the river. He became the association's official record keeper and analyst. I'd give him a report once a week as would other fishermen. His calculations showed that approximately five percent of fly-hooked fish died in comparison with a 40-percent-plus mortality rate for bait-hooked.

Fly-hooked fish generally were hooked in the lip, Hills found, while bait-hooked trout usually swallowed the entire hook and worm. The mortality was based on the physiology of the trout: All of a fish's vital organs are in the throat. A hook in the heart or liver was usually fatal.

A lot of fish were being caught on the Mainstream — 19,000 one year from May 1 to Labor Day between Stephan's and Wakeley's Bridge. That had kept up from 1938 to 1950. I caught more than 600 legal trout, but I returned virtually all of my catch to the river as did a lot of other good fishermen.

Based upon our reports, we pressured DeBoer to fin-clip trout differently so we could determine the year class of fish being caught. With that as a basis, Hazzard discovered that 75 percent of hatchery-reared trout didn't live a month and less than four percent lived a year. A few planted trout would learn how to feed in the wild, but very few would ever grow back to their planted weight of about seven to the pound at six to seven inches long.

Eddy, a fly-fisherman, fished with me the last year of any-bait rules on the AuSable. We counted 186 fishermen during our float, 181 using flies.

* * *

Flies-only regulations for the AuSable came before the commission in 1952.

We debated for months. Many fishermen appeared, and others wrote letters opposing the rules. One letter-writer even quoted Jesus Christ as saying flies-only was against the tenets of the Bible. However, based on the evidence Hills had assembled for the association, we approved a three-year flies-only experiment, increased the legal size from seven inches to 10 inches, and reduced the bag limit from 10 to five trout.

"Next year we'll have a bad year," guides said, "but in two years we'll take as many fish as now." They were wrong: During the first year of flies only, fishing was better, catches were larger, and more fish were caught than during the last year of heavy plantings.

Three years later Westerman had finally retired and A. B. Cook was acting chief, but DeBoer was still running the Fish Division. A vote on making flies-only permanent was due. Despite its known success, the published agenda included a recommendation for termination over Cook's signature.

Higgins Lake Training School was overflowing when Cook stood and repeated his published statement:

"Experimental flies-only regulations on the AuSable River have had no beneficial effect and we recommend that they be allowed to terminate," he told the commission.

When Cook set charts up on an easel and began explaining them, people began muttering in obvious disgust and walking out of the room. Everyone, including the commissioners, knew the figures were DeBoer's, not Cook's. Several people stopped me en route to lunch. The Higgins Lake chef was known for his delicious meals, but I could barely stomach lunch.

"Let's adjourn to the staff house, rather than discussing anything at the dinner table," suggested the chairman. Many of the fishermen had joined us in the dining hall.

We held a brief meeting. The chairman polled the commission. When the informal meeting resumed at 1:30. The chairman announced that, since so many people had attended the meeting, we had decided to make an exception and act on the flies-only issue now rather than wait until the formal session. He polled the members. It was unanimous. Everyone carried the message home and Mort Neff announced it to the state that night from Detroit during his *Michigan Outdoors* television show.

Flies-only regulations for the South Branch came up a couple years later. At first there was so much political pressure that I wondered if it would pass. Then the secretary said a telegram had just arrived from George Mason:

"The owner of ninety-five percent of the water of the South Branch is in favor of flies-only," he read. Mason had swung the vote. By 1957 flies-only was established, and we had a proposed bill in the Legislature calling for 200 miles of flies-only water on trout streams wherever the commission wanted it.

Harry Aldrich was cool to the bill and anything I proposed or supported. I hadn't pushed him in his candidacy to be director. Dorias Curry, who had earned my respect as the Conservation Department boss in the U.P., said, "If you're going to have flies-only, I want some in the Upper Peninsula, too." I saw no objection to that.

The bill was in committee and Gay Walker, liaison between the department and Legislature, testified the department's position.

"What is your personal opinion on 200 miles of flies-only trout water?" a lawmaker asked when he was done.

"Personally, I think 100 miles is enough," declared Walker. The bill was amended.

* * *

Ruhl was insistent that he be named to head the new Research Division. He pressed me to support him for the post.

"Harry, you're too controversial. You would have made a good director, and you could be a good research chief. If I thought I could get you the votes, I would work my ass off. But, Harry, you know as well as I do that I can't."

Ruhl practiced what he taught me to do — work behind the scenes. He would have liked me to have told a couple of the outdoor writers that he was the best man for the job. Jim McKenna of the Booth's Grand Rapids Press and Jack Van Coevering of *The Detroit Free Press* were the best-informed and least-biased writers and I was safe talking with them. But all the writers were fair with me. I couldn't float Harry's name — they knew as well as I did that, powerful as he was, he would never go higher in the Conservation Department.

We approved Dr. Justin Leonard as the Research Division chief.

Glassen and I usually voted together. Calcatera and Gotschall joined us in voting for Eddy.

Gotschall was for buying lands for public use, even if it was in his backyard where it would be taken off tax rolls and he might lose an opportunity, as a broker, to develop or sell it. He was a bait fisherman and opposed including a seven-mile-long stretch of flies-only water on the Pere Marquette downstream from his native Baldwin.

"I'm never going to tell anyone that he can't fish with worms," he said. Despite its effect on the economy of Lake County, the poorest in the state, many people echoed his attitude a decade later, especially when "the 10-inch rule keeps the kids from taking 'riffle rainbows,'" their name for young steelhead who hadn't yet smolted and migrated down to Lake Michigan.

On the other rivers, instead of 200 adamantly supporting flies-only rules, we had about 50 supporters and 50 who went along with the rules. On the Little Manistee, Corny Shrems was for it. His club had 20 to 25 members. The other 175 men who fished the river regularly were luke warm to the idea. They were not too happy with private clubs.

Harry Gaines fought the Nebeshone Club for years one and one of the first big victories for MUCC was a Supreme Court decision that kept the club from closing the river to other fishermen. Nowhere was there a solid percentage. A lot of people opposed flies-only on the South Branch simply because George Mason, who had money, wanted it. But they wouldn't write a letter or stand up in a commission meeting and oppose the rules. On the North Branch we had trouble, partly because the designation meant that Crawford County had 75 miles of quality trout water. There was some disagreement on the Boardman and other streams, but the rules finally won sufficient support to win commission approval.

Calcatera was a very active deer hunter from a big camp his family used during the summer. He knew more about lands than anyone else on the commission. Calcatera had a great respect for Ruhl, but that didn't necessarily mean he would vote for antlerless deer hunting in the U.P. He wasn't a fisherman, but he usually could be counted for a logical vote on fish matters.

Fletcher had a big camp on the South Branch just above Chase Bridge. Fletcher was both an ardent fly-fisherman and deer hunter. He also hunted birds, but his legs couldn't stand the long days of tramping behind bird dogs of his younger days.

McLouth was a great fly-fisherman and bird hunter. He was generally supportive but strongly opposed to buying more state lands, even at $5 or $10 an acre. He had a Grumman Goose in which he would fly into remote Canadian waters to hunt waterfowl. He could fly the plane, but he had his pilot take him in to wilderness lakes and apparently hunt with him.

Rahilly was a staunch supporter of anything that he thought would help the U.P. economy, but I never knew whether he hunted or fished. He didn't always disagree with Ruhl, but he enjoyed embarrassing the Game Division chief. He routinely stamped a question mark on anything the staff did. He often acted more like a feisty legislator defending his region from all who thought of the U.P. as a playground. Ironically, Rahilly's stance often pitted him against those who would send tourist dollars over Big Mac. The Williams administration built the five-mile-long suspension bridge across the Straits of Mackinac to link the Lower Peninsula with the Upper Peninsula.

I never changed from being an independent, despite my admiration for Soapy as both governor and friend. Nor did I accept the idea many residents had that I was Grayling's commissioner, and that it was my duty to get things for them. Both Helen and I were slighted at times because I tried to maintain an independent position and avoid local politics.

However, during my second year on the commission I brought the governor up to Grayling to be master of ceremonies and square-dance caller. Soapy was the life of the party and fit into every group. Being a peddler, I could sense that there were times when it was in my best interest as a businessman not to be the governor's choice. I explained this to him one day and he appreciated it.

Rep. Emil Peltz of Rogers City said management of the deer herd was the most controversial and most time-consuming subject during his 20 years in the Legislature.

"It was not our decision. It was the Conservation Department's baby."

At time sportsmen were less than civil about deer.

During a Saturday lunch in the early '50s at the Grayling Game Club with the governor and several game men present, I was forced to quiet the sportsmen.

"Gentlemen, in our role as hosts, it is our duty to treat our guests as the good sportsmen we are when addressing them."

Williams told me he had to leave for Drummond Island to attend a sportsman's club's dinner.

"Why don't you come along? You're the Game chairman."

I rushed home, got Helen's permission, grabbed a hat and mackinaw, and met the governor's party at the airport. Ben East and James A.O. Crowe joined us. It was a fun evening for Soapy — after a brief meeting, he called square dances until midnight.

* * *

Despite my respect for him, I could get mad at Ruhl. Damned mad. We fought frequently, but our quarrels were quickly forgotten. When we created the new position as research coordinator, Ruhl wanted the job.

"George, you know I'm the most qualified," he insisted.

"I agree, Harry, but you're too damned controversial."

He pressed me further.

"Harry, if I thought I could get the votes, I would work my ass off to get them for you. But I simply can't."

"I suppose you'll vote to feed deer. Your research man will not handle game research."

"If that is how you feel, I may vote to feed deer."

I was still furious as the chairman called the formal meeting to order. I heard someone make a motion to feed deer. I heard a second. Hal Glassen, with whom I shared beliefs in conservation, suggested that feeding was a waste of money — starving deer could not be saved with corn or hay. Ordinarily, I would have echoed his comments. But I was mad ... that damned, conceited Ruhl ...

A moment later the chairman called for a vote. I made a serious mistake and gave a frustrated "yes." I regretted it before the vote was complete, but I was too mad to try to change my vote. Feeding passed 4-3.

I was ashamed when Hal Glassen approached me after the meeting.

Fondling his pipe, he said dryly: "George, conservation was just set back 20 years this morning."

"Hal, I apologize. That damned Ruhl has been on me for two days. He wants to be research chief. You know we can't get him the votes. The best might be you, Calcatera and me."

Hal smiled out of the corner of his mouth. "Just try to not let it happen again. You're the only commissioner I can count on to make a logical decision."

Ruhl was talking with Whitlock and MacMullan. I motioned that I would like to see him.

"Harry, I apologize. There was no excuse for my vote. I would like to eliminate the new research position rather than lose your confidence."

"I accept. I guess I had you really worked up."

In a couple of months, we were back on the old basis of respect. With Ruhl, I always knew where I stood. If it had been another division chief, I might have never known.

My most difficult position had been during Fred Westerman's days as Fish Division chief. I played cards with Fred and he trusted me. He was about 80 when he told me about some stream-improvement work done by Horace Clark and his crew.

"Horace Clark is a dangerous man," Fred said. "He opposes our trout-planting program.

"The structures he builds don't have any more trout feeding around them than natural sites."

"Fred, there's more to it than more feeding fish; for one thing, there's water temperature."

He held up his hand to halt me.

"Commissioner, if you say so, we will keep it up."

I sensed that he had been convinced by DeBoer that stream improvement was a waste of money. Fred was a grand gentleman. If I had talked to him as I talked to Ruhl, he would have offered me his resignation.

*   *   *

There was a chill in the air. Duck season was only a couple of weeks away.

"Honey, the governor's office is on the phone," called Helen. I climbed the hill from the river. I was spending more and more time at home because of Helen's health. I often had to quietly tell her to go and sit down while I cooked meals or straightened up the house. It hurt her pride that high-blood pressure, which was first noted in her teens, kept her from caring for her home. She loved to play golf but gave it up on Dr. Moe Henig's orders.

"George, I want to bring my son, Gery, up duck hunting," Soapy said. "Can you set up a blind for us on Houghton Lake? Give me two days' notice. Nancy will have to send a note to his teacher."

I knew Gery. He was a friendly, extremely well-mannered teenager, and I admired Soapy for taking time out from being governor to instill in his son his own love for the out-of-doors.

"I'll call Bill Hines and get back with you as soon as possible," I said. Blinds on Houghton Lake were leased from the federal government. If you weren't in a blind by 8 a.m., you lost your right to it. Hotel owners had five or six blinds apiece. Our party had three blinds: Soapy and Gery; Hines, "Sailor Bill" Hudelson, who started the first canoe livery in Grayling; Dr. Roy Van Vleck; three others I don't recall, and me — three per blind a mile apart along the northeast shore of the huge, shallow lake.

The hotel owner took us to our blinds in a motorboat. He had decoys laid out in front of each blind.

"I'll bring you coffee at ten o'clock," he said. And he did. Just before 10 we heard a motorboat, then several flights of ducks came over our blind. En route with our coffee, he had motored through resting birds that we would never have seen. He had not guaranteed us shots at ducks, and he neither acknowledged nor denied that he had planned his route to send birds our way.

*   *   *

Don McLouth was dead. His death in 1954 was the second major shock of my two terms on the commission and left the commission Fish Committee chairmanship vacant.

SOAPY AND THE COMMISSION

Gotschall was chairman in a line of succession based on seniority. Larry drew me aside after the meeting.

"George, I can't give you both Game and Fish," he explained. "Which committee would you prefer?"

"I think Game can take care of itself, but the Fish Division needs help. I'll take Fish."

*   *   *

Horace Clark and Dr. Wayne Tody, Stream Improvement Section chief, were held back in their programs first because of DeBoer's domination of the aging Westerman and then his handling of his successor, Cook. Because of his hatchery orientation, DeBoer still didn't recognize the importance to a fisherman of catching a wild trout rather than one whose dinner was tossed to him.

Ruhl urged his men to keep bird dogs and to hunt so they would know the taste of the grass on both sides of the wildlife fence — from the hunter's as well as the biologist's viewpoint. Most of his men also were good fishermen. In contrast, few of Westerman's and Cook's men, dominated by DeBoer's hatchery orientation, were sportsfishermen. Most viewed their mission as producing numbers of fish rather than quality sportfishing.

I hoped, in my new role as commission Fish Committee chairman, I could breathe new life into the hatchery-smothered, stream-improvement program. Many gravel spawning beds on prize trout streams were covered with sand released by poor land use by riparians and rowdy livery canoeists. On the Pere Marquette and Manistee, some high banks were turned into raw sand slides. Most popular streams needed some help to withstand the worst use they had seen since the days of the timber barons.

By 1959, other outdoor writers had experienced Van Coevering's disgust with fat browns that didn't have the muscle to catch flies nor the brains not to strike at an artificial a second time. They joined in the growing criticism of rearing and releasing legal-sized but stupid hatchery trout.

Pollution was becoming a problem, but we were not fully aware of the many heads of the dragon. Some streamside property owners' sewer systems dumped directly into streams. Almost everyone chopped back tag alders and other

152

streamside growth and used pesticides to battle mosquitos and fertilizers to grow lush riverbank lawns. Few, if any, recognized that they were a part of the problem. Meanwhile, cities like Grayling dumped partially treated sewage into the river, which was growing filamentous algae and other aquatic plants at an alarming rate.

Pere Marquette tributaries in the Baldwin area, which boasted of having more than 150 lakes in Lake County, were dammed with U.S. Soil Conservation Service funds to create new lakes and ponds. Overflow dams warmed the water about 10 degrees. One small trout nursery stream dried up downstream from the fourth dam.

"My favorite pheasant territory is nearly devoid of birds," Dick Fletcher told me one day. I went to look at the area with the commissioner. It was tabletop level farmland with large fields of beans or sugar beets, no fences, and farming up to the gravel of the roads. There were traces of open drainage ditches that had long since had been replaced with tile and had come under the plow.

We drove a few miles then returned to where we had started.

"Well, what do you think, George?"

"Dick, just as any good game manager would ask, when did your hunting go bad? Now be careful to remember details."

He thought for a moment. "I would say about five years ago. It was when my present dog was a puppy."

"Was there any water in those old ditches?"

"Yes."

"Were the banks of the ditches covered with weeds? Was the land ever fenced?"

"Now, goddamnit George, you sound like Harry Ruhl."

"Dick, if you brought me here to hunt pheasants, I wouldn't take my dogs out of my car. Let's take a ride."

We were in my car. I drove about 30 miles to an area where there were wet spots, uneven ground, more game cover, and fences that were in ill repair. The crops didn't look very good.

"Dick, this is where I would release my dogs. I would guarantee that they would find birds here."

Fletcher said little as we drove back to his office.

"Come in and have a drink, George."

"I would like to, but I want to be in good bird cover by dark."

That final jab was a mistake. He was embarrassed, but we continued to be friends, and at times we supported each other. However, he never again brought up his theories on game or fish. I never knew whether he followed my advice and found pheasants to hunt. I had failed to sell him on scientific game management.

"Damnit, George, why do you have to be so all-fired cocky?" I asked myself. You sure wouldn't have sold stockings with that attitude — even if you knew you were right.

* * *

Planting of the best trout streams was done monthly during May, June, July, and August. When the Institute for Fisheries Research proved — as had been suspected — that most hatchery trout lived three weeks or less, DeBoer didn't admit failure. Instead, he scheduled heavier plantings twice a month.

"George, my client caught eight trout while I was getting ready to start a float," said Ted Stephan, Jay's father. "He asked me where they come from. I told him during some falls we have a false migration of trout, and that this was one of them.

"They were all those dumb hatchery fish, but he's a new fly-fisherman who will probably come for several years. I didn't want to tell him that the trout he was catching were dumped into the river two days ago. They were migrating, all right. They were making a run back to the hatchery for dinner."

With the cooperation of residents and guides, we determined that 19,000 legal trout were caught. In May, 10 percent were hatchery fish; in August, 55 percent.

Despite listening to countless misinformed, biased, but sincere people who wanted more hatchery trout, and feeling like I was riding herd over interdepartmental squabbles, I enjoyed being a commissioner. However, Helen accused me of taking a negative stance whenever I was approached. I tried to rock and roll with the tide, knowing I couldn't win them all.

John Kronenberg, president and chairman of Wayne Knitting Mills, and his wife, Edith, came to visit us. Kronenberg had grown up in the West and he had a large territory when Vassar produced men's underwear as well as ladies' girdles. They were both better-than-average anglers and were fascinated by the river. He had brought a case of Scotch. I engaged Earl Madsen to guide them. We fished days and partied nights, especially with the Roy Vandercooks and Major Hawkhursts.

On Monday night, Helen went with Edith to say goodbye to the Vandercooks. John and I had a Scotch, then a second.

"George, how would you like to come inside the organization?"

"I don't feel that I could be happy working with your sales manager or your vice-president on a daily basis. May I make a counteroffer?"

"If I can have another Scotch."

"John, you are aware that I have become a member of the Conservation Commission. Since Michigan produces more than half of my business, if my territory were reduced to Michigan plus Cleveland and Toledo, Ohio, I would be just as valuable to you and have more time for the commission."

He sipped his drink and pondered the idea for a moment.

"I'll arrange it for you. However, if you ever work for us more than half of your time, you'll be a damned fool. Furthermore, if you ever tell anyone I said that, I'll say you are a liar."

I was going to have more time for trout fishing, hunting, and being a part of resource management. This meant more time to be at home. Helen was going along on many of my trips, and I didn't have to worry about her being at home alone.

* * *

I first heard the name Trout Unlimited in 1950, during my first year on the commission.

I was waiting to put in my boat at Burton's Landing, where the Holy Waters start. There were four boats ahead of me: George Mason, president of American Motors, with his personal guide, John Stephan, and three of Mason's guests with guides.

Mason came over to greet me.

SOAPY AND THE COMMISSION

"George, I'm sure that your crowd will want to put their new commissioner in the proper position in the line."

Mason's huge frame shook in a belly laugh. Stephan, who was a good friend, answered for him: "We sure will, commissioner. Right at the end of the line." That called for handshakes with Mason's guests.

"The three of you get going," Mason told his guests. "I want to visit with Griffith for a few minutes." Their guides were glad to get in the lead ahead of Mason and Stephan.

"As you know, George, I have been national treasurer of Ducks Unlimited since it was organized. But my first love is trout fishing. I have been thinking about a similar organization. Trout Unlimited."

"It sounds good," I replied.

"My idea is to have one hundred twenty members who, of course, will know the fish people. Once a year we could wine and dine the director, staff and commissioners at the Detroit Athletic Club and tell them what we want."

"George, I can see that you are not a politician. We can't tell them anything. Fish and game managers want to be pushed into just what they already want to do, but are afraid to suggest.

"That list of one hundred twenty prominent fishermen may only fuel a bonfire built by one hundred thousand fishermen who are neither research- nor regulation-minded."

Stephan and Jerry McClain, my guide, said all aboard.

"Hold Friday evening open," said Mason as Stephan began poling him downstream.

That chance meeting changed my life.

* * *

GEORGE MASON AND THE SOUTH BRANCH

I invited Al Hazzard, Opie Titus, Jim McKenna and Don McLouth to attend the meeting Friday night at Mason's home on the South Branch.

Mason was one of many successful leaders of business and industry who was finding that spending time on a trout stream with a fly-rod was the ideal therapy for the high-blood pressure and ulcers that go with corporation board chairmanships.

We barely got started before the fur began flying, but it was the mating act that spawned the egg that hatched years later as Trout Unlimited.

"Gentlemen, I am treasurer of Ducks Unlimited. I would like organize one hundred and twenty prominent fishermen to fight to protect trout streams," explained Mason, who was the first treasurer of DU and owned the land through that flowed 14 miles of the South Branch of the AuSable River.

"Once a year we could wine and dine the fisheries biologists and tell them what we wanted."

McLouth jumped onto Mason's idea.

"George, you're thinking as I am — someday trout fishing is going to be just for those who can afford it."

Opie's weathered face heated a cherry red that matched his red and blue-plaid flannel shirt. Opie had spent too many years out-of-doors to care much for style.

I started to explain what I had told Mason — that a group made up of prominent fishermen might seem to control the Fish Division and fuel resentment in other fishermen.

Titus' hair trigger was cocked. He fired both barrels of a verbal blast at McLouth's idea that only the rich should be able to afford to fish for trout. I recognized that their clash was a replay, except for the subject, of other disagreements Opie said he had with McLouth when he was a commissioner.

"Trout fishing is not just for the rich," Opie declared. "The working man has just as much right to fish for trout as corporation presidents."

"Opie, you sure know how to crucify me," said McLouth, laughing. McLouth was the founder of McLouth Steel.

GEORGE MASON AND THE SOUTH BRANCH

"You can catch all the trout you want, Opie, if every fisherman carefully releases every fish he hooks," said Hazzard.

"Opie, I wasn't thinking of creating an elitism on the river," Mason explained. "I want the South Branch to be open to fly-fishing. I'm told that flies-only regulations should help perpetuate the wild trout in streams like the South Branch and AuSable for all anglers and for future generations."

His comments drew no blood, even from Titus. Mason wanted what we wanted — to halt planting of trout and to protect streams, partly through flies-only regulations.

McLouth and I came to an agreement everyone finally approved: At the next commission meeting, Don and I would ask Hazzard some leading questions about survival of hatchery-reared fish. That would give Hazzard an opportunity to report on the results of his research, which had been bottled up too long in the Fish Division.

Fish Division chief Fred Westerman was nearly 80 years old. He was a great gentleman, and fun to play cards with, but he was from the era of Michigan's Wolverine railroad fish hatchery car. We had fish hatcheries everywhere and the Wolverine played a role in the introduction of not only trout fingerlings, but various warm-water species.

If a legislator or a lake organization complained about the fishery in a certain lake or stream, Westerman would send the Wolverine with some hatchery fish. Perhaps that was why he was dominated by hatchery chief Marsten DeBoer and why he viewed men like Horace Clark and Wayne Tody of the Stream Improvement Section as dangerous to the fish-planting program. Perhaps that was why he had little faith in Hazzard's research — he believed in DeBoer and let him lead him.

Sensing the beginning of change within the Conservation Department, McKenna pleaded for a look at our questions before the meeting. He wanted to use them as a basis for his outdoor column for the *Press* and the other Booth Newspapers on the Sunday before the meeting.

Mason was strangely quiet as we planned our strategy. A crown prince widely respected in business and industrial worlds, Mason, privately, was a shy man who loved the woods and waters, but knew relatively little about the natural world.

Biologists, including Hazzard, held Mason in awe as the rich president and Chairman of the Board of American Motors who virtually owned the South Branch. Few suspected that behind the imposing six-foot, three-hundred-pound-plus image there was a man who hungered for their knowledge and was almost paranoid lest he betray his ignorance. Few also knew Mason avoided asking questions if he thought that they might belittle someone in authority.

Flies-only had been a subject for 10 years. Don and I decided to wait a few weeks before promoting our long-range plans: Flies-only regulations, a larger legal size, and an elimination of hatchery trout plants in quality trout streams. Several articles on flies-only had been written by Ray White and other scientists. We were wise. When we unveiled our plans through McKenna and other outdoor writers, they triggered letters, appearances at commission meetings, and feuds between property owners who had not fished for many years.

We expected, as with other controversial issues, no more than 35 percent of the residents would favor new restrictions.

Emotions ran high when the chairman called the informal commission meeting to order at the Higgins Lake Training School south of Grayling. The log building that had been built on the large, deep-water, inland lake by Civilian Conservation Corps youths during the dim '30s days of the Great Depression overflowed with fishermen and, surprisingly for the time, several women anglers. I was buttonholed by at least a dozen people before the meeting.

Larry Gotschall reminded: "When you make that motion, you're going to find that not everyone agrees with you."

A number of property owners and guides asked to speak during the informal session Thursday afternoon.

"Our catch will decline for the first year, but improve after that," veteran guide Earl Madsen predicted. Other guides echoed his testimony. Most of the guides who spoke supported flies-only regulations.

Not all approved. One property owner complained: "You're going to make a violator out of my nine-year-old grandson. He likes to dangle a worm to trout from my dock!" he cried.

"Why can't he dangle a fly?" I asked.

"He's too young to do that."

"What does he do now with the undersized trout he's now catching?" I continued.

The crowd sighed with relief.

Presentations, most emotional, continued all afternoon.

* * *

We were tense Friday morning when we sat down for breakfast at the long, rustic dining room tables and open benches that seated six to a side. I could overhear grumbling undertones among staff members who usually supported me. Gotschall was right. Not everyone in the department was in favor of setting flies-only regulations, but I couldn't let that stop us.

The chef placed steaming platters of pancakes and others mounded with eggs and bacon on each table. Two jugs of maple syrup stood sentry near each end of the table.

"Eat up, gentlemen," he smiled. "we have lots more coming."

It wasn't the Ritz, but the scent of the dew on pine needles wafted through the log structure and blended with the odors of frying bacon and eggs emanating from the kitchen. It was a breakfast fit for a king in a setting few kings could duplicate.

At 9 o'clock, the chairman gaveled the meeting to order. We called for a report from Commissioner Pete Calcatera on the Lands Division. Calcatera called on Charlie Miller, chief of the Lands Division. He explained the proposals. We approved about 40 purchases for the Parks, Forestry and Game divisions.

Then the agenda moved to flies-only regulations on the AuSable. The chairman turned to Don McLouth, chairman of the Fish Committee. Meanwhile, Fish Division chief Fred Westerman was being coached by hatchery chief Marsten DeBoer.

"Fred Westerman will make a statement," McLouth announced.

"Flies-only regulations on the AuSable. What does the Fish Division recommend?" asked the chairman. The proposed rules were over Westerman's signature.

160

"Mr. Chairman and Commissioners, we are reluctant to recommend permanent regulations," explained Westerman. "Since the commission appears to want to try flies only, we recommend a three-year experimental flies-only regulation between Burton's Landing and Wakeley's Bridge. We will conduct a study and report back after the second season." Stan Cain, a University of Michigan professor of fisheries and wildlife, told the commision he felt that the Fish Division was being overly cautious. Experimental regulation were unnecessary.

Hazzard had written an article in 1946, in which he said the answer to good trout fishing was to catch all you want but not keep any.

"What does the Institute for Fisheries Research have to say?" I boomed. Westerman looked surprised, and I sensed he was hurt. I had said nothing about Hazzard during our card game in the staff house Thursday night. Fred yielded the microphone to the young fisheries researcher from Ann Arbor.

"Our research shows that trout swallow worms completely, while fish tend to be hooked in the lip with flies." Hazzard gave a creditable report.

Discussion followed on the experimental aspects of the Fish Division proposal.

"Mr. Chairman, I don't favor experimental regulations on something that has been proven," McLouth said. "I move that we set flies-only regulations on the AuSable from Burton's Landing to Wakeley's Bridge.

"I second Commissioner McLouth's motion," I said.

The rules passed, although not unanimously. I believe Gotschall voted no. But in the excitement, I'm not sure if he was heard; he wasn't either.

"Mr. Chairman," he said, "I want to go on record as saying I'm against flies-only regulations. I will never vote for a motion that makes it unlawful for a man to fish with a worm."

The outdoor writers surrounded me after the meeting.

"When are you going to press for an end to hatchery plants and larger legal sizes, George?" asked McKenna.

"As soon as Hazzard can give us statistics to justify the action. From the information we have collected on the river and given to Hazzard, we know that the survival rate is poor. But he's the scientist, and I'll respect whatever he tells us."

I was positive Hazzard would support us.

* * *

When the same regulations were proposed for the South Branch two years later — in 1953 — Mason sent the commission a telegram stating that the owner of 94 percent of the property to be included (from Chase Bridge to Smith Bridge) favored the suggested regulations. The rules passed unanimously.

* * *

Mason and I were close friends. I spent at least one evening a week listening to his plans and dreams.

One night he talked about building a chapel in Hartwick Pines State Park.

"I'm not a religious man, and I don't attend church," Mason confided one night, "but my parents were pillars of their church. I am doing this in memory of them. I don't want the other commissioners to know about it." I wasn't sure he could keep it from them.

"You must have a permit from the Conservation Department to build a chapel in Hartwick Pines," I explained. I told him how to go about getting it as discretely as possible.

"I don't believe it will have to have commission approval," I told him.

* * *

Mason used to keep two or three expensive cars, all European, at his lodge. He would drive them through the woods at high speeds to try to find what made them strong. Then he would have the cars shipped to American Motors' factory in Kenosha, Wisconsin, where engineers tore them down and inspected them part-by-part. Mason was always looking for ideas that could be adapted to his cars.

Mason was very excited when he drove a Mercedes into our yard one Sunday morning. We were eating breakfast with Jim McKenna and his wife, Marie, who were our weekend guests. Mason didn't seem concerned about making his announcement in front of the *Grand Rapids Press* outdoor editor.

"George, the Chapel in the Pines is finished. It will be unveiled at eleven a.m. today. I want you to see it." He welcomed the McKennas to go along.

It was a private showing of the small Norwegian log chapel. Mason, who never allowed anyone to take his picture, finally consented to pose for McKenna's camera after extracting a promise that the negatives would be given to him, and the picture would not used again. Mason didn't pretend to be modest — he *was* modest. His accomplishments spoke for themselves. Nothing at the chapel site hinted that he had it built.

Mason didn't understand people who did not appreciate beauty. The chapel was some distance from the park entrance. Within a week, parents were standing guard while their children used the chapel as a toilet. Fortunately, Mason was never aware of that, but he did see initials carved in the log wall, prompting me to have the following reminder placed at the park's entrance:

Do not let it be said,

And said to your shame,

That all was beauty here,

Until you came.

Mason conceived a second wilderness chapel, the Fisherman's Chapel on the South Branch. Bill Jenson helped him select the site for the structure, also known as the Fisherman's Shrine. The shrine was built of Indiana limestone and logs on a high bank in a stand of pines overlooking the South Branch miles from any other buildings. It was completed after the land was transferred to the state.

* * *

Mason and D.B. Lee bought 14 miles of frontage on the then-remote South Branch from Cliff Durant, son of automotive pioneer William Durant. They agreed that the survivor would buy the other's half interest in the tract at the original price. When Lee died, Mason bought Lee's interest from his estate. He held the property, which he referred to simply as the "South Branch," in a strange reverence. I think I was one of few with whom he shared his feelings for the land.

"I've never cut a tree on my property for fireplace wood," he once said proudly. He wanted me to praise him. I couldn't.

"Cutting of some trees can be very beneficial, especially for deer," I told Mason. I had tried to be diplomatic, yet I knew that my statement irritated him. At that time I couldn't understand why. Later, he explained: "George, I realized that you probably knew what you were talking about, but I didn't want to appear ignorant. I'm ashamed that I've devoted so much of my life to mere machines and so little time to the beauties God has given us."

*   *   *

The South Branch was already steeped in history before Mason came, as Margaret Jenson, Otto Failing's sister, wrote in a booklet, *The South Branch of the AuSable*." I have quoted extensively from the booklet with her permission.

Lake St. Helen empties into the South Branch, which flows through Roscommon and under three bridges en route to its confluence with the Mainstream: Steckert Bridge in Roscommon County and, downstream in Crawford County, Chase and Smith bridges. No one knows when its recreational use started.

"Mrs. Roy Fuller, whose father was a druggist in Roscommon at one time, told how her family would float down the river on rafts to the Oxbow Lodge from Roscommon," she wrote. "They would haul the raft back to Roscommon using a team of horses."

"About 1902 John Failing had a sawmill just below the Downey House. They would float logs down the river from what is known as Failing's Landing to the sawmill. At this landing, Jessie Failing Bunker, at the age of two years, fell into the river and would have drowned if her brother, Otto, and her dog had not held onto her until help arrived and pulled her out."

She is unclear when the Downey house was built. Downey, who owned the Downey Hotel, where members of the Legislature stayed during sessions in Lansing, died in 1921. He and six other men had owned a large tract from Chase Bridge to Smith Bridge except for one 40-acre tract known as Forest Rest. The seven built the Downey house, which was named the Wolfville Lodge because at one time a wolf was killed near the site.

"Five of the men sold out to Mr. Downey and Mr. Woods and they divided the property. Mr. Downey took all the 40s touching the river, with hunting and fishing rights on all of the property. Mr. Woods took all the rest of the land, with agriculture rights to all of the land. Mr. Woods made a sheep ranch out of his (land) and built seven houses for his sheep herders and his home, which was known as the South Branch Ranch. The Sauders became caretakers of the ranch.

"The South Branch Ranch was built about two miles from the Downey house. Orlando Barnes started it in about 1909. He also organized a club made up of either seven or nine men," including Watson, Smith, Woods, Downey, Zimmerman, Vosbert and Barnes.

The Sauders moved from the sheep ranch, near Hay Marsh Creek, back to their home above Chase Bridge. Meanwhile a clubhouse was built of logs just below the Jenson house on what was later known as the Downey Place. Seven tenant houses were also built and the clubhouse was later used as a barn after the big clubhouse was built, she writes.

"Mr. Smith and Mr. Vosberg both tried farming, but the land was not good for that…a 100-acre field was cleared, but that, too, was mostly blown sand.

"About 1920 Mr. Sauders moved back to the main ranch house and a man by the name of John Wiynn had some Holstein cattle brought in…they were still trying to raise sheep, not having very good luck with either."

By then, all but Downey and Woods had dropped from the club and they divided it. Woods was killed in an automobile accident in 1922, and his widow kept the ranch with Sauders as the caretaker.

A story, not in Margaret's booklet, said a log building known as the Chin Whisker Club, which may have been the clubhouse, was built on the river and used largely as a place for a select few who played poker.

When they decided to divide the ranch, they organized a poker game with the 40-acre tracts divided among the members and used as poker chips. Forty acres had a value of $40. By the middle of the second day Woods and Downey had won all of the 40s.

"The ranch house burned down in 1924 or 1925, but Mrs. Woods had it rebuilt," Margaret recalled. "Harry Sauders can remember bringing in feed (for livestock) by a team of horses ... shipped in by the carload when it was so cold it would take hours to rub the ice off the horses before he could go to bed. They still kept about 125 sheep and quite a few head of cattle.

"After Mrs. Woods' death, the ranch went to her brother, Mr. Lincoln, and he sold all but 1,200 acres to the federal government. He lived in one of the tenant houses for a few years. Mr. Sauders left the ranch in 1933. Someone tried raising turkeys once on the ranch, but later it was sold to someone else.

"Mr. Sauders and his son, Harry, worked at the (Durant) Castle and had a horse drop dead from sunstroke. They built the dock and also helped when the 100-acre field was cleared."

Carl Babbitt was hired as Durant's guide in 1919 and he and his wife, Jessie, were hired as caretakers that fall and served until 1927, when his illness forced him to retire.

"Carl would take the long riverboat up the river in winter to Steckert Bridge and walk on to Roscommon for the mail or any supplies they might need. In an emergency, they would have Mr. Sauders take them in to Roscommon with his team of horses and sleigh.

"Otto Failing, Bill Jenson (Margaret's husband) and Dad (Horace) Failing were hired to terrace the lawn and build a stone retaining wall and steps going down to the river. They worked there in 1921, then Dad and Carl built the little cabin that was known as the pest house."

Horace Failing was caretaker for Durant and Otto and his brothers, Horace Jr., Pete and Rolland; they spent their youth there and much time fishing in the stream. They poled a boat upstream to the Castle site and floated back home.

"We saw an average of four fly fisherman a week," Otto told me. He said Mason, whose lodge was several miles downstream, floated the river two or three days a week and may have done 40 percent of the fishing done on the then-remote river before 1935.

Margaret recalls moving to the Downey Place in May of 1926 and working for Mrs. Downey for about three years before it was sold. Durant's friends included author James Oliver Curwood of Owosso, who had his own home at Chase Bridge. Dad Butler, coach of the University of Detroit, also visited Durant and brought some of his football players to hunt and fish.

* * *

Cliff Durant started to build the Castle on what was called Head's High Bank. Part of the old buildings were given to Fred Baldwin and moved to the mouth of Hay Marsh Creek. Durant gave him a life lease on that property.

"The Castle was built of red brick and stone, a sprawling two-story building of 56 rooms in all. The inside of the tower room was painted sky blue with stars and a moon painted on the ceiling. There was a huge basement gymnasium, and two large vaults, plus storage space. (It) had eight gables and seven fireplaces."

The Castle was completed by fall 1930, except for painting and decorating, she recalls. A crew of painters and artists painted vines with grapes on the walls of the dining room "and they looked so real that one felt he could pick them." The bathrooms were decorated with swans and ducks in ponds. The music room included the piano Durant played, also his drums, saxophone, clarinet and coronet. The Durants moved in despite the ongoing work.

"On Feb. 5, 1931, the painters were working…in the music room area and had lowered a light fixture that had about 50 bulbs in it while they painted the ceiling. That night the painters all went to Roscommon for the dedication of the new high school. When they returned, they noticed smoke coming from the house and awakened Bill Jenson, but by the time they got to the house, nothing could be done…the floor was covered with building paper and the fire spread from one end of the house to the other. Bill notified Mr. Durant and he had the fire marshall come from Lansing…(He) said the fire started in the music room…an electrical short circuit…or it could have been combustion from paint cloths left in the attic by the painters."

Durant returned in the spring to the Downey Place, where he spent his summers. He was something of a daredevil. When he was young, he raced in the Indianapolis 500. He owned five cars and an airplane and built air strips near both the Downey Place and the Castle. He had a pilot, but he also flew, and once landed his plane on its nose in the river in front of the Downey Place. He was uninjured but a passenger was hospitalized.

In the fall of 1931, another tragedy occurred. Lightning struck the building that included the caretakers' quarters, an eight-car garage, five Delco plants and a barn for saddle horses and a cow.

"Mr. Durant continued to spend his summers at the Downey Place. In the fall of 1936, he returned to California and died in October of a heart problem. His widow sold the property to George Mason and D.B. Lee; they kept it just as it was until Mr. Lee died, then Mr. Mason bought Mr. Lee's share."

Bill and Margaret Jenson worked for Mason for 10 years, living until 1945 at the Downey Place, then at his summer home five miles down the river. The lodge was large, with dark beams crossing the ceiling, and it had two furnaces. He also had a private river cabin with a boathouse under it that was his private quarters.

* * *

"One of our sons was married in the chapel," Margaret Jenson recalls. "The wedding was simple and small, but what a lovely wedding it was, with the wind singing through the trees, the river rippling over the stones and birds singing in the treetops."

The shrine was beautiful, but the secrecy in which Mason tried to cloak both chapels points again to his innate shyness. Memorials or no, I doubt if he really understood why he built the structures.

Mason gave the state 80 acres instead of a 40 the second time with the understanding that they would remove the three-story stucco Downey house and the caretaker's house within two years. I told him to do this.

"George, they won't do that."

"Do me a favor. Make it part of the offer."

A few months later he came in laughing.

"They're tearing the buildings down. They sold the buildings for $15. He couldn't believe anyone would do it for the lumber.

* * *

When George Mason said he was going to give the first of 29, 40-acre parcels to the state, I asked him what kind of restrictions he was going to place on the use of the land.

"Why do I need to place restrictions? You fellows on the commission feel like I do."

"Because I won't always be on the Commission," I replied.

George accepted my suggestions. But for those restrictions, the Mason Tract would have been treated like other state forest lands, and the beauty and solitude would have been carved into roads, campgrounds and snowmobile and off-road-vehicle trails.

*   *   *

George Walter Mason, who was born in Valley City, North Dakota, on March 12, 1891, had a flair for mechanics at an early age. He helped the mechanic at the Maxwell dealer's garage after school without pay. He first drove an automobile — a two-cylinder, 10 horsepower Maxwell — in 1906 when he was 15. During the summers he raced motorcycles on the flat dirt tracks in North Dakota.

He entered the University of Michigan in 1909 and studied engineering for three years. During his college years, he founded and operated a distributorship for the Briggs-Detroiter automobile in Valley City. He turned to business administration in his final year and was graduated in 1913.

He accepted a position with Studebaker in 1913, joined Dodge a year later and, in 1915, became purchasing agent for the American Auto Trimming Co. in Detroit. A year later, he joined Wilder Tanning Co. in Waukegan, Illinois.

During World War I, he coordinated activities at the U.S. Army Ordnance Department's Rock Island Arsenal. In 1919, he was placed in charge of business extension for the Irving National Bank in New York. He returned to Detroit in 1921, joining the Maxwell-Chalmers Corp., then being reorganized by Walter P. Chrysler, and became general works manager. He continued in the post when Chrysler Corp. was formed in 1924 and supervised production of the Chyrsler car, the automotive sensation of that year.

In 1926, he became vice-president and general manager of Copeland Products Inc. in Detroit, a leading refrigeration manufacturer, and became president in 1927. He resigned in 1928 to become president of Kelvinator Corp. Charles W. Nash offered him the presidency of Nash Motors of Kenosha, Wisconsin, in 1936. Instead, they merged into Nash-Kelvinator, with Mason as president and Nash chairman of the board.

Mason was elected president of the Automobile Manufacturers Association in 1946.

He also became chairman of the board of Nash-Kelvinator upon Nash's death in 1948, and led the company through a merger with Hudson Motor Car Co. on May 1, 1954, becoming chairman and president of the expanded corporation.

*   *   *

GEORGE MASON AND THE SOUTH BRANCH

Mason died in Detroit on October 8, 1954. George Romney, who assumed the presidency, recalled not Mason's industrial and economic accomplishments but the spiritual and moral lessons of his life. He cited Mason's innate modesty, deliberate restraint and his trait of giving himself freely and fully to friends and loved ones.

"While his spirituality did not express itself in the usual practices and was largely concealed by his varied activities and habits, he was a deeply religious man," said Romney. "The Bible was at his bedside and he read it regularly.

"George Mason did not seek the motes in the eyes of his friends, associates or others. He constantly sought the good and the true. He was never known to discuss the weaknesses of others, let alone to belittle or accuse them falsely.

"His consideration and concern for others was exceptional. He never lost the common touch or distinguished between his friends and associates on the basis of worldly position.

"He did not overlook the human consideration in decisions and programs. In acts affecting the lives of others, he would frequently say, 'Remember, we are dealing with a human being, the most important thing of all.' His highest compliment was, 'He is a great human.'"

I was one of six friends most quoted in his daily life selected to give brief taped tributes about Mason for The Detroit Round Table of the National Conference of Christians and Jews' 26th anniversary dinner and tribute to Mason November 14, 1954. Helen and I attended the dinner at the Masonic Temple.

John S. Bugas, vice-president of Ford Motor Co., was chairman, Edgar A. Guest, the poet, was master of ceremonies, and Romney gave the principal address, praising Mason's work with the Boy Scouts of America, Path-Finder Guide Dogs, Ducks Unlimited and Goodwill Industries. His tribute was interspersed with the six tapes.

*   *   *

The remainder of the parcels of land was given to the state of Michigan by Mason's estate in 1955, with restrictions I suggested:

A. The state will accept the gift within two years.

B. The land shall be left in its natural condition.

C. Canoeing will be allowed with a lunch area at the Castle site, and a second canoe stop at the chapel. Canoe camping will be allowed at the canoe campground. (At that time, the canoe campground was on national forest property, which became part of the Mason Tract in a trade.)

The key value of the gift was a blue-ribbon trout stream. Mason suggested for that reason that the property be managed by the Fish Division.

The terms of the gift stated that if the restrictions were not enforced, the property would return to Mason's estate — in perpetuity. The property was reportedly appraised at $1,125,000 in the settlement of Mason's estate in 1955.

I was a member of the Conservation Commission. We accepted Mason's gift with restrictions unanimously. Within days, canoeists were camping illegally on the banks. Strangely, the Law Enforcement Division refused to enforce the restrictions the commission had accepted with the gift of the property.

Mason deprived his family of a large portion of his estate to give the Mason Tract and access to the South Branch to the state in trust for tens of thousands not yet born who would share his love of the river and the wild forest land through which it flows. Ironically, fewer than 20 percent of those who fly-fish or canoe the South Branch have any idea who George Mason was or why he gave away his most important possession.

* * *

Four of us floated the South Branch from Chase Bridge to Smith Bridge, with a quiet hour and a half below the Castle for lunch and philosophizing.

We got home after seven and it was 10 before dinner was over and I could crawl into bed. It was a hot muggy night, and I tossed restlessly.

Suddenly, a voice called outside the window, saying, " I want to float the South Branch with you."

"Who are you?"

"The ghost of George Mason."

As dreams are inclined to do, Mason and I were suddenly at Chase Bridge, floating the first 100 yards. As the stream widened, there were rising brook trout dimpling the water as far as we could see, with a few trophy browns leaving rings the size of automobile tires.

GEORGE MASON AND THE SOUTH BRANCH

"Oh, George, what is this?" he asked, pointing to a large pile of ashes under a group of white pines and Norway spruce. The fires had exposed the roots of the stately trees within 20 feet of the water and erosion had silted what had been a beautiful fish run.

"You agreed there would be no camping and only four lunch spots. Here, less than 1,000 feet from the bridge, that campsite is killing those beautiful trees."

He reminded me of the state's original agreement that no new campsites or lunch areas would be allowed in the Mason Tract.

As I was trying to think of a way to explain how our highest-quality resources were being overused and polluted by people because of the lack of money, manpower and adequate legislation to protect them, we passed another well-used campsite. I described the situation in Grayling, Roscommon, and other communities where three state agencies were charged with enforcing pollution laws, but they were handicapped with confusing laws that failed to clarify the responsibility.

Mason was silent as we floated along.

We passed Forest Rest. George looked surprised.

"I hear a car! How did it get there? I closed that road twenty years ago!"

How could I explain that it had been reopened to accommodate a few fishermen. I knew the real shocker was just ahead. At the end of a road was the first lunch spot to which Mason had agreed. A woman sat in front of a car in a lawn chair, reading a book; a man was starting a fire; and in one of the stream's famous pools, two children and two dogs were playing. Their behavior would have been acceptable on a populated lake, but not on a wilderness trout stream.

The entire bank, as well as the forest Mason wanted to preserve as he knew it for hundreds of years, was eroding sand and littered with an assortment of cans, bottles, paper and other debris. Someone had even discarded a tire.

Mason shook his head. His weight shook the riverboat as we passed two more illegal camping spots in the next mile of stream. Eroded banks and silted streams were the landmarks.

"Look at those beautiful elms," he said. "They're dead."

"Yes, George, all of the large elms on the South Branch and the lower Main

Stream are dead or dying. Something must replace them if our waters are to be kept shaded and cool."

The Castle was around the next bend. Mason hung his head. He couldn't bare to look. Most of the trees he had preserved were gone; the bank and shoreline were eroding sand; and the log jam at the Failing cabin was gone.

His head moved slowly back and forth as we floated. In my repeated explanations, I think he sensed my misery in having failed in my commitment to carry out his wishes to preserve the river into perpetuity.

We discussed his reasons for wanting to found Trout Unlimited: fishing regulations aimed at full creels, more planted trout, smaller fish, and how his hopes for quality trout fishing, habitat improvement, larger size limits, and lower creel limits were being ignored.

"Still have flies-only regulations here?" he asked.

"Yes, George, we do, but they are only part of sound regulations."

"Well, that is one battle you won," he said.

"No, George, we have not won a battle. Rather, we, like a prize fighter, have been winning a round at a time."

"What do you mean?"

I explained that we had hired a new Fish Division chief a few years earlier and his first act passed on recommendations from his fisheries research section that all special restrictions be removed from the South Branch.

"What?" The boat shook.

"Their reasons were that predator populations of large brown trout and northern pike were hurting the smaller hatchery trout. I asked him for proof.

"We met at Roscommon. The new chief asked his men where he could float the stream at night with jacklights to see the predators."

"'I haven't been on the stream this year,' the regional fish man said. The season was over. The district biologist said that he hadn't been on the South Branch either, but that he had interviewed fishermen at access sites.

"These were the men who recommended drastic changes in regulations, supposedly based upon fact.

"They floated from Chase Bridge to Smith Bridge that night with jacklights.

GEORGE MASON AND THE SOUTH BRANCH

They saw two brown trout over twenty inches. The river was full of feeding trout from twelve to seventeen inches, but there were no pike. The smaller trout apparently were crowded out."

"Are you sure this happened?"

"George, I was with them."

I shuddered as we approached Fisherman's Chapel on the stream bank. I tried to prepare Mason. Near the upper dock lay 14 pieces of slate torn from the roof to shield a fire. As we looked up the steps, which had been carved out of the bank, to the chapel he had conceived before he died, we saw a 10-foot section had been torn out, apparently for firewood. In the chapel entrance were remains of another fire.

"It must have been raining," I said.

"Let's move on," said Mason.

On a steep bank below the site of the Downey house we heard a car start.

"How did that car get there?" he asked. Buildings were demolished and roads were to have been closed to all traffic.

Dog Town looked as he had hoped to see it. He was relieved. He didn't glimpse the parking area 100 feet from the bank.

Canoe Harbor had been turned into a bathing beach rather than a trout-stream pool. We counted 18 children churning up a cloud of sand and silt that was floating downstream. The bare, eroding banks were marked with dead trees. Campsites where grass had struggled to grow were barren from overuse.

The last few bends above Smith Bridge would have satisfied the dream of any trout fisherman. George smiled for the first time since we put in at Chase Bridge.

As my eyes gazed into a deep pool, I felt as if a heavy burden had washed away. Mason knew what I had dreaded telling him if we met again on a trout stream in the Great Beyond — how ungrateful people had mistreated his gift to them and future generations.

I turned to ask: "George, do you have trout fishing up there?"

He was gone. My wife was shaking me.

"George, you've been talking in your sleep."

*   *   *

George Griffith Named To Fishing Hall of Fame

George Griffith, one of the founders of Trout Unlimited, has been named to the National Fresh Water Fishing Hall of Fame. The award, one of just three presented annually worldwide, honors Griffith for a lifetime of achievement and accomplishment in the realm of fresh water. According to Bob Kutz, the founder of the Hall of Fame, Griffith's induction is "the angling fraternities highest honor."

Griffith was named along with two others, R.V. Gadabout Gaddis, and Carl Lowrance. Decreased inductees included David Starr Jordan, Joe Brooks, and Peter Mallock. The three living inductees will be honored recipients of the National Fishing Hall of Fame's "Time Eternal" awards while all six selected will be enshrined in photo and display in the Hall museum's Hall of Recognition Building in Hayward, Wisconsin.

Griffith makes his home at "The Barbless Hook" located on the famed "Holy Water" on the mainstream of the AuSable in Grayling.

Stream improvement on the Upper Manistee River near Cameron Bridge in the early '50s by Horace Clarke and his aides.

L to R: Stuart Udall, Secretary of the Interior; Ralph A. MacMullan, Director of Michigan's Department of Natural Resources; George A. Griffith, Chairman of the Board of TU. Aspen, Colorado, August 1965 at TU annual conference, MacMullan was Toastmaster and Udall Keynote Speaker.

Commissioners: L to R: Unknown; Harold (Opie) Titus; Pete Hoffmaster, Director; Unknown; Joseph Rahilley; Harry Whiteley Sr.; Harry Whiteley Jr. His nephew followed me on the Commission. He was a frequent hunting and fishing companion.

14-Mile Au Sable River Stretch Sought for George Mason Park

By JAMES A. CROWE

Starting with a million-dollar bequest of land by the late George W. Mason of Detroit, the State Conservation Department wants to keep a 14-mile stretch along the South Branch of the Au Sable River in its nautral state.

The gift of 1,450 acres of land covers most of both sides of the river from the Chase bridge downstream to the Smith bridge. The Chase bridge is four miles northeast of Roscommon.

George A. Griffiths, of Grayling, conservation commissioner, is leading a movement to get commission approval to purchase enough land to widen the strip to three miles.

FOR USE OF PUBLIC

The whole land and water area, which will cover a mile and a half on each side of the river, would be dedicated to public hunting and fishing uses and be permitted to remain as nearly in its natural state as possible.

Mason, president of American Motors Corp. when he died Oct. 8, left 35 heavily timbered 40 and 50-acre parcels of land to the Conservation Department. The broad, rushing river, one of the state's leading trout streams, runs through each of the parcels.

The will was probated without contest in Wayne County last week.

The late president of Nash-Kelvinator Corp. for many years before its merger into American Motors, also left two $25,000 grants from his life insurance to the department.

TO RESTORE FISH

One of them is to be paid out at the rate of $1,000 a year "to restore the fish to this stream that the grantor, over a 25-year period, has derived so much pleasure from catching."

The other $25,000 is to be spent to build a rustic chapel on the stream to be modelled after the chapel opened this year in the Hartwick Pine State Park, near Grayling.

Mason owned two luxurious lodges downstream from the property he left to the state. Shortly before his death, he told Griffiths, an old friend, that he had missed only two week ends of trout fishing there during the season in 26 years.

During that time he accumulated the land he dedicated at his death to the people of Michigan. He left the two lodges to his sons, George Jr. and John.

LAND SURVEYED

The plans to widen the land strip along the river have been surveyed by the department's land division. Charles E. Millar, division chief, said that the state will have to buy about 4,500 acres of privately owned land to realize the dream.

The balance of the needed land is part of the Lower Michigan National Forest, which until recently was named the Huron National Forest. The U.S. Forest Service is receptive to the idea of trading land it holds in the strip to the state for state-owned land elsewhere.

Griffiths said his proposal to the commission will be to permit full public hunting, fishing and other use of the land, but to forbid overnight camping, as Mason always did.

The only possible development of the land he might suggest, Griffiths said, would be the placing of picnic tables, stoves, firewood and wells in a special area somewhere near the middle of the stretch, where canoeists and fishermen could stop for lunch.

WOULD RELEASE TROUT

The $1,000 annual grant for trout restoration, Griffiths added, would pay for the release of about 1,000 trout in the stretch for 25 years.

He said, however, that in talking with Mason on Labor Day about the grant, it was clear that Mason would not have objected if the money were spent on trout projects of longer range benefit than the planting.

Thus, Griffiths said, there is a possibility of using the money for a project to improve the spawning beds in the stream, for example.

George W. Mason, who first conceived the idea of Trout Unlimited.

Crawford Co.

LOVELLS

NORTH

GRAYLING

AuSABLE

STEPHAN BRIDGE

WAKELEY BRIDGE

RIVER

BRANCH

SOUTH

ROSCOMMON

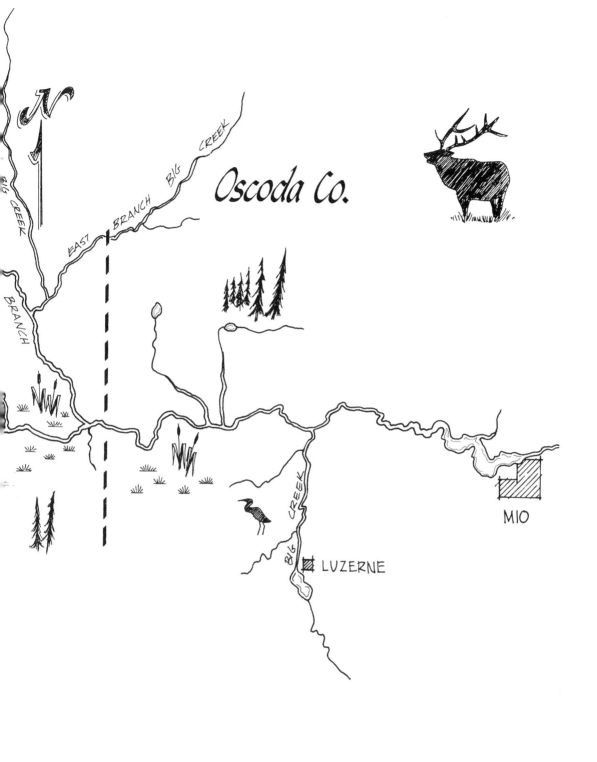

Oscoda Co.

BIG CREEK

EAST BRANCH BIG CREEK

BRANCH

BIG CREEK

LUZERNE

MIO

STATE OF MICHIGAN

OFFICE OF THE GOVERNOR

LANSING

G. MENNEN WILLIAMS
GOVERNOR

February 13, 1957

Mr. George A. Griffith
Grayling, Michigan

Dear George:

Congratulations on your confirmation
by the Senate as a member of the Michigan
Conservation Commission. I was very pleased
indeed to have them take this action.

Sincerely,

Governor

L to R: myself, my wife Helen, and Governor G. Mennen (Soapy) Williams.

April 10, 1969

Mr. George Griffith
Grayling, Michigan

Dear George:

What with pesticides, bond issues and all the other problems swirling across my desk
of late, your letter endorsing our new trout fishing regulations as "very modern and
progressive" arrived like a breath of fresh spring air.

Your approval means a lot, coming as it does from a man who is both a top trout
fisherman and a top representative of Trout Unlimited. I'm sure you know, George,
that we've heard some criticism of the new rules, and I imagine we will hear more as
the season progresses and people begin to feel the impact of the changes. It's
therefore mighty comforting to know we have the backing of an outfit like TU.

Actually, I wouldn't have expected anything else from Trout Unlimited because I've
learned over the years that I can expect TU to stand firmly on the side of progressive
management based on sound biology. You people understand, as so many
unfortunately don't, that maintaining a resource depends on how well we maintain its
base. We can't have trout unless we protect the kind of water that produces trout.

I think TU has tremendous potential for helping to secure good, sound conservation
legislation, not only in the states but also in Washington. I'm impressed by the *kind* of
people who belong to the organization, people who have the know-how and the
prestige to be influential when and where it counts. The Michigan TU group has helped
us out many times on critical legislative issues and I believe it will do even more once
it realizes its own strength. One of the hardest things I have to do is to convince
sportsmen that they can be influential in the political process.

Another kind of contribution that TU can make is, to put it bluntly, money. We never
have enough money to do all the things we need to do, and probably never will have
as much as we think we should. When we get a windfall like the 1,000 shares of
Connelley Corporation stock to buy a choice piece of trout water for management and
research purposes, it most certainly adds to our effectiveness.

Frankly, I've come to feel a pretty strong kinship with Trout Unlimited. Part of the
reason, I suppose, is that you invited me to speak on a couple of your programs and
then asked me to be your master of ceremonies out at Aspen. During my five years as
Director I've learned that an outfit will invite me once out of curiosity, but the real
acid test is whether they invite me a second time. Those second invitations always
give me a warm, friendly feeling.

To most of the people in this country a trout is just another fish. To the members of
TU trout are a way of life. As a resources administrator, I value and respect the
opinions of people like that and am comforted by knowing they are organized and
ready when the going gets tough.

Sincerely,

Ralph

Ralph A. MacMullan
Director

TROUT UNLIMITED

Pierina M. and George A. Griffith

are hereby acknowledged as

CHARTER LIFE MEMBERS

of Trout Unlimited and are recognized for a
lifetime commitment to Trout and Salmon
Resources Conservation

CHARTER NUMBER

1

George A. Griffith
Founder

J. Leon Chandler
Chairman of the Board

August 15, 1980
Date

TROUT UNLIMITED IS LAUNCHED

A small stone with a bronze plaque sitting adjacent to my dock commemorates the birth and birthplace of Trout Unlimited in the living room of The Barbless Hook, overlooking the lower Holy Waters of the AuSable River.

TU, as a growing movement, actually had its beginnings as early as the early 1940s. Dedicated conservationists were becoming concerned about the AuSable, its several branches and its trout, but World War II got in the way.

However, until that chance meeting at Burton's Landing when George Mason suggested an organization resembling Ducks Unlimited, the movement never had a name.

Unfortunately, Mason didn't live to see his dream for trout, his first love, come true.

It was July 1959 and I was in my second term as a member of the Conservation Commission. We had been planning TU, but not all members of the commission favored seeing the organization formed and two were outspoken opponents. It did not seem feasible for me to lead the organization of TU, and serve as its first president, while I was a member of the commission. My role as a commissioner outweighed — for the moment — my becoming an activist fighting the department. Governor Williams agreed. TU was still on a back-burner in my mind.

But Fish Division infighting had made Dr. Al Hazzard's position in, fisheries research intolerable and prompted him to accept a better job in Pennsylvania. His imminent move made launching of TU appropriate before he left. He had played a key role in all of our gains, including flies-only regulations. The movement had already lost two stalwart supporters in the deaths of George Mason and Don McLouth. I didn't want to lose Hazzard's input too.

I went to the governor's office and explained the dilemma. Soapy countered by revealing his decision that he was not going to seek another term. He warned me that the next governor would want to appoint his own man when my term ran out in 1961.

"George, you have my blessing to start Trout Unlimited," the governor said.

TROUT UNLIMITED IS LAUNCHED

"I'm not going to give it public support, but I won't ask you to resign from the commission if you help organize it."

We invited 60 men to that first meeting, but it was mid-summer, and many had already taken their vacations, or had vacation plans made. Only 16 people showed up, and some of those were vacationing guests who accompanied their hosts but either didn't join or never played a role in the organization.

The prime participants included Fred Bear, president of Bear Archery, Chuck Piper, his vice-president, and Vic Beresford, who had just been fired as editor of *Michigan Out-of-Doors* for an editorial criticizing the Republican-dominated House for not giving the Conservation Department legislation it needed.

Beresford had much organizational experience from his days at the *Detroit News*, MUCC and other sportsmen's organizations. He was a qualified, respected writer who knew the state's hatchery-oriented trout management, and he needed a job. Although he was somewhat abrasive, Vic had years of newspaper and business experience and a drive to get things done.

I had at least 15 months to serve on the commission, so others would have to obtain exposure for TU. We hired Vic to work as executive director half of his time for $350 a month.

That first meeting in our living room led to an organizational meeting September 5th, when we incorporated with Casey Westell, the much-respected forest scientist for Packaging Corp. of America at Filer City as first president. Westell loved to fly-fish, and managed forest lands through which the Little Manistee River flowed, but, as with many busy executives, he didn't get too much time to cast a fly.

However, Westell gave TU status from the beginning. He developed our scientific advisers' board composed of leading authorities in fisheries management and research. Whenever we were faced with a major issue such as stream improvement, mortality of bait-caught trout, or flies-only, size limits, catch-and-release and no fishing rules to protect spawning populations of wild trout, we could pass the questions on to Westell's scientists. All were happy to serve and many were eager to have a reliable organization to promote their findings. The board, alone, assured Westell's place in TU's Hall of Fame.

We had $815 in our treasury and Chuck Piper helped round up members. Our total membership swelled to 175 by the time we organized as a non-profit corporation.

Beresford sent press releases to the Associated Press and United Press International, which gave the fledgling organization early national recognition and sparked interest. TU mail multiplied overnight while our budget remained skimpy. Beresford often worked 75-hour weeks for 20 hours of pay and paid expenses out of his own pocket!

Outdoor editors in Minneapolis, Baltimore, Pittsburgh and Columbus, Ohio, called asking how to get involved. Vic's efforts were soon bearing fruit in letters and frantic calls for help from New York and Pennsylvania. National articles about fly-fishing by Joe Brooks, Ernie Schwiebert, Lefty Kreh and others, the advent of fiberglas fly-rods, and Leon Martuch's invention of Scientific Anglers plastic fly lines were all making fly-fishing more popular.

During the last few weeks before our formal organization of TU, we discussed dues. We should have spent more time on the subject. We recognized that we would not have as many members as the Michigan United Conservation Clubs, for example, because they covered all conservation issues and we were specializing in trout, trout streams, trout habitat and trout management.

Others were busy, too, including Rolly Burrows and Art Newmann, who organized a chapter in Saginaw; Charlie Fellows, who started one in Flint; Cornelius (Corny) Schrems and Bob Evenson, who founded the Grand Rapids chapter; John Keen in Big Rapids; Dr. John Spencer in Traverse City; Fred Bear, Chuck Piper and Carrol Wert in Grayling; Harry Bugbee and Duane Stranahan in Toledo; George Ewing in Pittsburgh; and Herbert Moore of Evanston, Ill., who was our Chicago representative. His fishing was done with the Waders of the Wolf on the Wolf River in Wisconsin. He couldn't afford to travel, but he wanted to help TU expand outside Michigan.

We agreed to pay Moore's expenses to Pittsburgh where George Ewing and Al Rockwell had arranged a meeting with a large group at a country club. As Ewing was asking Moore for suggestions about how to get men in the audience to sign up, he recalled someone else was suggesting he test the quality of the bar. By the time Ewing was able to get his attention, the crowd of potential members was dispersing. No one was even handed a TU membership application that night.

The next day Moore was addressing a luncheon meeting of the Theodore Gordon Club in New York. Martin Bovey, a longtime member of the club, tried very hard to persuade the club to join TU. But they were fly-fishermen and they wanted to be identified as such. Moore failed to recruit the club because TU didn't claim to be a flies-only organization.

Many TU members were — or were becoming — fly-fishermen, but it wasn't a prerequisite then or now.

However, Moore recalled that someone introduced Lee Wulff as a famous fly-fisherman and writer. He also recalled that Wulff handed him a new light-weight Tonkin cane fly-rod and asked his opinion of its action.

"Anyone would like one," Moore said. That was all he recalled saying a week later when he received a beautiful bamboo fly-rod and a bill for $165, a mighty stiff price at a time when bamboo fly-rods were selling for $15 to $35! Moore had been naive, but he learned a then-costly but valuable lesson. Along with Commissioner Lyle Kingston of the Wisconsin Conservation Commission, Moore helped open the door for TU with that state's Fish Division leaders.

Letters from anglers across the country seemed to have a common denominator: a general disgust with their states' management of trout resources. Beresford kept heralding TU as the rallying point for anglers. The message rippled over the borders and soon we were chartering chapters in Canada and Mexico. Members had only two things in common: a love for trout and a desire to improve trout stream management.

The TU movement was beginning to take shape.

* * *

O.J. "Wally" Wallis was the National Parks Service's fish biologist and the first outspoken professional leader to oppose wasteful hatchery practices. Wally served on the TU board for several years. Ken Peterson, outdoor editor of the *Flint Journal* and son of Hans Peterson, had grown up on the AuSable and served as the unpaid editor of Trout magazine for several years after Beresford left. He did much to help readers understand the role of trout habitat in conservation.

TU attracted many famous members. U.S. Sen. Philip Hart of Michigan, who was a lieutenant governor during one of Soapy's terms and became known as the "conscience of the senate," was an early member as was Congressman John Dingell of Michigan, whose father, John Sr., was co-author of the Dingell-Johnson federal excise tax on fishing tackle. John Jr. belonged to TU from its inception. Both Dingell and Hart drew fire from MUCC for giving TU more of their time but had to support them — both were dedicated conservationists with bipartisan respect. Dingell was a dear and respected friend of Hal Glassen and his wife, Jean, staunch Republicans, and a member of the National Rifle Association, which Glassen headed during the push for the Gun Control Act of 1968.

I met Martin Bovey in the press room of a Wildlife Management Institute meeting that I attended as a commissioner. Bovey overheard a conversation about TU between Hazzard, Paul Needham of California, and me.

Bovey, always aggressive, asked: "What is TU all about?"

Hazzard's and Needham's replies seemed to impress him. He turned to me with a smile.

"George, I'm going up to my room for an hour's nap. I'll call you afterward. Will you be in your room?"

"Could we meet in your room? Helen is resting for tonight's reception and banquet."

Bovey listened to my story about TU.

"If Hazzard and Needham support you, I will go by their judgment."

He wrote a check to TU for $100, which would be equal to $1,000 today.

At that time, the word "environmentalist" was virtually unknown. The first environmentalists were hunter- and fishermen-conservationists who saw the need and expanded their perspectives from the enjoyment of catching fish and killing game to fighting for a wise use of all natural resources.

Bovey was like a bull in a china shop. He had a frustrated youth. One grandfather was of John Deere agricultural equipment fame and the other was a founder of United Brands, a food conglomerate. Bovey's family wanted Martin to become a noted lawyer and politician.

TROUT UNLIMITED IS LAUNCHED

"I flunked law at Harvard and I taught law at Yale," he laughed. "My brother is a successful rancher and state senator in Montana, but I am a disappointment for the family. I used to take boys' clubs and Boy Scouts on long canoe trips across northern Ontario and Quebec. Now I fish for six weeks every summer on Montana trout streams."

Bovey was a member of both the New York Anglers' and Theodore Gordon clubs and quickly became an unpaid TU ambassador-at-large-without-portfolio for the nation. He was not geared to be a vice-president or a committee member. He saw himself only at the top. At times his ego caused friction, but Bovey had a close association with Ira Gabrielson and made many friends for TU among Montana trout fishermen. He became our third president and stands tall in the history of TU.

As we drove west out of Mexico City after the International Association of Game and Fish Commissioners' meeting in 1961, Helen and I passed a small lake just off the highway. There was a sign saying it had special regulations. We drove in and read: "Experimental trout lake — flies only, two trout daily, ten-inch limit."

The TU movement was becoming international!

* * *

During early years we often put on a brave front because we were afraid to admit to members — or sometimes ourselves — that TU had financial problems. Fortunately, we had board members who knew the score — men like Bob Evenson, Cornelius "Corny" Shrems, John Keen, Harry Bugbee and Bovey.

John Spencer of Traverse City, another friend, helped organize our first annual meeting at the Park Place Hotelin Traverse City. It was crucial to the success of TU.

However, a few months before the meeting, we realized that our financial report would be embarrassing. We were broke.

I joined Don Valley and his guide, Norval Stephan, for lunch on the South Branch. The topic naturally turned to TU.

"How does your financial picture look?" Valley asked.

"We are facing our first annual meeting with a minus balance in the bank," I explained.

"Could you possibly be in Detroit next week?"

"Our president, Casey Westell, and I will be attending a meeting at Haven Hill Monday and Tuesday."

"Could you two be in my office at 4 p.m. Tuesday?"

"We'll be there."

When a banker invites you to his office, you go.

* * *

Fund-raising was a perennial problem from the beginning. Fortunately, many top executives in business and industry share a love of trout fishing. That saved us.

Casey Westell and I went from a meeting at the Conservation Department's Haven Hill Lodge on the old Edsel Ford estate, now a state park, to The Detroit National Bank, the largest bank between New York and Chicago.

We were ushered into the executive offices and into the walnut-paneled office of Don Valley, the bank's impressive chairman of the board when he wasn't casting a fly on the Mainstream! A mounted trout and a painting of the AuSable revealed his true love. Alvin Macauley, vice-president of the bank and a charter member of TU, also greeted us.

Typical of a strong executive, Don opened the meeting: "Who is going to speak for you, George?"

"Our president, Casey Westell," I replied.

Looking at Macauley, he said, "Al has given me some background on TU."

Casey, an excellent executive, outlined TU's financial problems in less than three minutes. Valley was impressed.

"I will give you $100," Don said, looking at Macauley. "Will you match that?" Macauley nodded.

"I can see that this is a short-time emergency." Don called a secretary and started dictating a letter. When he completed the letter, he turned to Westell. "Do you have any vacancies on your board?"

"Of course," Casey replied.

"Macauley, how would you like to be a candidate?"

"I am not looking for work, and I am now on several boards, but none is as important as TU."

"Fine. Put Al on your list," said Valley. "By the way, would you mind if I used your stationery? Send me enough to write fifty letters."

As Casey and I were thinking how to say thanks, Don excused himself and stepped through a door near his desk. Macauley began asking questions.

"Let's see what Don thinks," said Westell.

Macauley laughed.

"Don is halfway home. That's his usual way of ending an important meeting." Macauley became an active board member and contributed much to early fund-raising.

I adopted Valley's tactic as my own.

I found the tactic of asking a potential donor, "Would you give to TU?" failed to get a donation more than half of the time. But, "Would you join me in a $500 contribution to help TU out of a financial emergency?" proved successful for me and saved us from many minus balances over the early years.

*   *   *

Frank Birch, managing director of the Detroit Sportsman's Congress, replaced McLouth on the commission and, during my second term, Shirley Allen, head of the University of Michigan Forestry School, and Stanley Cain, a professor of fisheries and wildlife at U-M and later assistant chief of the U.S. Fish and Wildlife Service during President John F. Kennedy's administration, were appointed and they helped me upgrade the role of research in Michigan's conservation effort.

Commission Chairman Lawrence Gotschall, Allen, and I were in the Michigan delegation to the International Association of Game, Fish and Conservation Commissioners in Seattle in September 1957. Allen and I met Dr. Ira N. Gabrielson, president of the Wildlife Management Institute in Washington, D.C., and learned he was completing a survey of the Iowa State Conservation Department. Larry, as chairman, approved our proposal to invite Gabrielson to evaluate the Michigan department.

Gabrielson's reports were complete. They pointed out the weaknesses of bureaucratic systems in most departments and the departments' failure to consult their own scientists. A close friend of Harry Ruhl, Gabrielson was especially concerned about the lack of scientific input in fisheries management.

When we returned to Michigan, Commissioner Joe Rahilly persuaded Gotschall to hold up the invitation. When Allen brought up the Gabrielson study, Gotschall could not remember it, recessed the commission meeting at the Higgins Lake Training School and pointed commissioners to the staff house.

We were in a heated discussion when two outdoor writers barged in. Despite Gabrielson's reputation as the most outstanding conservationist of the day, Rahilly, a 20-year veteran commissioner from Newberry, said he had no idea who Gabrielson was.

We explained that Gabrielson was perhaps the most outstanding conservationist in the nation with as much, if not more, experience in the operation of conservation organizations as any man in the country.

"At his own organization's expense, Gabrielson has made invaluable surveys of the operation of state conservation departments and those of several Canadian provinces," Allen pointed out. I echoed his statement.

"Michigan will be his thirty-fifth study of a state or provincial department," I added. "He has done some a second time by legislative request."

"Well, I fear any kind of evaluation will take on the aspect of an 'investigation' of the Conservation Department," said Rahilly. "I object to it."

Commissioners Pete Calcatera of Baraga, Bob Brevitz of Battle Creek and Gotschall supported him, making it four to three. We were forced to wait until we could determine what benefits, if any, Iowa and the other states had obtained from Gabrielson's evaluation of the way they managed their natural resources.

* * *

In January 1961, Lt. Gov. John B. Swainson was inaugurated as Governor Williams' successor. Later, he celebrated quietly over a cup of coffee with August "Gus" Scholle, fiery state labor leader, whom he had chosen for the Conservation Commission. Harry Whiteley, Rogers City newspaper publisher, was his Republican choice for the commission. My days as a commissioner were over. As

TROUT UNLIMITED IS LAUNCHED

Soapy had explained, each governor names his own men. Scholle was a staunch Democratic supporter of both G. Mennen Williams and Swainson and once related how he persuaded Williams to run for the Supreme Court.

"'Gus, I've never even tried a case,'" Scholle related.

"'Mennen, at one time you didn't even have to be a lawyer to be a Supreme Court justice.'"

Soapy won and served with distinction and became chief justice of Michigan's highest court. I was still an independent, but I was proud to have served as a commissioner during his Democratic administration.

* * *

Governor George Romney was a Republican and he was not anenvironmentalist. It bored him. The ex-American Motors president and chairman of the board was too well organized and too realistic to be at home in politics. However, he went along with Democrat Rahilly and the opposing commissioners and named a state Blue Ribbon Committee to make an evaluation of the Conservation Department rather than bring in Gabrielson.

* * *

Pacific coho salmon smolts were raised and released in Bear Creek, a tributary to the Big Manistee River, and at the old Platte River Fish Hatchery.

State biologists had been told by Western fish chiefs to plant the salmon in the state's best trout streams. The two streams also had rearing facilities and steelhead runs were returning. Michigan trout fishermen looked at the introduction of coho (silver) salmon and the planned introduction of chinook (king) salmon skeptically. They were told the introductions were intended to repopulate the "biological deserts" of the Great Lakes, consume overly abundant alewives that intruded from the Atlantic Ocean in ships' ballast water, and reduce fishing pressure on inland lakes and trout streams. However, they weren't told that the introductions were being financed from trout-stamp revenues at the expense of trout stream habitat improvement work.

Dr. Jim McFadden, briefly fish chief, conceived the idea; Dr. Howard A. Tanner, who succeeded McFadden, arranged for supplies of coho salmon eggs from Oregon and Washington, but Dr. Wayne Tody, who had spearheaded stream improvement, found himself defending the salmon program and taking the brunt of trout fishermen's criticism. His neglect of streams as he carried out first the coho then chinook introductions offended some prominent TU members who had nudged Dr. Ralph A. MacMullan to name Tody as their choice for fisheries chief. In Tody's defense, when he included stream improvement in his proposed division budget, Governor Milliken removed it.

At the same time, Tody was under fire from both commercial fishing and tourist interests for blocking plans to turn commercial fishermen's trawls loose on the Great Lakes to net the alewives that were dying on Lake Michigan beaches and costing the tourist industry hundreds of millions a year. There were numerous proposals for use of alewives from packing them like sardines to grinding them for fish meal or fertilizer.

Tody was counting on the salmon feeding on the alewives and solving the Lake Michigan die-off problem while providing a new source of income for the tourist industry. He persuaded Congress to delay trawling operations for 1967 and the first adult coho salmon run over Labor Day proved him right, spawning new interest, new income and a new charterboat industry. In a few weeks of the runs off Manistee and in Platte Bay, the new fish restored all that was lost all summer by the economies of shoreline communities.

Unfortunately, instead of relieving pressure on trout streams, the salmon spawned a new breed of fish hog — snaggers who tore up trout stream habitat in their crazed desire to hook the big fish in any way they could "because they're just going to die and go to waste." Tody's efforts to limit upstream runs only infuriated many who, overlooking that the DNR had provided the new fish, demanded legislative control of fish management.

Bear Creek and the Platte River both took a beating and coils of 50-pound and heavier monofilament fishing line fouled streams and banks, especially below dams as the salmon were spread to other rivers.

But the snaggers had a point. Tiny Carter Creek opposite Traverse City *Record-Eagle* outdoor editor Gordon Charles' writing cabin on the Platte River downstream from the hatchery stank with the carcasses of dozens of salmon lured to die in a few inches of fresh spring water too shallow for them to swim in.

TROUT UNLIMITED IS LAUNCHED

Tinkering with Mother Nature often yields mixed blessings.

* * *

Bob Evenson was chairman of the Kent County Republican Party and responsible for sending its monthly contribution to the state GOP treasury.

The new Natural Resources Commission, to which Republican Gov. William G. Milliken — son of my friend and mentor, Jim Milliken — had turned over most of the state's environmental responsibilities after Earth Day 1970, had a vacancy. Every conservation organization was eyeing it.

There were several candidates. TU needed a candidate. Evenson suggested Hilary Snell, a young Grand Rapids attorney and an ardent trout fisherman. Snell had a good head on his shoulders and a broad view of the environment, including trout.

"George, how do I go about getting Hilary appointed?" he asked as we met for lunch on the river.

"You send a pretty fat check to the party's slush-fund, don't you?"

"Yes, $12,000 a month."

"What would happen if you were to forget to mail the check — for a month or so?"

"I'd probably get a call from the governor's office reminding me."

"And that would give you an opportunity to remind the governor of our need for a commissioner."

Evenson smiled and nodded.

Bob's delay initiated a phone call from a Milliken staff member. Evenson gave an evasive answer. A few days later, the governor called "just to keep in touch."

"Oh, by the way, Bob, is there any reason why we have not received your committee's check?" Evenson said Milliken asked.

"Of course not, Governor. No more reason than you have had for not appointing Hilary Snell to the Natural Resources Commission."

A few days later the governor's office announced that Hilary Snell, a Grand Rapids attorney active in Trout Unlimited and concerned about the environment of the state, had been appointed to the Natural Resources

Commission. Money makes a way.

* * *

Development of the lands through which the Holy Waters of the Mainstream flow began in 1940. A few young businessmen in Grayling found heirs of these holdings anxious to sell.

Their development extended from Louie's Landing to Whirlpool Road, two miles of river frontage, with the lower half of it divided — without professional guidance — into small riverfront lots. The first to be divided was the Richardson property. The inept developers, not recognizing the value of riverfront land, foolishly sold the lots at prices comparable to lakefront lots on an average warm water fishing lake.

Most of the original owners were from Toledo, Ohio. Going upstream from Stephan's Bridge, there was the Marshall property opposite Edgewater. Jack, the son, died at a young age, leaving a widow but no children. Next was historic Wa Wa Sum, owned by Mrs. Duane Stranahan. Her sons, headed by Duane Jr. (Pat), an attorney who was settling the Marshall estate. Pat was a TU board member for eight years. The three Stranahan brothers paid higher than the asking price for the mile and a half of Marshall property and gave it, minus the buildings, to TU. Due to our tax-free statute, we couldn't accept buildings.

A short distance above Wakeley's Bridge was the Thunderbird Lodge, later owned by the Milton Knight family, also from Toledo. Milton died in his mid-sixties and his son Milton Jr. (Tony), guided by his friend, Pat Stranahan, gave Thunderbird to TU.

Finally, Mrs. Stranahan followed her sons' example and offered Wa Wa Sum to TU. But she wanted the huge historic family log lodge and adjacent buildings maintained, which TU could not do. Finally, she gave the property to Michigan State University which uses the land for forestry research and the lodge as a conference center. Restoration of the buildings is being done with donations from various TU groups, the Royal Order of Trout, and other trout and non-fishing groups that hold meetings there.

* * *

Helen's mother's death a week after her father's fatal heart attack in October

TROUT UNLIMITED IS LAUNCHED

1939 freed Helen from a life of around-the-clock nursing. Her mother, who was a heavy woman, had been an invalid for the last four years. Fortunately, the school board wanted our two-family brick home as a high school site. We bought a smaller home and Helen spent at least a week of every month on the road with me. She became popular with my customers and also became a familiar sight at conservation conferences and TU meetings.

With a reduction in my territory after I was appointed to the commission, I was able to spend more time with Helen at home. We rebuilt a large garage and ice house into a caretaker's house and began having someone living with us from 1950 to do the cooking and housework and to keep Helen company when she wasn't on the road with me. The Robinsons had just moved in when Helen had her first heart attack in 1961. Leona spent whatever time Helen needed with her and made it possible for me to continue making necessary trips when Helen didn't feel like going along.

Helen recovered and enjoyed entertaining both at home and in our winter home in Florida until she suffered a stroke while we were at the community of Crystal Lake in Pompano Beach, Florida, in February 1967. Her recovery came slow after seven weeks of hospitalization, and she never regained her strength.

Helen fell out of bed in 1975. Dr. Moe Henig, who lived a half mile away, arrived in minutes and persuaded Helen to go to the hospital for an examination. He called an ambulance, then gave me a stern warning: "George, don't expect her to come home."

During the next seven weeks I was at her bedside from 10 in the morning until five in the afternoon, when Henig insisted that I leave the hospital. Many days Helen did not recognize me. Those days helped prepare me and TU bolstered me for the worst.

Two weeks after her death and cremation, as we had agreed years earlier, I arranged a memorial service. A day later, several friends joined me for a float trip. Lunch was solemn.

"George, I'm planning another trip to Montana," said Charles Fellows. "I can go any time you are able to go." We had made a similar trip earlier, and the others joined him in urging me to go. I agreed.

Fellows and I headed for Livingston. Charles Cummins was to join us for our third week.

We stopped for lunch at a small Wisconsin shoreline park overlooking Lake Michigan. It was mid-August and traffic on the two-lane roads to St. Cloud, Minnesota, was heavy. The forests of the Upper Peninsula of Michigan gave way to the dairy farms of Wisconsin and Minnesota, and I felt a twinge of nostalgia as we saw cows returning to their pastures as lights went on in kitchens and milk houses. Momentarily, I was a boy again back on the family farm in Ohio.

Our conversation turned to politicians and we marveled at the number of our nation's leaders who had sprung up from farm roots with the moral values that came from being close to the land. Suddenly it was late afternoon and we were approaching Fargo, North Dakota. We were making good time despite the two-lane road traffic. We ate, then drove until dark.

I never tired of the scenery. There is a strange beauty in the Badlands of the Dakotas. The majesty of the snow-capped Rocky Mountains against the big blue sky held us in awe for 75 miles to Billings, Montana. The sky was beginning to take on its warm evening colors as we arrived at the Townhouse Motel shortly before six o'clock where we caught up on current news over dinner with George and Mary Ewing.

Dan Bailey's fly shop, with its huge picture window showing his fly-tiers at their benches, was buzzing at eight o'clock. Red Monical, Dan's partner, and several guides and a few fishermen were exchanging reports. Chester Marion, a popular guide on the Yellowstone River, had good news — the grapevine had it that Slough Creek was full of large trout going upstream to spawn.

We also heard that cutthroats were going upstream at Buffalo Ford on the Yellowstone. This was hopper season, when big trout become bold during the daytime.

George Ewing came in a half-hour later and we crowded into Marion's car for the long ride to Slough Creek in Yellowstone National Park.

The creek was beautiful, but Marion said fishing would be best in late evening. Since it was already five o'clock and we were 200 miles from Livingston, we started back. Midway, we stopped at Buffalo Ford where cutthroat trout were eager to take our flies.

We drove through Hayden Valley, where a 14-mile stretch of river was closed to all humans as a sanctuary in which grizzly bears, moose, deer and birds of countless species were never disturbed by man, even on foot. Marion suddenly pulled off the road in a dip and stopped. We watched as five elk cows crossed the road a hundred yards ahead.

"Look," Chester cried out as they passed. A large, bull elk was following the cows. Behind him, a young bull was boldly approaching, ready to mount a challenge. We watched for an hour, at times at less than 50 yards, as the elk battled for the harem. Finally, the old bull, nearly exhausted, proudly turned and slowly walked off in the direction from which he had come.

"That's the first time I've ever seen a bull elk give up and walk away," he said.

The Yellowstone was our favorite water. We were impatient. By nine o'clock the next morning, we had a car placed downstream from Mallard's Rest, a landing on the river, and we cast off in a McKenzie Riverboat. Chuck tied a hopper pattern on his tippet while I tried a trude pattern. Chuck soon had a good cutthroat, then landed a rainbow before I connected with a trout. We also were catching whitefish up to four pounds on the same No. 8 and No. 10 hopper and trude flies. With all the dry-fly action on the surface, we didn't try any streamers.

Some fishermen class the Yellowstone second-rate because of the whitefish, but we were well aware that smaller whitefish feed big trout and that streams such as the Madison and Gallatin, which lack whitefish, seldom produce trout over 18 inches on dry flies. Dan Bailey, Martin Bovey and other TU anglers echoed our opinions.

Unlike AuSable Riverboats, Western trout guides use the McKenzie Riverboat and sit in the middle for a 20- to 30-mile float, while fishermen cast from both ends. The Yellowstone has many islands and most fishermen stop on the islands to fish the riffles on both sides, which were productive, but we old men preferred to float while fishing the shoreline. Chester's advice was invaluable. Floating dry flies over runs shaded by willows produced our best trout. Montana has wisely zoned shorelines of streams so that the banks will not be disturbed. On average, two of us would catch 20, 12-to-14-inch trout, 20, 16-to-18-inch fish, and another 10 over or under those sizes.

With a good guide, you can expect more and larger trout. In those days, a guide cost $35 a day and he would furnish lunch. There are several areas with one-day floats of at least 100 miles of stream. Fishing quality varies, but the Yellowstone is all very productive from Jim's Canyon to Springdale, about 150 miles.

* * *

I went to Pompano Beach in November 1975 for the winter. I intended to go on down to Islamarada and fish for bonefish in the Keys.

George and Peri Martinette Kennedy of New York had been our neighbors and occasional dinner partners during the early 1970s. I knew that George, who had been my occasional golfing partner, had died and that Peri had spent the winter of 1974-75 with her children on Long Island instead of coming to Florida.

Peri and I met on the elevator. She smiled her usual vivacious smile. She knew of Helen's death. I sensed that Peri was lonely. Suddenly I knew that I was very lonely, too.

"May I call?" I asked as she got off the elevator. She smiled, and said yes.

Twenty minutes later I called her apartment and asked if we could have dinner together. Tonight.

She said yes.

Cupid's arrow hit and the survivors of two long, happy marriages found happiness neither of us expected to know again.

* * *

Peri, an artist, had never fished, yet with a few lessons, she took to fly-fishing like a duck takes to water and accompanied me on several trips to Montana as well as bonefishing in the Florida Keys and in Belize.

And over more than 15 years, she has become a familiar figure at TU's annual meetings.

Meanwhile, TU has grown to more than 66,000 members and is still growing in the United States and Canada, Mexico, Europe, Japan, and now the Soviet Union. In 1989, while many other conservation organizations were facing the loss of members, it gained six percent.

*   *   *

Joe and Mary Brooks spent four months a year in Montana. We saw them frequently at the then Island Resort. Later we all moved to the Parkway Motel with its large, well-kept rooms, some with cooking facilities. Our neighbors included Mary and George Ewing, Jack and Ellie Bannon, the Doctor McCarthys, the Max Stevensons and the Watermans. Dan and Helen Bailey and the Monicals would join us on Sundays, which came to be known as "ladies' day."

Armstrong Creek and Nelson's Spring Creek, owned by Ed and Mary Nelson, were oversold commercial streams. They charged ten dollars a day and fishing was fantastic. But by the early 1970s, Joe Brooks and others were suggesting flies-only and then no-kills regulations. We discovered several prize spring creeks within 150 miles of Livingston through Brooks, but we seldom fished those streams more than twice a season to avoid wearing out our welcome. We would spend a few days a year on the Big Hole River and two creeks as well as the Madison and Gallatin rivers.

As fishing grew in popularity, we tried to leave a tangible effort to be remembered for. It paid off later when a rancher welcomed us, but asked us to leave our car in his barn. He was afraid of neighbors, who had banded together and posted their lands against fishing because of a few thoughtless fishermen.

As I look back, as an old man is entitled to do, friendships made with anglers always seem to overshadow all others — perhaps because they are welded together with a common love and respect for fish and wildlife and the woods and streams.

*   *   *

TU is more than 30 years old, but new generations of dedicated trout fishermen continue to fight for the same goals we defined July 16, 1959 in the living room of The Barbless Hook as we watched the Holy Waters rippling on their way to Lake Huron.

*   *   *

Chapter Eleven

BAROTHY AND SALTWATER FISHING

A young man hurried down Chicago's Lake Shore Drive on a cold March night in 1916. He shifted a heavy canvas duffel bag from bare hand to bare hand as a bitter north wind lashed the southern shore of Lake Michigan.

When he reached the small harbor, he surveyed the few cargo boats docked with large pleasure craft. It was nearly midnight. In the dim light from a distant lamppost he made out a name, "Norway, Muskegon, Michigan."

His eyes warmed against the cutting wind. He saw no one on the deck of the small steamship. There were no lights.

He walked up the short gangplank and was aboard. He lifted his duffel bag over the gunnel of a canvas-covered skiff rocking like a hammock in a cradle on deck. His eyes swept over the deck again, then he pulled himself into the lifeboat.

He pulled his heavy dark blue jacket around him, stretched out on a pile of life preservers and placed two over his legs. He pulled his wool stocking cap over his face and buried his head in his duffel bag. He was frightened as he heard two men came aboard.

"Tonight was sure a bust," one said.

"Captain said we're going to cast off at eight." said the second. "I'm going to hit the sack."

"Me, too. It looks like everyone has turned in."

Then it was all quiet again.

The boy shivered and tried to sleep as the skiff rocked and the wind lashed the tarpaulin. His breath frosted the underside of the canvas. Would eight o'clock ever come?

*   *   *

An edge of daylight sliced across his eyes as the wind lifted the tarpaulin. He could hear the steady beat of the steam engine and sense the churning of the propeller. He peeked out. The vessel must be in open water. It was too late to turn back.

The youth rehearsed his story once again, then dropped out of the skiff. His duffel bag slapped the deck, startling a member of the crew.

"Where is Bill Long," he asked.

"Who the hell is Bill Long?" the sailor shrugged.

"A friend of mine. He told me he would take me to Frankfort today."

"How did you get aboard?" the crewman asked.

"This looked like the boat Bill described last night. I didn't see anyone on deck to ask, so I climbed into the skiff to wait for him. I fell asleep."

"Well, we can't take you to Frankfort," the sailor explained. "We're headed for Muskegon. But I think we can find you a ride. You must be freezing. How about some breakfast?"

The boy relaxed. His luck was still holding. The odor of coffee, bacon and hotcakes cut through the chilly air. He was away from Chicago and about to have his first breakfast on a ship.

"I sure could use some. My name's Vic Barothy. What's yours?"

"Nate Fry. I'm from Muskegon."

The captain wasn't used to stowaways. He was skeptical, but Barothy was a clean-looking lad. He accepted the youth's story. He might be as old as 18 or 19. If he were running away, the captain didn't want to know it. He wanted to get his boat home.

"Find him a bunk, Nate. Get him some breakfast, and then bring him up to the bridge."

In the distance, Barothy could see the Chicago shoreline. He visualized the posh section of Lake Shore Drive, where he was born and had lived the first 15 years as the son of a prominent doctor. Until last night.

*   *   *

The skyline of the Windy City disappeared in the blowing snow. Vic's mind turned to last night when he and two other boys were returning from a dull evening program at school.

"Mother has a new Pierce Arrow," he recalled saying as they neared the big house with the long drive sloping down to the cobblestone street. "The lights are out so she must be in bed. Let's go for a ride."

The car stood headed toward the street. Barothy released the brake. He didn't start the engine lest it awaken his mother. The big canvas-topped touring car with isinglass windows picked up speed. He saw the dim headlights of another car heading toward them. He couldn't find the foot brake. He pulled the hand brake and tried to turn. Too late! They hit almost head-on on the snow-covered bricks. All three boys hit the street, their leather soles slipping underneath their feet, as the other driver jumped out and uttered several oaths. His car appeared showroom new.

The boys' pace slowed as they circled the block. Barothy's friends veered off toward their homes. Vic was alone.

The youth entered the back door of the big house. All was quiet. His father was home, too. He could hear him snoring. He could make out his father's pants hanging over a chair. He found the old man's wallet, withdrew a handful of cash and tiptoed to his room. He closed the door and turned on the light.

"It's just a loan, Dad," he said to himself, as he counted $214. "Maybe a longtime loan, but I'll repay you someday. Someday when you're not mad at me."

He threw a few necessities into the duffel bag. He heard a pounding on the front door. His father's snoring stopped. The old man must be making his way to the door. Too bad, Vic thought. He seldom gets a full night's sleep. There's always a patient or someone from the hospital at the door at all times of night.

He'll feel like killing me when he learns what I did to Mom's new car. She'll be sick. It was her first car. Dad bought it for her birthday, and the carpenters had started building a big garage. There wasn't enough room in the old barn, where Dad kept his car ready to rush to a patient or to the hospital.

Vic rushed down the alley, expecting to wake every watchdog in the wealthy neighborhood, and down a neighborhood street to Lake Shore Drive. He looked back. He could see two figures around the cars.

Dad knows.

* * *

His mind returned to the present. He held onto the railing as he made his way forward on the deck with the hot mug of coffee. Icy mist hit his face. He might as well tell the captain he'll be glad to help.

"We don't have many guests," the captain explained as he sipped from the steaming cup. "Take the wheel while I drink this."

BAROTHY AND SALTWATER FISHING

Barothy folded his hands around the ship's wheel, and smiled as he looked ahead into the snow. He sensed the power he had at his command. What lay ahead?

"Hold her steady, boy," cautioned the captain. "Keep the arrow on north-northeast." He sipped the coffee and tugged on the bill of his cap, struggling to pull it over an obviously heavy head of gray hair. He was trim for his age. His hands were large and weathered and soft wrinkles led from his cheeks to deep-set eyes that squinted against the snow.

"I'll be happy to help, skipper," Barothy offered, fighting to hold the ship on course. "My name's Vic, Vic Barothy."

"Well, Vic, Cookie is always looking for some help in the galley. When I'm done with my coffee, why don't you go down and see if you can't help him? Tell him I said to ship me a mug of coffee from time to time. I don't want to leave the bridge."

Cookie welcomed help. The crew wasn't large, but there always were dishes to wash. Washing dishes wasn't a task Barothy was familiar with as a rich boy, but, as a young man suddenly on his own, it was a job to which he could adapt, even if the deck was rocking under his feet. He washed dishes, peeled potatoes and became popular by carrying steaming mugs of coffee to the captain and his crew. In bad weather, Nate explained, the skipper wanted everyone to stay at his post.

The blizzard softened to light snow that melted almost as soon as it hit the steel deck warmed by the engine room below. Barothy's mind was miles ahead. At Muskegon a few days later, Vic thanked the captain for an offer of a job in the spring and said goodbye to his newfound friends. Nate took him to the post office. The postmaster, who was a friend of the captain, said he could arrange for Barothy to help on the mail car that would be departing soon for Frankfort. It was a ride and it was warm. He helped sort letters. Vic left the train in Ludington, at the mouth of the Pere Marquette River. He sat his duffel bag down in the express office.

Barothy's father owned some land on the Pere Marquette near Wallhala. Vic had gone there with him once on a camping trip. He was wondering how he would get a ride there. He remembered a small storage building on the river's edge. It had a bed and some camping gear and a small stove. There was a well, he recalled, and an outhouse. He could get by.

A horse-drawn hearse was backed up at the express dock. He heard the man tell the agent that it contained the body of a businessman from Wallhala to be shipped home to Chicago. Vic offered to help the driver unload the casket.

When the driver learned Vic was looking for a ride to Wallhala, he invited him to ride along.

"You can put your things in the back of the hearse," he told Barothy.

"I need to pick up a few things at the hardware, and some groceries," explained Vic. "I won't be long."

At the hardware, he bought a double-bitted axe, a box of shells for his father's 12-gauge shotgun and some mittens. At a grocery, he added a side of salt pork, a bag of flour, a bag of beans, a bag of peas, a crock of butter, several tins of canned milk and some crackers. He sniffed the coffee beans beside the grinder and ground a couple of pounds. He seldom drank coffee at home, but it had sure tasted good on the ship.

"I'm new at this," he told the grocer. "Put in whatever else you think I'll need, and a recipe book, if you have one."

The hearse driver had heated two soapstones at the express office and wrapped them in old woolen blankets. Vic felt the heat as he put his feet on them. He had never seen soapstones. It was amazing how they retained heat.

At times, the matched bays were in a foot or more of snow. The hearse was relatively light weight. As they neared Wallhala, Vic offered the driver $5 if he could drive him to his Dad's place on the river. That was nearly as much as the undertaker's assistant made working all week.

The man agreed.

*   *   *

It was his second day at the camp. He heard a knock on the door. A visitor! Someone must have noticed the smoke from the fire he had built in the small cast-iron laundry stove.

Vic recognized Dan, the local handyman. Dan remembered the boy.

"Well, hello Victor," he said, removing his mitten. "What brings you here in the middle of March?"

Vic's mind leaped ahead. He had to persuade the man, who was also the caretaker for several other camps along the river, that all was well in Chicago.

"Have a seat on the bed."

Dan sat down.

"I've been unhappy in school. I pleaded with Dad to let me drop out of the spring semester. He said, 'If you're not going to school, you must do something useful like going up to the Pere Marquette and clearing a spot to build a log cabin.'"

"What is Eon, the Finnish carpenter doing this winter?"

"Not much, I'm sure," said Dan. "Let's go see him."

Now the boy was cornered. He had to make another move.

"I be looking for voork," said Eon. "This be goot time to start cutting logs for cabin."

"You're hired," he heard himself saying. Oh, well, Dad will pay him in the spring. If he comes up in the spring. Dad doesn't have any idea where I am.

"Let's build the cabin over here," he told Eon. "Build it so the front window looks upstream to the bend in the river."

Barothy found a couple of wide cedar boards and some paint. When he had the sign done, he nailed it to the outside of the building. The ground was too hard to dig a hole for a post.

The sign read, "Barothy's Lodge, Camp Sites, Fire Wood, Guide Service." The steelhead season was about to open and Vic arranged with a couple of local boys to keep firewood chopped and ready for sale. Fishermen were soon buying wood and paying him for a place to pitch their heavy wall tents.

"How about a guide?" one steelheader asked.

"My other guides are out," he lied, "but I'm available."

"How much?"

Vic thought for a moment. "I charge $5 a day."

"You're hired."

At times his client looked at the boy skeptically. He seemed young. A big female steelhead saved the day. The man slipped on the slick clay along the shore. Vic braced himself and extended his hand. He kept the man from slipping into the river, then helped the proud angler land his trophy. The fish was more than 30 inches long and her belly was full of spawn.

The once-doubtful client gave Vic the spawn to sell to other clients, and he sang praises of Barothy, the new guide, wherever he went on the river.

Barothy's Lodge was born.

*　　*　　*

It was March 1950. Vic related that story of his "misspent" youth to me while we were fishing out of Barothy's Caribbean Lodge at Islamarada Key in Florida.

Guy Means, a Cadillac-Buick dealer in Fort Wayne, had called from his winter home in Hollywood, Fla. Guy was an excellent fly-caster and hunter. He often called me from several hundred miles away with an invitation to join him for birdhunting or fishing, so I wasn't surprised. This time it was to tell me about a new sport — fly-fishing for bonefish.

"Bonefish are becoming very popular with spin fishermen," Means said. "They're even more fun on a fly. You stand up in the boat and shoot a fly to the fish.

"Only a couple of fishermen have done it," Means explained. "I've engaged Bill Smith and his wife, Bonnie, who is also a guide, to take the four of us bonefishing this weekend."

Helen and I packed quickly. I forgot to take a fly-rod or any tackle. We arrived at Miami airport the next night. At 8 the following morning we met Bill and Bonnie Smith.

Bill Smith explained that bonefish live in up to 30 feet of water, but they feed primarily on miniature shellfish on the bottom of "flats" that are usually less than two feet deep. They feed with their bodies in a steep angle, and their tails protrude from the water.

"That's called 'tailing,'" Smith explained. "That's how we find bonefish. You can tell which way they are headed by their tails. You cast about three feet ahead of a fish and retrieve slowly, a few inches at a time.

"But you must be very quiet. Bonefish are very sensitive to noise."

BAROTHY AND SALTWATER FISHING

I explained that in the rush to get here, I had forgotten to bring any fishing tackle with me.

"If you want to try fly-fishing, I have a fly-rod and three streamers a client left," explained Smith. "You can use it if you wish."

The Smiths took us out onto the flats in a 32-foot yacht towing two skiffs. Bonnie took Helen and Mary in one skiff and Bill took Guy and me in the other.

Bill quickly found bonefish tailing and pointed to where the fly should land. It was a long cast, I thought.

"Are you a good fly-fisherman, or just one of those guys that fish a few days of the year?" he asked.

"George is one of the best," Guy declared.

"I fly-fish all summer on the AuSable," I added. Smith's manners were beginning to irritate me.

"Well, these casts may be too long for you. My customer made long false casts, stripped all the line into a coil in front of him, then did what he called a 'double-haul.' He cast about 30 feet, but couldn't reach the fish. He said he was going to give up fly-fishing after he caught a few nice bones on spinning tackle."

I began to test the rod. It felt a bit stiff, but it should cast all right.

"Don't try to stop a bonefish," Bill warned. "The mouth of the fish is too soft. That reel is supposed to have about 200 feet of backing. Try to cast a few feet past and to one side of the fish, and if you get a strike, let the fish run."

It would be a long cast, but with two false casts to get line out, I shot the fly to just beyond the bonefish.

Guy gave Smith an "I told you so" grin.

"I would never have believed it possible that you could place a fly like that," Smith said. A moment later, I raised the rod lightly when I felt a fish strike, and held it high as the line spun from the reel. Suddenly the line went slack.

"Goddamnit, George, I told you not to try to stop the fish. You have lost my leader and one of my three flies." Bill was still dressing me down as I caught the end of the fly-line.

"Your line wasn't rinsed," I chided. I broke off a six-inch piece and a second and a third. Then I broke off pieces of rotten fly-line all the way to the belly, throwing them in his face. Fly lines in those days were made of coated silk and were delicate. They had to be rinsed after each use and kept clean and treated or they would rot — especially with a coating of salt water.

"The line appears to be strong enough here," I said. Smith grumbled, but he made a leader from ten-pound test monofilament line he unwound from a big spool, and I tied on one of his two remaining streamers.

The water was clear and full of feeding bonefish. I hooked a big one. The line was not completely off the reel when it went slack again. When he realized what he had done to the fly line, Bill became surly and insulting. I changed to spinning tackle. Guy landed a nice bonefish, and I reminded him what fun it would have been on a fly. Smith smoldered, but he said nothing.

Means had engaged the Smiths for two days. The next morning Bill said he would guide the Meanses and Bonnie would guide Helen and me. Helen didn't fish and Bonnie was pleasant to be around. She obviously knew the water.

Bonefish are exciting, even on a spinning rod. You feel the strike or see movement of the line then things begin happening all at once. The first run is 75 to 100 feet. Then the fish jumps and starts another run. A five-pound bonefish usually makes three long circles of the boat, pulling out every foot of line, and may swim straight toward you. Sometimes it may be behind the boat while your line is still on the water in front of you. When it's completely exhausted, a bonefish can usually be picked up.

Bonefish are good to eat; however, they're full of bones, including a big bone on either side of the backbone. Most are released. A shark often follows a hooked bonefish, and waits to catch it when it is released. To outwit sharks, stroke the fish in the water until it's breathing well, and it can outrun a shark.

To me, a tailing bonefish is as exciting as a flight of giant Canada geese waiting to drop into a layout of decoys.

* * *

As we were leaving for Hollywood the next evening, Helen cried stop.

"There's Barothy's sign. Mrs. Barothy is my niece's sister." We had met Betty Barothy when her sister, Joan, married Helen's nephew, Bob Hall, two years ago. Betty had married Vic about nine months earlier. She insisted that we stay over. Vic would be home tomorrow.

Guy said he couldn't stay.

"George, why don't you and Helen go back with us tonight, then you can come back tomorrow in our station wagon and stay as long as you like. I have my Cadillac here, too"

Barothy returned from a three-day charter and had two days free. About five-foot-eight, Vic weighed about 200 pounds. He had a leathery face behind a well-groomed beard that was the mark of an old salt. It was set with mischievous bright blue eyes.

We went fishing the next morning. Vic was anxious to talk. Soon, he was recalling what he referred to as his "misspent youth," and the creation of the first Barothy's Lodge on the Pere Marquette River.

"My brother, Fred, is now running the lodge on the PM," he explained, after relating his story about stowing away. For two years, he said his parents didn't know he was alive. When he was 16, he had parlayed his knowledge of boats into a job operating a high-speed motorboat for bootleggers. He out-raced federal agents to whiskey dropped by runners in certain Florida Keys weed beds.

"It was close a couple of times, but I was never caught."

Suddenly, Barothy whirled and pointed.

"There is the largest school of big redfish I have ever seen. There must be hundreds."

The school was swimming rapidly across a wide open flat. We tried to follow them. We searched for two hours without seeing them again.

Joe and Mary Brooks stopped to visit that night. Joe was manager of the Miami Metro Fishing Tournament and was "Mr. Fly-Fisherman" of the Keys. He held most of the records for big fish caught on a fly. I told him about my experience with Bill Smith. The two strikes interested him more.

"You really hooked two bonefish on streamers?"

"Yes," I replied.

We became instant friends.

Joe and Mary, who had been married only a few months, decided to stay. Joe was a big man, a lean 210 pounds on a six-foot-three-inch frame with a leathery-tanned face and penetrating eyes. His trademark was an Alpine hat sold by his friend, Dan Bailey, at his fly-fishing tackle shop in Livingston, Montana. Joe added a grouse feather and wore it everywhere.

Vic and I fished together the next day with spinning gear and caught bones, reds and snook. Joe fished with Mary, who was probably his equal with a fly-rod, although she usually stayed in the shadow of her famous outdoor writer husband. If she out-fished him, only a few close friends ever knew it.

Joe had his own fishing boat. On the second day I went out with him. Since I poled my riverboat in Michigan, I suggested that I could change off with him. We could both pole as well as fish. Joe agreed. He outfitted me with the finest fly-fishing tackle I had ever used, and we spent the week together fly-fishing for bonefish, redfish, ladyfish and snook.

We experimented with all sizes and patterns of flies and tippets and concluded that we preferred smaller flies and finer tippets. Joe averaged 30 bonefish a day, but I averaged about 15. With that experience behind me, I became an unpaid guide for Vic, taking out several of Barothy's good clients. Guiding furthered my education in saltwater fishing.

Vic, Joe and I were soon "Old Vic," "Jose" and "Middle-age." Vic was actually the youngest, but most people referred to him as Old Vic. I became Middle-age because I was the oldest, but they said I didn't act that way.

Over three decades, Joe painted a broad stripe in the lore and legend of fly-fishing. I had the good fortune of spending much of 25 years with him. I was impressed because he was equally well known in South America. While he made his living as an outdoor writer, he was best known to anglers everywhere as a fly-fisherman.

*　*　*

With each annual trip to Florida, we spent a little more time. Helen and I stayed away from the bright lights and golf and our wardrobes became smaller. After we started going to Barothy's Caribbean Lodge in 1950, we spent much of our time in swimsuits. My daytime fishing clothes consisted of swim trunks, a hat and tennis shoes. Helen usually wore a bathing suit or a short skirt with a sleeveless blouse. We dressed casually for dinner.

BAROTHY AND SALTWATER FISHING

Barothy pioneered houseboat trips at Islamarada for bonefishing.

"For the past two years I've been taking four fishermen out on four-day trips," he explained. "It's much more profitable than just running the resort where my income is primarily from board and room. At least one in four fishermen wants a guide. The guides were making more money than I was.

"I've been looking for another virgin spot. Islamarada is becoming too popular. Fly-fishing interest has increased and guide services have doubled and tripled in the last two years.

"I searched Belize, Central America and the Caribbean islands, including Cuba's Isle of Pines, for a place to establish a charter-boat system. I want to have four fishermen living on a houseboat and fishing two to a boat, each with several miles of good flats.

"Isle of Pines has all that plus thousands of oversize, non-migratory black ducks and a large population of quail. There are no fishing rods or guns on the island. It is a thirty-six-by-thirty-six-mile island, with enough bonefish flats for a dozen boat parties to fish without ever seeing each other."

How he managed it, I never knew. Vic met General Fulgencio Batista, the Cuban dictator, and they became friends. Batista made it possible for Barothy to buy eighty acres on the Hookero River, a large stream that entered the ocean four miles downstream from his landing.

Vic found the native population friendly, intelligent and ambitious. He recruited fifteen Cubans and brought two guides from Islamarada to train them. Half of them were named Pedro. He paid them $40 a month. A guide at Islamarada cost $64 a day for a fisherman and $36 for a non-fishing wife. It was a bargain. Where could a fisherman enjoy the finest bonefishing and provide his wife a comfortable trip for $100 a day?

Barothy operated out of tents until he found builders who knew how to make bricks. At the end of the first year he had a 40-by-40-foot building with a high dividing wall. One side was the dining room and the other, with a large fireplace, was the lodge's lobby-parlor.

Barothy was soon grossing $16,000-$20,000 a month from mid-November through June. Betty was flying to Miami monthly to deposit their take in several banks.

Helen and I spent several six-week vacations at Isle of Pines.

A mile back from the river was a large freshwater spring that was the camp's water supply. A stream drained a small lake two miles above the spring. The lake held a large population of baby tarpon ranging from eight to 25 pounds.

Helen went there with me one day. The tarpon were easy to catch on streamers. I hooked one and handed the rod to her on the middle seat. She didn't know what to expect. The fish jumped beside the boat, shaking water all over us. She handed the rod back. It was fun, and it was private. Vic said only five people had ever fished this lake.

From Key West to Q-Air Lines' own small airport near Havana was 125 air miles. The flight cost $32. Santa Fe was 11 miles from the airport, Barothy's camp was another three miles and the "Alcatraz" of Cuba was five miles beyond the lodge on a black marble mountain.

The marble was mined by prisoners for use in construction of public buildings throughout the world. The roads were built of marble gravel. Batista ordered a two-mile extension of the road built to Barothy's lodge, where he was occasionally guest of honor. The camp also had excellent telephone service. Later, Fidel Castro cited those instances of favoritism as examples as he built support for a revolution against Batista's rule.

Helen enjoyed the hospitality. We met many friendly people. Herb Johnson of Milwaukee, a founder of Johnson & Johnson, was an international fisherman who owned a home in Chile he used only for fishing. Johnson was one of Barothy's first regulars and Vic sold him a hundred feet along the river where Herb built a three-bedroom home. He invited me to go quail hunting with him and his guide. It was the start of a friendship. Johnson joined our fishing crowd and I arranged a trip to Montana for him. Herb, in turn, urged us to use his home on Isle of Pines whenever it wasn't occupied.

Helen and I went on one of Barothy's houseboats with Gene and Marie Andregg from New York City. Gene was the American distributor of German camera equipment. One of Vic's Pedros was my guide in the small boat.

"You know the clock, señor?" Pedro asked. I said yes.

"There is a bonefish at eleven o'clock."

My fly landed about four feet from the fish. I started to retrieve the fly slowly and nothing happened. It happened again and again — 70 times by my count.

"Pedro, I am doing something wrong!"

"Yes, sir. You do not cast far enough. There is a fish at seven o'clock. I cast, the fish struck and I landed my first Isle of Pines bone. As I landed my fourteenth sometime later, I suddenly realized that it was dark.

"Where is the houseboat?'

"Over there about three miles." Pedro pointed. I couldn't see the boat's beacon.

"Can you see to get there?" He nodded. "Si, señor." Weed beds were in all directions. I finally saw the beacon. Pedro guided the skiff up beside the houseboat about 8:30.

What can you say?

"Thank God we finally got here."

Turning to Pedro, I said, "Be sure to overhaul that motor."

A drink and a good plate of food revived me. When I finished, the atmosphere was again friendly.

Gene had caught five fish on spinning tackle and was back on board at 5:30. I explained the short casting I had started with, and was properly censured as the dunce. I turned to Pedro and reminded him again to fix the motor.

Gene smiled. "George, we were waiting for your motor to start. When you started it, it sounded like it was running perfectly."

My face felt flushed.

We headed out at nine the next morning, but we couldn't locate a bone in a two-hour search. Helen and Marie were disenchanted with the sun, so the other guide took them back to the houseboat. Gene got into my boat. We caught a few fish, but it was dreadfully slow.

"There's a white flag on the houseboat," said Gene. "What does it mean?"

"Lunch, señor," Pedro smiled.

We relaxed on the big boat until four o'clock, then fished until seven. On the third day we resumed fishing about 3:30 and were in for dinner at the lodge at seven.

The next morning, we saw Gene and Marie off. Joe and Mary Brooks got off the plane. The camp was full again. The Brookses and Griffiths covered the 200-mile island road system in Vic's Carryall, and we tried out several flies and various leaders.

Joe and Mary saw us off on Monday morning. I had an appointment on Tuesday in Detroit.

"Did you leave a down payment for a lot with Vic," Helen asked on the flight home.

I shook my head. I wondered why I hadn't. It was Paradise.

*   *   *

The political climate was changing in Cuba in the mid-'50s, and Barothy was seriously looking for a new site. He phoned me.

"George, meet me at Miami airport for a trip to British Honduras. Bring your fly-rod and six flies for a couple hours of fishing, but be prepared for a couple days of business."

On the way, he explained: "Castro is stirring up the natives in Cuba, and he has many followers. Not that my friend, Batista, is unpopular, but he has been a dictator for a long time and people always listen to unkept promises."

On our last trip home from Isle of Pines in March 1957, a crowd of 75,000 was expected for a Castro demonstration at the Havana airport. Every follower was supposed to wear a white shirt every day. Approximately 200,000 gathered. Luckily, Q-Air Lines got us out of Havana and to Key West. We took a bus north to Guy Means' home in Hollywood, where we had left our car.

It would be difficult for Vic to find a place as handy as Isle of Pines.

By early January, we were hearing from the Barothys frequently, but they were not receiving our letters.

We learned that Castro had two guards stationed on Barothy's property around the clock. Vic and Betty weren't molested, but they were prisoners in their own camp! Vic couldn't go to town for supplies without a guard. After hosting one group of fishermen, he canceled all reservations. His boats sat idle.

BAROTHY AND SALTWATER FISHING

The Hookero River had a strong tide. In March 1958, Barothy secreted extra gasoline, food, water, and bare necessities aboard a houseboat docked on the river. At two o'clock in the morning, during a high tide, the Barothys, their son, Vic Jr., and their top guide and his wife and son quietly boarded the boat and glided silently down to the river mouth before they started the motors. When they were 60 miles from Isle of Pines, they heard a plane and rushed to the safety of a bay of a small key. The plane circled twice, as though searching, then flew away. They went on to Jamaica.

Vic and Betty faced the loss of everything they had built up, but their cash assets were safe in Miami banks. A week later they were in Belize, halfway from Miami to Mexico City, and wealthy clients were offering to pay for materials and labor so they could set up a new camp and provide bonefishing for them.

Belize is a strip of land along the Atlantic side of the Yucatan Peninsula that Great Britain colonized 150 years ago to set up sugar plantations. It was the poorest country south of Mexico. The British enjoyed it that way.

Belize City was a city of 34,000 people, more than one third of the nation's population of 85,000. The country was primitive. Roads ran no more than 15 miles inland from the ocean, so most travel was by canal. The main street, Prince Boulevard, didn't live up to its name. It had an odorous open ditch on each side that slowly drained raw sewage down to the ocean.

Vic made arrangements to buy 40 acres on an island with an agreement by the government that it would not sell any more of the island. It offered bonefishing and scuba diving without the long boat ride at Isle of Pines; however, there was no fresh water and no possibility of drilling a well on the island. Barothy had to bring water from the mainland daily. He also collected rainwater.

Vic could offer few of the amenities of Isle of Pines, but he advertised it as being in the jungle. It didn't have a Castro threatening to take over privately owned business; however, England controlled the prices and the economy. British families owned all of the important franchises for commodities such as gas, oil, and automobiles. They set up private schools for their children, while native children could only go through the sixth-grade. About 100 British troops in knee-length khaki pants and short-sleeved shirts were always on guard at the airport.

208

Shakespeare sent the Barothys a supply of casting and spinning rods and reels. They soon had three trailer-type buildings and several skiffs. When we spent Thanksgiving in Belize, they were ready forbusiness. Within months, they were making a profit. They had three houseboats operating by March. However, they just couldn't duplicate the Isle of Pines fishing experience. Fishing was good, but the winds were strong in March and April, the months when I wanted to go bonefishing.

On the plane back to Miami, we started a conversation with a group of young folks from Montreal, who said they had been scuba diving at Paradise Place, 30 miles north of Belize City on San Gris Key.

"Was there any fishing there?" I asked.

"Oh, yes. We got well acquainted with four bonefish guides. The resort is small, but it can accommodate thirty-six people."

We flew to San Gris Key in 1977 with the Ebb Warrens of Gaylord and the Ben Wrights of New York. Ben was a retired publisher of *Field & Stream*. Ebb's wife, Betty, was a first cousin of Dolly Wright.

It was hard to locate baggage in the small airport at Belize City where we had to transfer to an eight-passenger plane. I noticed a good-looking native boy, whom I recognized as a baggage hustler on previous trips. He was a friend of Vic Barothy.

"Mr. Griffith?" he asked as he approached. I grinned and held out my hand.

"Going to Vic Barothy's?"

"No, six of us are going to Paradise Place."

"Give me all your baggage checks, sir. Go out that side door to that small plane. If you go through the regular line, you will be nearly an hour getting through Customs and Immigration."

I handed him a fiver, 10 dollars to him, and collected our crowd. A half-hour later we were unloading again on San Gris Key's main street, which also doubled as the runway for our plane. Our host was waiting with a large wheelbarrow for our baggage.

Paradise Place was a group of thatched huts that, from the outside, resembled cheese boxes. Inside, they were modern motel rooms. The main lodge had eight rooms and a rustic dining room. A separate building with a sawdust floor had a hanging sign that said "Bar." One of the guides was the bartender and he made very good drinks. On Sundays he flipped the sign and it read "Church."

San Gris guides were $55 a day, so we each hired a guide. Dinner was overwhelming: The first night the chef was disappointed because six of us ate only nine large lobster tails.

A beautiful beach ran the length of the key. There were no breakers. The tide hit a reef three miles from shore and the water only went up or down. Unfortunately, the beach also doubled as a dump. Every hundred feet of shoreline contained a large garbage pail of refuse.

A group of friendly teenage boys was paddling around in two canoes most of the day. They welcomed my offer of 50 cents for every 10-by-10-foot fish net of trash they picked up and took to the dump. It was a vacant spot our host had persuaded the city fathers to set up, but it was away from the beach. I hoped that when my $10 was used up, others would join the club, and that the people living along the beach would follow through, but I saw no effort to clean up anything. It was sad that a place so beautiful was so dirty.

* * *

From 1941 to 1960, we spent our winter vacations in Hollywood, Florida. We shifted to Islamarada, where we were staying at Jim Wiley's El Capitan Lodge. We made some lasting friends among the fishermen we met, including Bart Foth, a furniture manufacturer from Gettysburg, Pa., John Alden Knight, creator of the Solunar Tables, Lefty Kreh, outdoor writer who succeeded Joe Brooks as Miami tournament manager, and Billy Pate, well-known fisherman. We also fished with Cecil Green, Dixie Knowles, Ken Williams, and Clarence Rowe, all top guides.

Wiley's resort was next to the Theater of the Sea, a well-known porpoise show. The porpoises, who swam to music, were in a large pool of saltwater changed daily by the ocean tides. Helen occasionally became a part of their act. She stood on a platform 10 feet above the water, and held a mullet by the tail with her teeth. When the trainer rang a big bell, a porpoise started its run from the end of the pool, leapt out of the water, and took the fish without touching Helen. She enjoyed it.

In 1962, I entered the Greater Miami Metro Fishing Tournament with Dixie Knowles as my guide. I caught a redfish that weighed nearly 14 pounds on a fly and took a first place in the tournament. The catch entitled me to membership in the Islamarada Fishing Club.

However, that was our last year. Helen's doctor said the heat and humidity of the Keys were not good for her health. It was a shock to us. We both liked the Keys. We sought a second opinion, which was a weak agreement with the first. We felt there was an escape clause — he didn't ban a trip of a few days.

That reminds me of an old friend. A true story. Tom entered one of my favorite bars and sat down and ordered a glass of wine. I was surprised. Tom favored Jack Daniels.

"Tom, what's with the wine?" I asked.

"Doctor's orders. I had a checkup last week and the doc said, 'Bad news! Your drinking days are over. No more whiskey, no more beer, no more vodka ....' I ran like hell before he could say wine."

*   *   *

The Keys were hard to give up. Good bone flats on the ocean, great tarpon fishing around Key West, bones, tarpon and redfish in Florida Bay. We moved to Fort Lauderdale in 1963. Helen wanted to be there because two of her friends from Fort Wayne spent their winters there. However, her high blood pressure prevented her from joining in the activities they enjoyed.

We bought our first apartment in Pompano Beach in 1971, and a second in a new seven-story building that had an elevator and was the only structure of more than three stories in the area. That's where we met George and Peri Kennedy of Long Island, New York.

Helen and I flew to Belize in April for a long weekend with the Barothys. We didn't take a boat trip. Vic and Betty were losing ambition. Vic offered me $15,000 a year to take over and manage the camp from December through mid-June. I had been retired since 1959, and I could have taken up his offer. But, with Helen's health, I had enough to keep me busy. I didn't want a job.

Young Vic wanted to take over the camp from his parents, but he was still in grammar school. They sold out and moved to Coral Gables, Florida, where Vic died within two years.

*   *   *

When Vic Jr. finished the eighth grade, he quit. He was determined to go back to Belize. Betty reluctantly agreed. She bought him a large pleasure boat, which had twin diesel engines. The boat held six people, and had a 1200-mile cruising range. He outfitted the boat for charter fishing and was open for business.

Peri and I were married in the spring of 1976.

I called young Vic about a charter trip.

"I haven't had any clients yet, but I have a good crew, including Dad's old skiff foreman." I knew the man well. He was an excellent choice.

Peri had made about 10 winter cruises during which women changed clothes three or more times a day. She expected something like that. I suggested a very casual wardrobe, and stressed that this was a fishing trip with Vic Jr. She still packed two suitcases. When we got to Barothy's, she discovered that she was the only woman aboard. It was quite a shock for her. It was our honeymoon!

I had met the first mate when he worked for Vic's father and he gave us special attention. One morning I came out on deck as he was about to board a skiff.

"Good morning, Jose."

"Oh, Mr. George, I have a small gill net set out to catch table fish. Do you want to go along?"

Peri heard us. She wanted to go, too. It was less than a mile. The bottom was beautiful sand and Peri said that she felt like getting out and wading. It was deceptively deeper than she thought. When we neared a very small island with a sand bar that ran slowly out into the flat, I jumped out, lifted her out of the boat and stood her beside me in the ocean. The water reached her breasts. She screamed, at first, then she began laughing.

"What would my children think of their mother being this deep in the ocean?"

Jose waited until she had her bearings, then went on to pick up his catch. The water became shallow as we waded toward the beach. As we admired the beautiful sunrise, Peri screamed again and grabbed me, pointing ahead.

"Can we reach the shore?"

I looked and three sand sharks about four feet long were cruising. Since we had not disturbed them, they continued on their way. When Jose returned, she told him the story, and we all had a good laugh. She never liked sharks after that, but they seemed to like her.

A couple of days later we were enjoying an after-lunch snooze on deck mattresses when Jose yelled and waved his arm to the horizon. Hundreds of tuna, many weighing over 100 pounds each, were swimming past us about 200 yards away. We had only one heavy trolling rod aboard. Minutes later, Peri, Jose and I were trying to get ahead of the school. Jose put a foot-long fish on a hook and Peri let out line. Suddenly, she had a terrific strike. She could barely reel in the wire line. We were in thirty feet of water, waiting for her tuna to come into view. Suddenly, we realized that four sharks seven feet or longer were swimming around the boat. Her "tuna" was a shark!

She fought the fish and finally brought it close enough for Jose to gaff it. He dragged it into the boat and hit it over the head with a baseball bat. He finally managed to get the shark across the four and one-half-foot-beamed boat and we headed back to the houseboat with the shark's head hanging off one side and the tail off the other. Suddenly the shark came back to life and, with one great shake, it knocked the motor control from Jose's hand, and splattered all of us with blood. We returned to the boat with only a skiff full of blood.

* * *

I had gotten well acquainted with Dan and Helen Bailey of Livingston, Montana, during a trout-fishing trip to the Northwest in 1975, after Helen's death. I called Dan to tell him about Peri and also about young Vic. They had known Vic Sr. Dan quickly lined up a third couple, Stens and Laura White, and we flew to Belize.

We fished all day for four days about 30 miles offshore. Porpoises swam around us as we left the boat in skiffs.

Dan, whose Livingston fly shop was known to fly-fishermen across the nation, was to fishing something like Arnold Palmer was to golf, a determined competitor. We were taking turns fishing, a half hour or until you landed a bone. We had planned to be back at the big boat by five o'clock the last day so Vic would have daylight to take us through the narrow channel and back to camp.

"That's thirty-seven, Dan," I said as I landed a bone at 5 o'clock. "I guess that's it."

Dan had 36.

"No sir, I have half an hour coming."

I agreed. That was fair. Within ten minutes he had tied me with his thirty-seventh.

"Happy ending, Dan."

* * *

Bonefishing can be done by wading at Islamarada, but 70 percent of the bottom is too soft to wade at Belize. I gave up all wading after the loss of my eye.

The key to success in bonefishing is to do a lot of it. The bonefish's only protection is a lack of color and terrific speed. A good bonefish weighing five pounds or more will usually take a full fly line plus some backing in unbelievable runs, even with a reel's drag set. The school is easily spooked.

I like to fish for snook and redfish, too, possibly because of my first place win in the Miami tournament with a redfish on a fly with a six-pound leader in 1962.

* * *

Leon Martuch Sr., inventor-founder of Scientific Anglers, gave me some fly lines to try. At dinner one night at the fishing club at Islamarada, several guides began talking about the design of fly lines. Their suggestions for changes seemed to make sense.

I said nothing, but I called "Boss" in Midland, Michigan, the next morning.

"Boss, why does a fly line have a fourteen-foot tapered tip and twenty-two feet of belly?"

"I guess because we always have made them that way, George. Why? Is a change important enough to get me out of bed on Sunday morning?"

He always asked before you told him anything.

"Boss, the guides here say that, with a nine-foot rod, a nine-foot leader and twenty-two feet of tip and belly, you have only a couple of feet of regular line out in an average cast to a bone or redfish. Most casts are forty feet or less.

"They say the tip should be eight feet long and the belly only sixteen feet for casts from forty to fifty feet."

It was my most important contribution to saltwater fly-fishing. I could hear Boss repeating my words as he made notes.

"George, I'll have several lines made to those specifications, and I'll ship them to you within four days. If they work out, I'll order a production run."

The lines arrived as Boss promised. I wound one onto a reel and took my rod to The Tackle Box, an Islamarada tackle store that had a 100 foot wide casting pool. Most of the guides chartered out of this shop, which was on the water's edge. Dixie Knowles, Clarence Rowe and John Alden Knight were talking about their days of fishing as I arrived.

I handed my rod to Rowe and explained what was on the reel. Clarence stripped all the fly line off into coils, made two strong false casts and cast with all his strength. To his surprise — and that of all of us — the line laid across the entire pool, one hundred feet!

Martuch had sent me four different tapers. I kept the line on my reel and gave the other three lines to Knowles, Knight and Rowe. By then the store owners, a retired schoolteacher from Kansas, and her husband, were among several dozen spectators.

"Can you get me thirty-dozen of those lines," she asked.

"I sure can."

I called Boss that day. The weight-forward line was born.

That experience changed forever fly-line tapers for saltwater fishing. I brought the line back to the AuSable and found that a fast weight-forward line is also great on inland trout streams. Bass fishermen soon adopted it.

Since then I've used a weight-forward line for fishing from my AuSable Riverboat.

*   *   *

I recommended Vic Jr. as a charter skipper to Leigh Perkins, owner of the Orvis Company from Manchester, Vermont, and set up a bonefish charter with young Barothy for Perkins, his wife, Romie, and their daughter.

Lee called to say they enjoyed the trip and the mangroves, grasses, wildflowers and the many species of birds in the islands. And the hospitality of young Vic and his wife.

Wife?

"Vic married an attractive Cuban girl."

His father would have enjoyed knowing that his son was living a life that emulated his own.

A life of guiding that had its beginning on a bitter March night in 1916 when a fifteen-year-old stowed away on a cargo boat bound for Muskegon.

*   *   *

FATAL BEAUTY

It is the opening day of the 1991 Michigan trout season as I stand at my favorite station looking out the front window of the Barbless Hook down onto the Mainstream of the AuSable River.

Only two days ago, Peri and I had left the concrete jungle of our Florida condominium. And even though cave dwelling has become much more luxurious through the ages, we still consider our home in Florida somewhat of a cave compared to the scenic surroundings of the Barbless Hook. Many caves nowadays overlook a golf course and come with many levels. Our cave is on the fifth level and just one of a group of 10. Our particular cliff has almost 70 caves.

And while we are all crowded into relatively small spaces, we get along suprisingly well. Our neighbors are more than lenient with Peri and me considering we are past our allotted three score years and ten. Our Florida cave is a welcome retreat from the cold and snowy Michigan winters with a climate that more than compensates for the limited elbow space of cave living.

Our airplane trip from Florida back to the Barbless Hook has its destination in Traverse City, the "Jewel of Michigan," which gives us a 60-mile drive home to the AuSable. And although, through the years the countryside has changed, it has still retained the blue expanse of Lake Michigan and the vivid shades of green offered by the never-shedding pine, balsam and spruce. In the background of this greenery towers the drab gray of the aspen, oak, and maple trees that will show their glory in just a short period of time.

Nestled comfortably in the center of what was once a forest of giant white pines lies the historic town of Grayling with its attraction of the winding AuSable River. As we pass through, just a short distance now from home, we remark about the regrowth of the 10 foot jack pines that have reforested the depleted ground that experienced a raging forest fire just 10 years ago.

Three miles down the road, leading east from town, we pass the five foot high pines on the Trout Unlimited property, known as "Guides Rest," which also took a leveling blow from nature's fires just three years ago. As we cross the Stephan Bridge Road, again we see the damaged area that burned just the previous year. Here stands new growth that is yet to reach two feet amongst the remaining dead trees.

While this last fire was probably the most devastating in recent memory, like all of nature's disasters, there can be a good side. Much of the dead debris on the ground burned, giving new growth a better chance.

As we turned and traveled down Wakely Bridge Road, our resident flock of turkeys was there to welcome us. And again, as we turned into our driveway and proceeded to the house, there stood three suspicious white-tailed deer eyeing their "old friends" who were returning home.

The woods opened its arms at the end of the driveway and the old homestead looked as if we had never left. Craig Perry, our resident and efficient "overseer," had raked and manicured the lawn asif it was his own. Only a few dead stumps and downed trees gave any evidence of the winter storms.

We moved quickly through the house to the front window to greet the rushing waters of our precious AuSable. As usual for this time of year, it was a few inches high from the snow melt and early spring rains. I also recognized the slight red tinge that the runoff brings. But, for the first time, I saw a new invasion in the river that raised some suspicions and concern. A sandy colored, moss-like scum had attached itself to the larger rocks scattered amongst and along the river's flow. A sure indication of too many septic tanks and drainfields passing their refuse into the river. The scientist calls this aging. I made a mental note to explore this further as this process can cause a very quick demise to any free-flowing resource.

But first, I had to say hello to one of my oldest friends. My riverboat that stood at attention awaiting my arrival in the garage. Its heavy coat of varnish, built up through the years, shone anxiously to once again meet the rippling waters of the river. They too had become old friends that shook hands graciously upon each meeting.

Peri called from the house. The telephone had already started to ring. Yes, we were back at the Barbless Hook.

Rand Oslund called and would not be able to arrive with his wife Michele until Monday. Doctor Henig checked in but would not be able to join me on the river for a month due to some ill health. Bob Summers called from Traverse City to remind me that we would float the river on Monday morning. Our schedule was already filling up…but normal!

One more quick look at the river before the unpacking began. A few flies were in the air and the occassional one lit only to be quickly devoured by a rising fish. More of my friends letting me know they were still there and ready to challenge me throughout the summer.

By the next morning we had hastily unpacked so that I could get to the more important chores of the day. The first ritual of the upcoming season was to renew aquaintances with one more old friend…my #735, 7-foot, 3 weight "Summers" bamboo rod. A mighty able tool for our early season flies.

Peri joined me at the window as I added reel and line and reminded me that the "AuSable Hilton" behind the house must quickly be made ready to receive our guests who would be dropping in for the "opening."

Peri prepared lunch while I took on the chores of the Hilton. And as usual, my full stomach was a good reason to digest both my food and the warming sun in my most favorite chair overlooking the river. Soon the sun changed position and the trees' shadows caused me to doze off into a dream that recalled my first day of fishing a major hatch on the waters below the house. It was June 5th of the year 1938.

We had purchased our cabin in February and brought up the first truck-load of furniture in March. Business commitments had prevented my enjoying the first month of trout season.

We reached the cabin about 2 p.m., and as Helen unlocked the door and began her inspection, I made quick exit to the river. It was still there and running clear and smooth. Beautiful could not adequately describe it.

As I walked back to the cabin, still looking over my shoulder at the flowing stream, Earl Madsen, a guide we had met in March, was getting out of his car in the driveway. He had been looking after the property while we were away.

Earl was one of the best fly tiers around, so it was without hesitation that I asked him quickly what fly I should be using at that time of day. "Forget this afternoon," he replied. "We're going to have a heavy hatch of Brown Drakes at about 6:30 tonight. Be on the river about five hundred yards above your dock and fish very slowly down to your landing. You should have more good trout than you can use in just a couple of hours."

I was on time with one of Earl's drake pattern flies. The water was nearly waist deep and slow. Two live flies floated down past me, then a good trout fed on my left. As I was working line out for a cast, two more good fish surfaced.

I had caught a few strong leaping trout, but all on large streamers. Suddenly my rod tip was letting me know that I was into something even bigger. I struck back at the boil of water at the end of my line. It had to be a lunker. As Earl had advised, I let my prize carefully wear itself out. Finally Allah was good, and my trophy glided almost willingly into my net. With more than slightly trembling hands, I admiringly inspected my catch from every angle and reluctantly placed it into my creel.

Amazingly enough, my battle had not disturbed any of the other feeding fish. Another one shortly took to my fly and buried itself under some small logs before my line was even under control. I tried to bring it out, but my fly came shooting through the water without as much as a shake of the trout's head.

I tried to light up a cigarette twice, with a hand that was shaking so badly I couldn't even singe the tobacco. Back on the river's bank, I could finally steady myself well enough to light up and inhale deeply. It was becoming quite a night on the river.

In two hours I had number five on my line and four in the creel all over 15 inches long. That meant two meals for Helen and me. So after a few caresses and a less than casual goodbye, I released Mr. Number Five back into the water.

By the time I reached the dock it was after 10 o'clock and I had released five more fish.

As I stood on the dock reflecting on my accomplishments, Mr. and Mrs. H.B. Smith stopped their float briefly to compare notes and welcome me to the river. They were the familiar owners of the Ginger Quill Camp and ultimately became our neighbors when we moved into the Barbless Hook.

Helen, being the patient listener she was, endured my detailed description of the evening for over an hour until she finally pushed me into bed.

The next morning I could hardly wait to reach the Madsen's and confirm Earl's instructions to me the previous afternoon. Earl's delightful wife Alice was already serving coffee to Earl and Walt Shaw, another well-known guide on the river. Three other fishermen had also stopped by to buy some of Earl's flies. It didn't take much encouragement for me to relate in great detail my experiences of the night before.

That night still stands out as my most thrilling fishing adventure. While that drake hatch lasted a couple of weeks and the fishing continued to be good in the evenings, for me it still never compared to that first night. Nor probably will it ever.

Earl remained busy with his regular customers, but squeaked me in a few times to float fish with him in his riverboat. But after that first night, it was difficult to convince me that wading wasn't the best way to fish. Earl told me that if I was going to continue to fish here, I would have a boat in two years. You know, he turned out to be right!

In late August of 1939, Earl Madsen was helping me build a small shed. And as we were resting after lunch he said, "Fishing is about over and I want to offer you a proposition. Let's spend six days together. Three of the days you'll pay me thirty-five dollars a day. The other three will be free. The days I get paid I'll guide for you. The other three days you'll guide and I will teach you how to handle a riverboat."

I was not aware that he knew that I had turned over twice and also landed several times in a log jam.

This was the best money I ever spent. He was facing me from the front of the boat most of the three days while teaching me the secrets of handling a riverboat. He taught me to let the river do most of the work. And today, I enjoy guiding the boat as much as fishing. There also was a bonus in that six days we spent together. He showed me some excellent grouse cover that belonged to Mart Winnie up around Traverse City.

After those six days, I was fishing to some spots that I had never looked at before and my average trout was becoming at least two inches longer.

FATAL BEAUTY

We also met Bill and Helene Brand and Vic and Grace Garbutt. Both had homes on the Recreation Club property. Many nights were spent with them around the bridge table in heated competition.

Dr. Garbutt had purchased a new riverboat from John Stephan two years earlier. It was really the many trips down the AuSable with the good doctor that convinced me that this was one of the most effective methods to explore and fish the river. I think that my success in freeing us one time from a forbidding log jam during the 1939 trout season finally convinced him of my boat-handling prowess and was the secret in cementing our longtime friendship. When he found out I was in the market for a riverboat, he finally admitted that he could no longer handle the chores in the poling seat and made me an offer for his boat that I couldn't refuse. There was a method to his madness, however, because the sale was stipulated with the agreement that I would continue to take him fishing.

It was one of the best deals I ever made, as his friendship and talent on the river will always be remembered.

The boat enable us to enjoy many days on the river, to McMaster's Bridge and from Steckert's Bridge to the mouth of the South Branch.

Our friendship was even nurtured further with our common interests for the future of the AuSable. We had become extremely concerned with the large number of trout either being fin clipped or tagged. We had been told that after three weeks in the stream, the hatchery trout were dying at an alarming rate. The fisheries people told us that they were now planting every two weeks because of the high mortality. A few of us were getting acquainted with our fisheries research people. They also made us aware of how much our precious cover for large trout was disappearing. The canoeists were pushing to having more channeling done in the stream so they could navigate their canoes more easily. At that time, aluminum canoes were not available. Cedar construction was the most desirable but more costly and not as durable.

I was also fortunate in meeting Otto Failing at a sportsmen's club meeting one evening. Like Earl Madsen, who was a close friend of Otto's, he took an interest in me. He was the first one to suggest to Harry Ruhl that I would make a good Commissioner.

When I asked him in 1943 what happened to the generous population of grouse on the Wakely Lake property, he came down for a close look. I told him of the high number of grouse once there and questioned why there had been a drop in the population.

He looked over the grounds of the property very carefully and then said, "Wherever you look there are well-worn deer runs crossing each other. Were they there when the grouse were plentiful?"

I took a long look before agreeing that they were not.

"George, your answer is ground cover. Grouse like to move from one small bush to another while feeding. They have a greater fear of air predators than ground predators. A good example is a hawk rather than a fox."

What I should have observed myself, he had quickly pointed out to me. His lesson was very similar to what Earl Madsen had carefully taught me: Good cover is the secret, whether in the woods, the field, or in the river.

It's interesting to note that the AuSable and other streams should really be called watersheds and not rivers.

Suppose if we were to call the AuSable "Holy Waters" a watershed ... bordered on the south by South Down River Road or state road 72, and on the north by North Down River Road. Call Burton's Landing the west boundary and Wakely Bridge Road the east boundary. The distance between South and North Down River Roads on the west is one and a half miles; the distance between the two roads on the east boundary is just less than three miles.

When I moved to the river in 1938, there were seven buildings on the road from Wakely's Bridge to Burton's Landing. Today that number approaches almost 500 buildings. The same applies to the north side of the river.

There were less than 15 buildings directly on the river where we have 180 today.

Today, we also have over 1000 septic tanks draining into our watershed called the AuSable River.

Historically, the stream doubles in size every three to five miles. In 1940 the temperature of the stream was lower at Wakely's Bridge than at Stephan's, while double the size with only one tributary. This was the result of the spring water coming into the river through the springs. These springs also fed billions of larvae of all kinds and made a constant picnic for the fishery.

All of the original owners are gone and their properties have been subdivided, except for Wa Wa Sum, Marshalls, and Knights Camp Thunderbird. Through the years there have been an increasing number of additional homes and cabins built on a great many of the most productive spring beds that feed the river. Now, that cool, pure spring water resource has been filtered through the wet lands and redirected, adding harmful, not beneficial, nutrients.

Let me relate an example of what has been happening along the beautiful and "attracting" AuSable.

"Dick and Marie" are a happily married couple with interests in all the usual hobbies. Dick is invited by a friend to enjoy a weekend at his camp on the AuSable for some "outstanding" fly-fishing. Although Dick is not a fly-fisherman, he accepts the invitation just to do something different and to "get away from it all." As often happens, Dick falls in love with the sport of fly-fishing. Let's admit it, it doesn't take long. And like with most of us, the fishing trips become longer in duration and more frequent.

Marie's curiosity finally gets the best of her, and Dick is forced into including her on one of his new-found adventures to the AuSable.

In planning their trip, Dick has included the inspection of a couple of summer home building sites he has secretly been admiring on the AuSable.

In an effort to "sneak up on them," and probably his wife too, what better way to "see the river" than by canoe on a bright sunny day? Maybe even with a little picnic lunch.

After a short period of time, they come upon a beautiful bend in the river with an "undercut bank that just has to have a big one feeding there." "An undercut run for good resting lies." See, already he's even learned the language of the fly-fisher. I'm sure that Marie was quite impressed. Suddenly, Dick shakes the canoe, half scaring Marie to death, as he points to a spot along the undercut bank that has a feeding trout "that must be at least 18 inches long."

"Oh, that's nice" was Marie's reply, "but I don't see it."

Then the water suddenly bulged with a tiny whirlpool. "See...there it is! It's feeding!"

Not waiting for her to join his excitement, Dick was already tying a new fly on the end of his tippet.

He cast his fly above the bulge and as the fly drifted past there was another bulge. (Isn't that always the case?) He cast again, almost throwing Marie out of the canoe. Another bulge and Dick jerked his fly rod high into the air. A trout was jumping all over the water as Jim tried to bring it to net. Dick had finally conquered the prize that was flopping all over the bottom of the canoe. He placed it into a sack full of wet leaves.

"Put it back in the water," said Marie! "He belongs in front of our new home. Is this lot for sale?"

"I don't know," said Dick, barely able to keep a straight face.

"Seems strange you don't know," said Marie. "It appears to be the one you were talking to the livery man about earlier when you didn't think I was paying attention. Maybe we ought to talk to him again to make sure."

Well, a deposit was made ... a builder was found ... and the next day they started making their plans.

Could some of the low spots on the lot be filled? Could some of the logs and stumps be removed along the shoreline so that the lawn can go all the way to the water's edge? (On their canoe trip they had passed two homes with beautifully manicured riverside lawns.)

Later that week, Dick secretly took the day off work and met on-site with the builder to continue making their plans.

"We've selected this spot because of the shoreline and the trout cover out front. Great fishing here!"

On the contrary, what Marie had envisioned was beautiful, but not suitable for a pristine trout stream. With her expectation of a concrete seawall and a golf course-like lawn made lush green with bags of fertilizer, the disappearnce of the trout cover out front was inevitable.

This all happened a few years before I met Dick on the stream one day. We were both having a very good day. His description of the various small insects would have made Dave Whitlock envious. His casting was superb!

"How's Marie," I asked in passing?

"Well, she started to play golf ... better than average at it, too. She doesn't fish, you know. When I refused to make a country club out of our riverfront, we kind of drifted apart. Our differences finally caused us to separate. So three other flyfisher friends and I joined together and formed a club. While we still have some differences, we at least have a common interest in the trout. **Fatal Beauty**."

Recently, the shoreline of the AuSable "Holy Waters" is being replaced by seawalls and lawns at the rate of 100 feet a month. The springs they replace are no longer contibuting to the hatch of larvae and insects at the rate of billions a day. And we all know how important these insects are to the trout population.

While this is illegal, the Grayling Township Zoning Board makes no continuing effort at halting it.

Along with Fisheries Chief John Robertson and his able research staff, we can correct this. It's a challenge. And one that must be taken seriously if we are to maintain the great coldwater fishery that the AuSable River has been known to be. We will lose this great resource and the many other coldwater fisheries across the country that we have all enjoyed so very much through the years. It's time to stand up and be counted! Each and every one of us!

All waters are holy. But that which have been historically labeled the "Holy Waters of the AuSable River" begin at Burton's Landing and continues to Wakely Bridge. A mile of that river frontage was owned by the Richardsons from Toledo, Ohio. It was one of the first to be subdivided. And while there are some beautiful, quality homes on the property, the lower portion has been further divided into lots of only 100 riverfront feet. Each with it's own septic system and it's own idea of what pretty landscaping is all about…not necessarily with the quality of the river as the top priority. And so it goes on down the river.

But let's not ignore the opportunites that have been availalble at various times. Sometimes taken advantage of…and sometimes not!

Wa Wa Sum was originally owned by Mrs. Duane Strahanan, Sr. and George Bell. The property has a large log lodge with several other substantial buildings. This property was offered to Trout Unlimited provided that the buildings would remain and be maintained intact. Unfortunately, Trout Unlimited's non-profit, tax-exempt status would have to have been violated.

In turn, the property was donated to Michigan State University with the management of only the riverfront becoming the responsibility of Trout Unlimited. To date, this arrangement continues.

From Wa Wa Sum to Stephan's Bridge, the riverfront was owned by another Toledo family by the name of Marshall. This was ultimately put up for sale. Again, the Stranahan's stepped forward and purchased it, immediately turning it over to Trout Unlimited for its protection and maintenance.

Incidentally, the elder Stranahan son, Duane, Jr., served three terms as a National Director of Trout Unlimited.

Below Stephan's Bridge down to Pine Road was owned by the Stephans, long time residents, guides, and riverboat builders in the Grayling area. From there to Black Bend was owned by the Youngs. From there to the Recreation Camp was Camp Thunderbird which was owned by another Toledo family called the Knights. This property was also donated to Trout Unlimited by Milton Knight, Jr., and remains today in their custody as a public fishing access and research area.

None of these properties are still owned by the original families, but have been developed or subdivided in some form or another.

Some of them fortunately by people sympathetic to protecting the resource of the river. Unfortunately, over 51% of the shoreline now has some form of seawall that in most cases has destroyed the natural cover and habitat for the trout population. Most of the valuable trout habitat frontage borders the river side of the Trout Unlimited property. I point this out, because the constructed seawalls are probably the most dangerous threat we have to the survival of not only the AuSable River but most other coldwater fisheries we are trying to protect throughout this country. Most of them block the natural spring drainage into the rivers that are so important to the streams healthy life. Instead, the spring water is warmed and polluted before it drains directly across the land surface into the river …without the benefit of any natural cooling and filtration.

I state with great pleasure, however, that more and more fishermen are becoming aware of the many problems that are confronting the AuSable River as well as the other thousands of streams in this country that we all enjoy so very much. "Catch and release" is becoming a way of life for many fishermen and women.

Unfortunately, too many of those sincere people are crediting this "no kill" policy with too much too fast ... while overlooking many of the other problems that can and will damage our rivers and kill off our fish population at an even more alarming rate.

As an example, for the present, the City of Grayling has corrected its pollution problem attributing to sewage drainage into the AuSable River.

When the sewage disposal plant was built some 25 years ago, it was adequate. However, we must look to the future. The number of new homes in the watershed has more than doubled. And where we had less than 25 septic systems draining into the watershed in 1940, today we have nearly 1000 homes or cabins.

The past and proposed expansion of the Michigan National Guard facility (Camp Grayling), in the heart of Crawford County, has caused a great uproar amongst many residents and visiting fishermen and women as well. Where is the guarantee that the National Guard's activities and facility expansion will put the protection of the river at the top of their priority list? And who within our governing system is willing to step up and take on that responsibility? The watershed of the AuSable River is not something that can be repaired like a broken down tank. Damage in most cases will be fatal.

BUT ALL IS NOT LOST...

People are still discovering the AuSable River today as I did so many years ago. In many cases they feel as if they have found Utopia. And they may well have!

What you never experience you do not miss.

Once, while fishing with my Pastor, who incidentally was not a fly fisherman, I witnessed an experience that maybe will eventually put it all in perspective.

The good Pastor, through no fault of his own, was fortunate enough to entangle his fly with a beautiful little brown trout. Finally, after he had brought the fish to net and the excitement was over, he looked up at me and smiled.

"George," he said in his Sunday morning voice, "I am once again convinced that the Lord does work in many ways His mysteries to perform. Only with His help did I land that trout."

Another explanation might be that "Nature, with God's help, does perform some miracles."

Surely he has plans for such a miracle as the AuSable River again. The river will double its size between Stephan's Bridge and Wakely's by adding cool, pure, oxygenated water filtered through some kind of spring beds, or an equally effective substitute.

Like the decline of our grouse population on the Wakely Lake property. I know that it was caused by an unnatural population of deer that browsed the habitat that was cover and a food source for the grouse. It was nature's plan to overpopulate the deer herd. It was contolling fires that suddenly caused an explosion in the deer population, while nearly wiping out the grouse population. But, now both deer and grouse are beginning to stabilize their populations once again.

We will always have a selfish, but well-meaning number of people.

My answer to these many questions and problems is that research programs must be accepted rather than be the misconceptions of the past.

Controlling pollution and getting rid of the problem rather than floating it into and down the river is up to those who want to continue the natural process and be able to enjoy our coldwater fisheries forever. The natural resources we love can and will respond to us with equal love.

It won't happen overnight. But given a chance, the AuSable River and the many rivers just like it will not cease to be the wonderment they are overnight either.

Someone...working in mysterious ways, will guide us with great wisdom and instill in us the desire to accomplish the goals that nature sets forth.

FATAL BEAUTY

"Don't let it be said,
and said to your shame,
that all was beauty here,
before you came."

George Griffith